CLASH OF LOYALTIES

WEST VIRGINIA AND APPALACHIA 3
A SERIES EDITED BY RONALD L. LEWIS

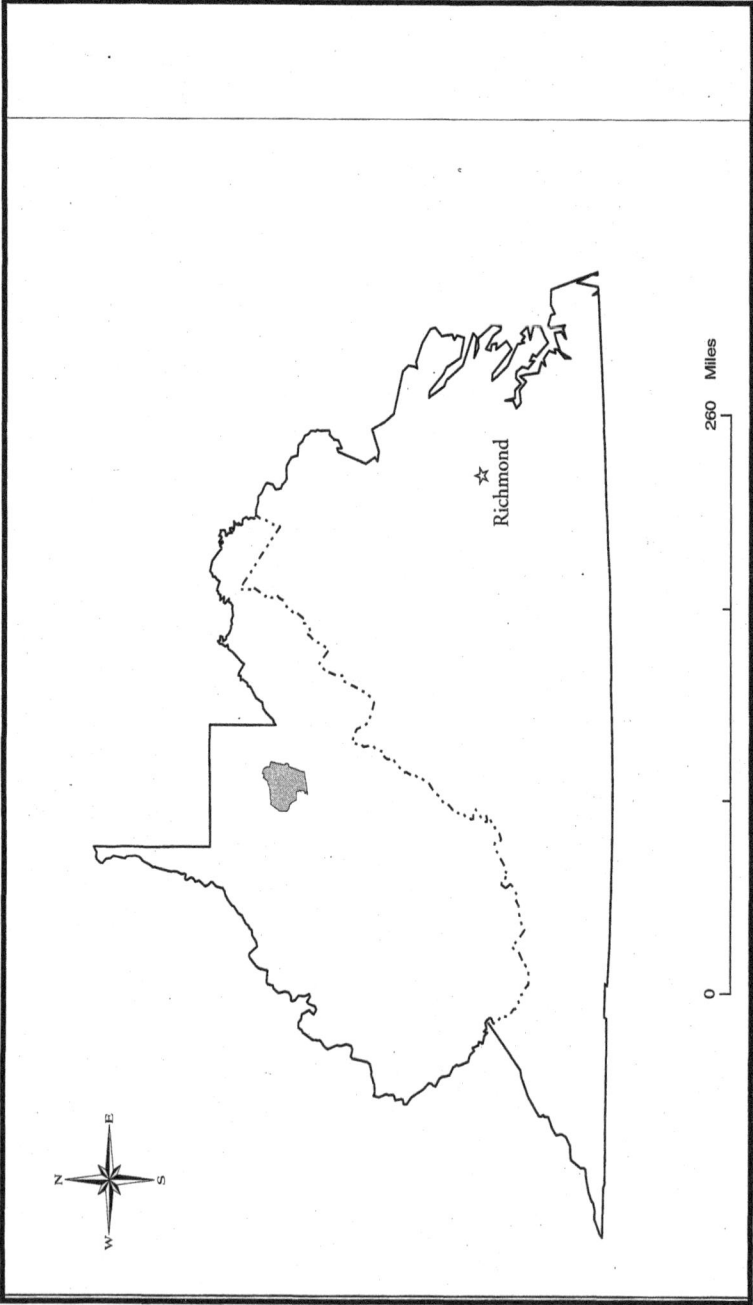

Pre-war Virginia, showing the present-day West Virginia and Barbour County

CLASH OF LOYALTIES:

A BORDER COUNTY IN THE CIVIL WAR

BY

JOHN W. SHAFFER

West Virginia University Press
Morgantown 2003

West Virginia University Press, Morgantown 26506
© 2003 by West Virginia University Press

First edition by West Virginia University Press
Printed in the United States of America

10 09 08 07 06 05 04 03   8 7 6 5 4 3 2 1

ISBN (cloth) 0-937058-73-4 (alk. paper)

Library of Congress Cataloguing-in-Publication Data

Shaffer, John W.
    Clash of Loyalties. A Border County in the Civil War / by
    John W. Shaffer.
        p. cm. — (West Virginia and Appalachia; 3)
1. Barbour County (W. Va.) — United States—History—19th
century. 2. United States—History—Civil War, 1861-1865—
Virginia. 3. United States—History—Civil War, 1861-1865—
West Virginia. 4. United States—History—Civil War, 1861-
1865—Regimental histories—West Virginia. 5. West
Virginia—History—Civil War, 1861-1865. I. Title. II.
Shaffer, John W. III. Series
IN PROCESS

Cover illustration: Courtesy of Library of Congress—
gmd/g3894p.pm010080. *Town of Phillipi, Barbour County,
WV. 1861.* Sketched by Mrs. M.D. Pool of Virginia.

Design by Connie Banta
Cover design by Lisa Bridges Design
Printed in USA

TABLE OF CONTENTS

LIST OF TABLES

INTRODUCTION

In the spring of 1864, a brigade of United States cavalry set off from Martinsburg, West Virginia, on a raid aimed at Dublin, Virginia, a major Confederate rail center and supply depot over a hundred miles to the south. Successfully eluding several Confederate columns, the Federals reached their target and promptly set about destroying bridges, supplies, and rolling stock. They then struck out west towards the headwaters of the Kanawha River. Near Blacksburg, a brigade of Confederate cavalry threw up hastily-prepared positions along the Federals' path, but after a brief skirmish the raiders escaped back to Union lines. The Confederates were able to capture only a handful of the cavalrymen, mostly stragglers found plodding along behind the tail of the column.

One of the soldiers captured that day was eighteen-year-old Henry Stockwell of Barbour County, West Virginia, who had joined the Third West Virginia Cavalry only a few weeks earlier. As the prisoners were escorted to the rear, a Confederate officer who had been a neighbor of the Stockwell family witnessed what he later described as "a rather pathetic scene."

> Among the prisoners was one by the name of Stockwell and nearby was a brother, a Confederate. I saw them meet, first with a sad look at one another, then a smile and salutation with a handshake. They then turned away from the rest and rode side by side a few paces and entered into an earnest conversation, seemingly paying no attention to what was going on around them.[1]

The little drama played out on a mountain backwater seemed to the officer to sum up the tragedy of the war, for the two armies that had fought that day were composed largely of West Virginians. Now here were two brothers, sworn to fight one another, calmly sharing news of home and family. Perhaps unspoken was the realization that their own fates were yet to be decided by the war that had placed them in opposing armies. As it turned out, Henry, the youngest, would die in Andersonville prison before the year ended. His Confederate brother William would be severely wounded at Hatcher's Run only a few weeks before Lee's surrender at Appomattox.

The most moving symbol of the Civil War is that of brother fighting brother. It is an image as powerful as it is poignant, for it reduces to simple human terms the tragedy of a nation split by war. Nor is the image mere romantic fantasy. The American Civil War was by no means a strictly sectional conflict between northern and southern states. Between these two extremes lay a vast stretch of territory in which sentiment was neither completely pro-Union or pro-secessionist. Encompassing the states of Maryland, West Virginia, Kentucky, Missouri, and Kansas, the border area included 15 percent of the country's land, population, and resources. Whichever side could seize and hold the borderland stood a good chance of winning the war, and both the Federal and Confederate governments expended a considerable part of their energies trying to secure this goal. Ultimately, success depended largely on the people of the border states themselves, and at the war's beginning in 1861 it was by no means clear where their allegiances lay. Often the boundaries separating people of opposing loyalties were nothing more than the property line between two farms, or a table over which members of the same family argued and ultimately chose sides.

The importance of the border states in the Civil War has long been recognized. Though the region was largely Southern both socially and geographically, vast numbers of its citizens remained loyal to the Union and fought to preserve it. Without question, these Unionists turned the tide against secession and assured the defeat of the Confederacy. At the same time, many within the region just as wholeheartedly supported the Confederacy, and fought against both Northern invaders and local Unionists they declared to be traitors. As much as their Unionist enemies from the border tipped the balance of forces against the Confederacy, border state secessionists ensured that the war would be a protracted struggle lasting not a few months, but four long years.

Union loyalists of West Virginia represented only part of a broad movement across the border region. Yet they were unique in one crucial respect. When Virginia seceded, citizens of the Western portion of the state not only refused to follow the Old Dominion into the Confederacy, but seized the opportunity to create a separate state for themselves. The birth of West Virginia was thus inseparably linked to the war that created it. Wrested as it was from a seceded Virginia, the new state inevitably became a principal battleground of the war. Union and Confederate armies fought scores of battles within its borders in a bloody struggle for control of the territory. Many of the Confederate soldiers were themselves West Virginians, for as in the rest of the border region, the inhabitants of northwest Virginia were by no means unanimous in their support of either the Federal government or the new state it had accepted into the Union. Theirs was as much a fight to prevent the dissolution of Virginia as it was to secede from the Union. The result was a civil war within a civil war, which marked the establishment of West Virginia as one of the most violent beginnings in the annals of statehood. Certainly no other state was created amid such turmoil, had so large a segment of its own population fighting bitterly against its formation, or so much owed its survival to the survival of an undivided United States. It is with considerable justification that West Virginia came to be known as "The War-Born State."

There is no question that West Virginia owed its existence to military necessity. The impossibility of getting Federal troops into distant Unionist strongholds like eastern Tennessee left loyalists there at the mercy of the Confederate army. Western Virginia was a different matter entirely. Bordered by the Ohio River, it presented Washington with both a greater threat and a greater opportunity. A Confederate government in Western Virginia could seize the Baltimore and Ohio Railroad, Washington's only link to the West. It could tap the considerable manpower and industrial resources of the region and carry the war across the Ohio. Conversely, Federal control over the same territory not only preserved control over a vital rail line, but offered the ability to strike deep into Confederate Virginia and Tennessee. In the final analysis, recognition of West Virginia by Washington—in effect, of the right of secession against secession—may have flown in the face of the Constitution, but was justified on the grounds that it would ultimately preserve the country. Any constitutional questions over the legality of West Virginia's creation were ultimately decided at Appomattox.

But beyond military necessity lay the equally important fact that the majority of the people of the Northwestern counties were opposed to secession and strongly supported the creation of the new state. Virginia's ordinance of secession was overwhelmingly rejected in the Northwest and over the course of the war West Virginia furnished some 25,000 men for the Union army against perhaps 15,000 who enlisted in Confederate regiments.[2] These facts have caused historians to treat the history of West Virginia from a very particular point of view, retrospectively shaping the entire historical perspective of the region's development up to 1861. A review of these arguments is instructive, for they continue to influence current historical research.

Early historians, many of them direct participants in the events they described, saw the state's creation as a culmination of a half-century of struggle between two radically different societies—the slave-based plantation economy of the East, dominated by aristocratic oligarchies, and a society of small independent farmers in the West. The earliest of these historians was Theodore Lang, a native of West Virginia and a Union veteran, whose work set the tone for interpreting West Virginia's history for decades. For Lang, the people of the western counties were "hardy frontiersmen. . . . They had few slaves and depended upon their own labor for a home in the wilderness. A population thus originating . . . was naturally uncongenial to the aristocratic element of the Old Dominion."[3]

Most historians of the nineteenth century were, like Lang, outspoken apologists for the Union cause, and the thrust of their work emphasized the distinctions between Eastern and Western Virginia. All shared the view that the differences between the two sections were so deep-rooted that separation of the West was inevitable. Granville Hall, a reporter for the pro-Union *Wheeling Intelligencer* and later West Virginia's Secretary of State, declared that "The connection between east and west was an unnatural one from the first. It grew to be a union of force which only awaited its opportunity to be broken."[4] "Western Virginia belonged, by nature, not to Virginia, but to the Valley of the Mississippi," said William P. Willey, son of the new state's war-time senator. "Its natural outlets were south and west with Cincinnati and Chicago, with Pittsburgh in the north, with Baltimore in the east."[5] Geography, it was argued, dictated that from the region's earliest settlement, commercial ties would be directed away from Eastern Virginia. "Mountain barriers had been reared by nature between the two sections," wrote Hall. "Commerce divides with the watersheds and flows with the streams. The interests and purposes of men follow commercial lines."[6]

Agriculture in the Western mountains was likewise molded by geography. With a shorter growing season, labor-intensive crops like tobacco and cotton could not take hold outside of a limited area along the Kanawha River. Instead, the agrarian economy of the West was geared toward a mixture of cereal production and stock raising which precluded reliance on slave labor. Not only were there fewer slaves in Western Virginia, their numbers were growing smaller as the war approached. In 1850 the slave population of Eastern Virginia totaled some 452,000 compared to only 25,000 in what is now West Virginia. Ten years later the number of slaves in the East had increased by some 20,000 while in the West it had decreased by 2,000.[7]

But nineteenth-century historians attributed the relative absence of slavery in the Western counties as much to social and religious influences as to purely economic considerations. Thus Willey claimed that "The population of the Western Section had come largely from the neighboring states of Pennsylvania, Maryland and New Jersey. They constituted the 'Yankee' element of the State. They had nothing in common with the population of the Eastern Section, and the enforced isolation only served to make this fact more evident and the unnatural alliance more odious."[8] The same ideas were echoed by Thomas Conduit Miller, like Lang a veteran of the Union army: "The influence of the churches in Western Virginia was powerful in its opposition to slavery, and did much to keep the institution out. . . . Immigration came from the North. . . . The people were different from the slave-holding aristocracy of lower Virginia. They were Scotch-Irish Presbyterians, German Lutherans and Moravians, and English and Welsh and other nationalities who were not in sympathy with slavery."[9]

In assessing the role of religion on the early history of the state, historians have almost universally credited the Methodist-Episcopal Church with exercising the most pronounced opposition to slavery. The prominence of ministers such as Gordon Battelle and Robert Hagans in pushing for the elimination of slavery during the war led many to ascribe to the church an influence beyond that which it may have deserved. In 1910, Charles Ambler went so far as to assert that the strength and location of pro-Union sentiment was virtually synonymous with that of Methodist-Episcopal membership.[10] There is no question that its influence was considerable. Of 26 ministers serving as chaplains in West Virginia regiments, 19 were from of the Methodist-Episcopal Church.[11] The influence of Methodist-Episcopalianism in limiting the extension of slavery and fostering pro-Union sentiment among its members is usually explained by the prewar history of the church. After its division in 1844 into northern and southern branches over the slave question, an acrimonious struggle for influence and members erupted between the two in West Virginia. The bitter contest intensified the controversy over slavery and served to crystallize antislavery tendencies already inherent in the northern branch. When war finally came, large numbers of ministers and laymen, hardened by more than a decade of struggle, were unflinching in their support of the Union.

Geography, religion, and the social origins of West Virginia's people may have created a society markedly different from Eastern Virginia, but by themselves these influences did not account for the animosities that grew up between the two sections of the Old Dominion. The political history of Virginia in the half-century before the war was seen as a struggle by the West to expand democratic rights in the face of Eastern oligarchies intent on retaining control of the state's government and economy. Much was at stake. As the population of the West increased, the demand for internal improvements grew, improvements that could only be financed by the state legislature. Since political representation was apportioned on a basis that included slaves, and the right to vote was restricted to those paying specific amounts of taxes on real property, the majority of those living in the West were effectively without a voice in the legislature. To many in the West, the clamor for investment in roads, canals, railroads, and public schools seemed to fall on deaf ears. "The people of western Virginia felt the injustice keenly," wrote Hu Maxwell. "The eastern part of Virginia had the majority of inhabitants and the largest part of the property, and this gave that portion of the state the majority in the Assembly. This power was used with small respect for the people in the Western part of the state. Internal improvements were made on a large scale in the East, but none were made west of the mountains, or very few. . . . The door was shut on them."[12]

Although the West's demands for greater representation, internal improvements, and a more equitable tax structure forced two revisions of Virginia's constitution, first in 1830 and again in 1851, the aims of the West were never fully realized. The fight was as bitter as it was protracted. Declarations such as that of state senator Benjamin Leigh in 1833 that the "peasantry of the West" could not expect to share in the affairs of the state did nothing to soothe the sentiments of the Western people. Lang asserted that from his earliest recollection, any candidate running for political office in the West had to declare himself a supporter of the division of the state if he expected to be elected.[13] Seen from this perspective, the outbreak of the Civil War afforded an already disaffected population the first real opportunity to achieve its goals.

Though historians like Lang, Hall, and Miller clearly acknowledge the secessionist sentiment in the Northwest, their treatment of the events of the period portrays a people overwhelmingly anti-secessionist and pro-Union in outlook. Typical is Lang's highly romantic description of the first response of the West to the passage of Virginia's ordinance of secession. It was, he declared, akin to "a shot fired in their midst" that "awoke a peaceful people into a frenzy of war."

> Men went to enlisting, officers to organizing companies and regiments, following which came the mighty gathering of our heroes. The doors of workshops were closed, the fields were deserted, armed men poured down from the hilltops and surged up from the valleys; the middle wall of partition was broken down between classes until it seemed like the good old days of old, "when none were for party, but all for the state."[14]

The myth of Western unanimity has been shattered by subsequent research showing that in many sections of what would become West Virginia, the sympathies of vast numbers of people were decidedly pro-secessionist. One of the most important revisionist interpretations of West Virginia's origins is that of Richard Orr Curry.[15] His work clearly demonstrates that the majority of the population of the Shenandoah Valley and Southwestern counties, areas which together encompassed half the territory of the new state and 40 percent of its population, by and large supported the Confederacy. Examining voting returns on the ordinance of secession and subsequent elections, Curry narrows the Unionist sections to those counties along the Ohio River and the Pennsylvania border, and along the line of the Baltimore and Ohio Railroad. Even within this stronghold of pro-Union sentiment, large numbers of people remained loyal to a seceded Virginia.[16]

The thrust of Curry's argument was that the secessionist-minded sections of West Virginia were consciously incorporated into the new state by Unionist Democrats fearful of Republican domination of postwar West Virginia. However, his explanation as to why the people of the extreme Northwest repudiated secession echoed the emphasis of previous historians: the long tradition of political struggle waged over representation, taxation and internal improvements; the social and ethnic heritage of the people who settled in the Northwest; and the influence of the Methodist-Episcopal Church. In the Southwest and the Valley, people rallied to the cause of a seceded Virginia precisely because of the relative absence of these influences, coupled with a conscious effort by the Virginia legislature to convert the population of the two sections into "good Virginians."[17]

So much has the traditional view evoked by Lang and others been discredited that the link between sectionalism and secession itself has been questioned.[18] It is certainly true that a fair number of prominent champions of Western rights came to support Virginia's secession in 1861. Edward Johnson of Lewis County and Edward J. Armstrong of Taylor represented Western interests at the 1850 constitutional convention; both fled south in 1861. Before the war, David Goff of Randolph County championed the cause of the West in the state legislature and swore he would take up arms in defense of Western rights. He eventually did arm himself, fighting for a seceded Virginia. Samuel Woods of Barbour County, elected a delegate to the Richmond Convention in 1861, hoped that support for Virginia's secession could be traded for a redress of Western demands. He too served in the Confederate army.[19]

How then do we explain the movement that led to the creation of West Virginia, or the divisions that pitted its people against one another? Research focusing on the leadership of the new state movement has greatly contributed to an understanding of the sentiments, ambitions, and goals of those who tried to direct the course of events during this period.[20] Yet the Civil War was above all else a popular movement, or rather two movements, one in favor of secession and the other bitterly opposed to it. Curry's invaluable analysis was the first attempt to investigate the extent and pattern of sentiment in West Virginia, but ultimately failed to directly link these sentiments to the social, economic, political, and religious influences which have for so long been employed to explain them.

More recent studies addressing border state Unionism and secessionism are of particular relevance for West Virginia. One of the most important is the work of Michael Holt.[21] In Holt's view, the key to understanding both movements lies in the crucial role played by political parties in antebellum America. In the decades before the war, the interplay between Democrats and Whigs had largely deflected sectional controversies over slavery. Each westward expansion of the United States provoked renewed controversy over the extension of slavery into new territories. So long as both parties maintained national, cross-sectional political bases, party leaders had managed to work out compromises which, while not satisfactory to all Americans, nonetheless prevented the disruption of the Union. With the collapse of the Whig Party in the 1850s, especially in the deep South, and the concurrent rise of the Republican Party in the North, the inability of political parties to unify the country exacerbated sectional conflict. The division of the Democratic Party in 1860 between supporters of Stephen Douglas and the States Rights candidacy of John C. Breckenridge crippled the last party to claim broad national support, and war became inevitable.

This aspect of Holt's thesis to a large extent repeats traditional interpretations of the political crisis confronting Americans in late 1850s. Holt's principal contribution lies in his analysis of the essential role played by political parties. Enthusiasm for the political process was widespread among antebellum Americans, as is evident from the regularly high rates of voter turnout. No doubt the theatrics attending local electioneering explains much of the interest shown by voters, but something more fundamental was drawing people to polling places. Holt argues persuasively that, however divided Americans may have been geographically, socially, and economically, the great mass of voters shared a common devotion to liberty and republican ideals of democratic government. Political parties served to channel these aspirations into concrete goals, whether they were the extension of suffrage, government support for transportation, banking or education, or, above all, protection from threats to republican values.[22] Political contests were thus often portrayed as battles to save the right of self-government and liberty from despotism, whether in the form of corrupt government, foreigners, banks, aristocratic oligarchies, or unbridled mob rule. In the context of sectional conflict over the extension of slavery, Southern political leaders, Democrat and Whig alike, portrayed the contest not simply as pitting slavery against abolition, but as a struggle to protect the rights of Southerners in general from the despotism of Northerners bent on the subjugation of the South. Restrictions on slavery in any form constituted a denial of basic liberties and of southern equality.[23]

In this context, the collapse of the two-party system confronted cotton-state Southerners, slave owners and non-slave owners alike, with the threat that control of the government by the Republican party would relegate them to an inherently inferior status. That Republicans themselves declared the defeat of the slave power as essential to protecting Northerners from enslavement was an argument completely lost on most Southerners. When Lincoln was elected in 1860 by a purely Northern vote, Southerners lost all faith in the political system and believed they had no choice but to secede. The central impulse behind secession was thus not so much the protection of slavery, but the perception that it afforded the only means to escape enslavement by Republican tyranny.

In the border region, however, the Whig Party and its various evolutions as Know Nothing, American, and Opposition Parties retained the loyalty of large segments of the electorate. The continued interplay of political parties, especially in the form of contests within each state, preserved voter faith in traditional political processes. And to the extent that both parties within the region could lay claim to being local extensions of national political parties, voters were presented with the possibility that crises could be resolved through normal political means. It was thus no mere accident of history that the principal efforts to effect a compromise to the secession crisis were generated by political leaders from the border states.[24]

In a study extending Holt's argument, Daniel Crofts's examination of the secession crisis in Virginia, North Carolina, and Tennessee not only concludes that Unionism in these states was a far more powerful force than previously acknowledged, but also seeks to establish the sources of Unionist and secessionist sentiment. When the Cotton States of the South left the Union immediately upon Lincoln's election, these and other border states hesitated, refusing to secede. Despite strong secessionist movements within each state, Unionists managed to prevent secession for over half a year. Like Holt, Crofts sees the contest between the two as being in large part an extension of prewar party struggles, arguing that Unionism drew its principal strength from Whig leaders and voters while secessionist sentiment was most pronounced in those areas where support for Breckenridge had predominated in 1860.[25] Crofts further argues that similar party loyalties in the other border states played a crucial role in shaping reactions to the secession crisis.

This model tends to break down in the composition of upper South Unionism. As Crofts readily admits, the movement was by no means exclusively Whig-based, but represented a broad coalition of Unionist Whigs and Democrats, including significant numbers who had supported Breckenridge. In fact, the secession crisis provoked a complete realignment of the previous two-party system, transforming the contest into one in which Unionists—Whigs and Democrats alike—struggled against secessionists who drew support not simply from both states rights Democrats and Whigs.[26] As Crofts's own analysis reveals, the main base of secessionist sentiment lay in areas where slave owning predominated, while Unionist strength came principally from non-slave owning upcountry counties. Statistically, the degree of slave ownership was a somewhat greater predictor of secessionist sentiment than party affiliation.[27]

Beyond this lies the more basic issue of how parties actually conducted campaigns. While voters may have viewed political parties and their leaders as the embodiments of their own aspirations, the mission of party campaigners was to get their candidates elected. Those who stumped local precincts had to adhere to the general platforms of their candidates, yet these positions could be tailored to meet local conditions. In the Virginia gubernatorial contest of 1859, both Whigs and Democrats emphasized the pro-slavery stances of their candidates in the East, while downplaying the issue in the West. There, leaders from both parties campaigned on issues more dear to the hearts of Westerners: internal improvements, more equitable taxation, and a redress of representational imbalances.[28] A similar two-fold campaign developed during the presidential election in 1860, in which supporters of Breckenridge stressed his state's rights stance in the East while arguing in the West that a victory for him represented the best means of preserving the Union.[29] Finally, Crofts's thesis appears to have only limited relevance when applied to Western Virginia. In the 1860 presidential election, counties of the extreme Northwest, which would become the main bastion of Unionism in the new state, not only voted overwhelmingly Democratic, but many returned majorities for Breckenridge. In the Southwest, several counties that had long voted Whig, and returned majorities for the Whig-based candidacy of John Bell, became strongholds of secessionist sentiment after 1861.[30]

Ultimately, Unionist loyalty in the upper South proved to be insufficiently entrenched to oppose secession. Many Unionists, regardless of their party allegiances, conditioned their support on the refusal to accept the right of the Federal government to use force against secession. After the fall of Fort Sumter, when Lincoln called upon the states to contribute men and arms to suppress the rebellion, Unionism collapsed throughout most of the upper South. Many of those who had worked against the secessionist tide pledged their loyalties to their states and joined the Confederacy. In only a few regions within each state (Northwestern Virginia, the Western upcountry of North Carolina, and Eastern Tennessee) did Union loyalists carry on the fight against secession.

Crofts's study stands as a major contribution in establishing both the extent of Unionism in the upper South and the political and social foundations of its strength. Because this work is limited to the period up to the actual secession of the three states examined, no attempt is made to explain the resilience of Unionism after secession. The question remaining is why Unionists in regions such as Northwestern Virginia remained steadfast in their loyalty to the Federal Union while their erstwhile allies abandoned the cause and flocked to the secessionist camp.

The purpose of this study is not simply to recount the role of Barbour County in the war, but to explore the basis of Union and Confederate sentiment within the county. Barbour was selected because its people were nearly evenly divided in their sympathies, making the county a kind of microcosm of the divisions that separated the population of West Virginia as a whole. Information was gathered on the social, economic, and religious backgrounds of those individuals who enlisted in armies of the two sides, served in public office, or whose allegiance could be determined from available sources. Fortunately, a wealth of biographical material exists. Beginning in the late nineteenth century, local historians began compiling the histories of thousands of West Virginia families. The foremost of these historians—Hu Maxwell, Oren Morton and Thomas Conduit Miller—lived in counties bordering Barbour, and the bulk of their work dealt with the people of the immediate region. Their studies constitute an invaluable source on the history of Barbour and its people.

Using military service records, biographies, contemporary newspapers, public records, diaries, and letters, it was possible to identify 718 Union loyalists and 509 Confederates. (The total number was actually 1,207, as 20 men switched loyalties during the war. For this study, these were included in the analyses of both sides.) The vast majority—three-quarters of the total—were men who served in the armed forces. The remainder were persons who held public office or whose sympathies could be determined through source material. The most glaring omission is that of women, with only 23 included in this study. Local histories, written by men, paid virtually no attention to the important role of women in the conflict. On the other hand, the men included in this study total nearly half the male population of Barbour County, and without question represent the hard core of Union and Confederate sentiment in the county.

Curry identified the area of which Barbour was a part as the zone separating the strongly pro-Union Northwest and the secessionist-dominated Southern sections of West Virginia. Barbour was a border county in a border state, and it is precisely this fact that makes it worthy of close examination. Neighbors who had lived together for decades suddenly found themselves enemies. Friendships were torn and families divided. Brother quite literally fought brother. For the people of Barbour, the conflict was in every sense of the term a civil war. How its Union and Confederate sympathizers acted on their convictions constitutes the history of Barbour County during the war.

When the fighting ended, these same people were forced to deal with the almost equally difficult problems posed by peace. Wars never end when the fighting stops. Many who survived military service returned home with wounds that would serve as constant reminders of the conflict. Others who had escaped shot and shell were struck down with diseases from which they would never fully recover. Beyond these were countless others for whom the very experience of war had changed their lives forever. The fear, hatred, elation, and sadness men and women experience in every war live on long afterward, burned into their hearts and souls. The Civil War was no exception. In 1890, Federal census workers made a special count of war veterans and asked each if they had been wounded or injured. "Wounded in my character" is how one Barbour veteran answered them. All this was true for people throughout the country. What was different for the people of Barbour was that former enemies returned to the very same community, sometimes to the same farm. The cessation of a fratricidal struggle compelled Barbour's people to lay aside bitter animosities created by four years of war and learn to live in peace with one another. How that peace was finally achieved is as much a part of Barbour County's history—and the nation's—as the war that shattered it.

- 1 -

BORDERLAND COUNTY

The topography of Barbour County is typical North-central West Virginia, a mountainous, forest-covered, sparsely populated region of often breathtaking beauty. The dominant geographic feature is the Tygart Valley River, flowing through the center of the county. Along its banks lie some of the most fertile land in Barbour County, excellent for crops and grazing, and it is here that the largest and most productive farms are to be found. The eastern third of Barbour is more rugged, encompassing the western spurs of the Laurel Mountains. Soils there are fertile enough, but the steep, heavily wooded hillsides limit cropland to narrow bottomlands along streams and creeks. Although by the standards of the day Barbour was considered "largely settled" when it was formed in 1843, vast sections of the county were an effective wilderness and remained so well into the late nineteenth century. At the war's outbreak, over half the county was still covered in forest.

Barbour's social structure also was typically agrarian. Fully eighty percent of the families listed in the 1860 census were headed by farmers or tenants. The rest of Barbour's population consisted for the most part of artisans—wheelwrights, coopers, blacksmiths, etc.—whose livelihood depended directly on the farm-based economy. Although large coal deposits existed, they remained virtually undeveloped for most of the century. An iron foundry established in 1848 at Valley Furnace manufactured pig iron that was shipped to Pittsburgh, but within six years was forced to close down due to prohibitively high transportation costs. While the foundry operated it had provided a source of extra income to scores of local farmers who dug and hauled coal to the foundry. By 1860 only three men earned their living full-time from mining.[1]

The only urban element in Barbour society was the few dozen families residing in Philippi, the county seat. These residents included six lawyers, two doctors, and two ministers, who rubbed shoulders with three merchants, two hotel keepers, and various artisans and tradesmen. The town itself was less than 20 years old in 1860. Situated at a ferry crossing on the Tygart River, it had been little more than hamlet of a few farmsteads when the county was created in 1843. Locating the county seat there—on land owned by one of the first county magistrates—hastened its growth. Philippi's importance was further increased with the construction of the Staunton-Parkersburg turnpike in the 1840s and the Philippi bridge in 1852. Even so, by 1860 its population totaled only 387. Contemporary descriptions of the town varied widely. One Indiana soldier in 1861 thought it "beautifully situated in the river valley locked in by hills." Other travelers the same year referred to Philippi as "God forsaken" and "the last outpost of the barbarians."[2]

While Barbour County's social structure cannot be described as egalitarian, neither was it marked by extremes of wealth and poverty. Instead, wealth was graduated. Based on the values of real and personal property reported in the 1860 census, the predominance of the family-operated farm is readily apparent. Fully two-thirds of the families were headed by landowners, over a third of whom owned property worth between $500 and $2,500. This category generally corresponds to farms of between 50 and 200 acres—the minimum needed to provide subsistence and the most that could be worked by a single family. Farms of this size were by far the most common unit of production in Barbour, while those with no land at all constituted another third of Barbour's families. However, this figure is misleading for it consists mainly of tenant farmers—twenty percent of the total population—as well as merchants and professionals who, while not owning land, were nonetheless fairly well off. Most important, it also includes the married children of landowners, most of whom could expect to inherit a portion of the their parents' estate. Day laborers, the bottom rung of Barbour's social ladder, numbered only 30, all of them young men.

Every county had its wealthy element, and Barbour was no exception. Fifty-four families possessed property valued in excess of $10,000; collectively, this group controlled 34 percent of the total wealth of the county. Only seven held property worth more than $25,000. The richest of Barbour's residents, John H. Woodford Sr., owned land and property worth some $77,000, almost twice that of the next wealthiest individual. Barbour's elite hardly compared to those of neighboring Randolph, Harrison, and Preston counties, where many owned property valued in excess of $100,000.

These relatively wealthy families did, however, dominate Barbour's political life. When Barbour was created in 1843, all county officials were appointed rather than elected—the justices of the peace by the governor, the sheriff and court clerks in turn by the justices. It was a system designed to restrict office holders at the local level to only the most prominent men of the county, and for ten years it served the elite group well. In 1850 only 27 men in Barbour—less than two percent of the 1,470 households listed in the census that year—owned land valued in excess of $5,000. Yet between 1843 and 1852, when a new state constitution requiring the election of county officials came into effect, these same men all served as county officials in one capacity or another, together accounting for a quarter of all Barbour's office holders. The important positions of sheriff, prosecuting attorney, surveyor, and county and circuit court clerks were invariably held by these most prosperous citizens.[3]

Wealth was by no means the only prerequisite for public office. Barbour's magistrates commonly submitted the names of their own sons, brothers, or in-laws to the governor as potential appointees. Those who ran the organs of local government were thus linked not only by bonds of class, but by close ties of kinship. The hold on public office maintained by Barbour's elite was only somewhat loosened with the introduction of direct elections under the 1851 constitution. In the elections that followed the next year, a number of men of more modest means were voted into office, many of whom had never before held office and only one of whom was directly related to current office-holders. Yet the principal offices of the county—sheriff, prosecuting attorney, and court clerks—continued to be the possessions of the wealthier families.[4]

Barbour County was formed at a time when the economic life of the region was undergoing fundamental changes. From the era of the first settlers and well into the early decades of the nineteenth century, society in Northwest Virginia retained the essentials of pioneer life. Farms were of necessity self-sufficient, rarely exceeding 50 acres of cropland.[5] Homes were little more than crude log cabins, with few windows and with floors of rough-cut wood or packed earth. What could not be grown or made on the farm—cooking utensils, farm tools, and guns and powder—were secured by trading ginseng, maple, furs, and other products that could be easily transported by horse or mule to towns on the South Branch of the Potomac, or in the Shenandoah Valley.

Reliance on pack mules was necessitated by the virtual absence of roads in the region. Most "roads" were in fact trails that generally followed earlier Indian paths, sometimes widened to allow passage of mule trains. As one local historian put it, "A path which could be followed by pack-horses without scraping the packs off against the trees, was considered a great convenience, if not a luxury." [6] The first man to bring a wagon into the area, one Thomas Parsons, was able to do so only because slaves repeatedly dismantled it every few miles, carried the pieces around and over obstacles, reassembled it, and started the process again at the next obstruction. Trails only slowly became passable for wagons—during the dry season, anyway—and only for short distances. The first road in present-day Barbour County was constructed in 1800 and ran but seven miles east from the present site of Philippi. It would be another three years before it was extended east to Beverly and west to Clarksburg. Even then, the man who built it decided to save money by avoiding any grading, with the result that the road went straight up one hillside and down the other. About that time Randolph County, of which Barbour was then a part, ordered the construction of a wagon road through that portion of the county later to become Barbour. However, because local farmers were loath to cede rights of way, the road meandered around corn patches and through swamps.[7]

Better roads were beyond the financial means of impoverished counties or single individuals, and Western leaders for decades demanded the state intervene. Their outcries were largely ignored until the 1820s, when the Virginia Assembly finally began voting money for improvements.[8] The appropriations were grudgingly made and the roads themselves a long time coming, but when they were finally constructed, the economic isolation of Western Virginia was broken at last. The penetration of roads, together with a marked increase in population, brought about the beginnings of a market economy that would forever change the pattern of life in West Virginia.

In 1827, the legislature authorized the construction of a road from Winchester to Parkersburg, the famous Northwest Turnpike that is today U.S. Route 50. Its completion in the 1830s opened the territory to more concentrated settlement. In 1838, the Assembly began passing a series of funding measures for the Staunton-Parkersburg Turnpike, that would run directly through Barbour. Construction began in 1840 and would continue for over ten years before the fully macadamized road was completed and rivers bridged. The crowning pre-war transportation achievement was the completion of the Baltimore and Ohio Railway. In 1851 it reached Grafton, only 11 miles from Philippi, and by the following year was completed to Wheeling.[9]

Farmers quickly took advantage of reduced transport costs by gearing production for the markets now being opened to them. No direct figures on production exist for this period, but the effects of the road and railway can be seen by examining the evolution of wheat and corn prices recorded at Morgantown. Corn, which remained the staple for local consumption, remained largely unaffected; prices hovered between $.25 and $.30 a bushel in the 1820s, and remained fairly stable for the next two decades. Wheat, which became the grain for trade, went from $.50 or $.60 a bushel in the 1820s to over $1.00 in 1834, finally leveling off at $.75 in the 1840s. When the rail line reached Morgantown in 1850, wheat prices doubled and within five years doubled again. Clearly, market forces were at work and the county was no longer a strictly subsistence-farming area.

Improved transportation not only affected cereal production, but spurred the growth of stock raising. Livestock had been an integral part of Western Virginia's economy from the time the region was first settled. Tax records from the late 18th century attest to its importance. Of 191 households recorded in the 1787 tax list for Randolph County, three-fourths owned cattle, a fifth of them possessing ten or more.[10] Early pioneers tended to select rich bottomlands for corn production, and they found the land's productivity astonishing. One writer in the 1870s described bottomland that had been continuously in production for over 80 years and still yielded 80 bushels of corn per acre without the use of fertilizers.[11] Yet bottomland was a rare commodity. As population increased during the early decades of the century and fewer fertile hillside lands were brought into production, farmers were forced to introduce crop rotation to prevent soil erosion and preserve fertility. Newly cleared lands were sown in corn or wheat for two or three years, then left in pasture for another two or three years. With the increase in pasture came increased use of cattle and sheep.[12]

Reliance on livestock was also largely due to the lack of means for transport. Not being able to move grain to distant markets in bulk compelled farmers to raise cattle and sheep as the only way to ship farm surpluses. "Feeding surplus grain to stock is widely preferred to selling it," explained one early commentator, "not only because it thus transports itself to ... market almost without trouble, but because a large percentage of its value is returned to the soil as manure."[13] With the growth of markets created by improved transportation, stock raising accelerated.

Travelers in the 1840s remarked on "the immense herds" being driven each year to markets in Pittsburgh, Philadelphia and Baltimore.[14]

An 1840 government survey of agriculture reported a total of 15,000 head of cattle for Harrison and Randolph counties, the two counties from which Barbour would be formed. A similar survey in 1850 showed 44,000 head in the same area, including 10,339 in Barbour.[15] Ten years later, the number of cattle in Barbour had increased to 12,990 head. These surveys also show a rapid expansion of farming. In the decade prior to the war, the total farmland in the county increased from 181,031 to 281,914 acres, while the total number of farms increased by 18 percent.[16]

Nearly half the new farmland originated from the acquisition of state-owned land, forfeited to the Commonwealth due to failure by the owners to pay taxes on it. The origins of these lands date to the years immediately following the Revolution, when the westward expansion which was effectively cut off during the war resumed on an unprecedented scale. Tens of thousands of settlers streamed into Ohio, Kentucky, and Tennessee, where cheap land abounded. In its eagerness to populate its own Western territories, the state of Virginia adopted a relatively simple plan: give its land away. In 1788 the legislature dropped the price at which it sold state-owned land from $5.80 to $1.00 an acre, and in 1793 to two cents an acre. Anyone willing and able to survey claims and file patents for them could acquire as much land as they wished.[17] Within a few years, millions of acres were patented in Western Virginia. The scheme, however, did not have quite the effects the legislature intended. The haphazard manner in which the patents were issued, often without proper surveys or with no surveys at all, resulted in countless land disputes, often lasting for decades and producing a profitable living for generations of lawyers. Moreover, the vast majority of patents were filed by wealthy speculators who quickly claimed tens and hundreds of thousands of acres for themselves. One study estimates that over 90 percent of the land patented after 1793 was claimed by non-resident owners.[18] In many instances, the tracts remained undeveloped for decades or more, passing through successive owners who hoped to eventually profit from timber and mineral rights.[19]

The state's land scheme not only discouraged settlement in the West, but it also failed to generate the revenues the legislature had envisioned. Many speculators, having acquired their land-holdings for a pittance, aimed at keeping their outlays to the mini-mum by refusing to pay the taxes. The state clearly recognized the problem, and repeatedly tried to redress it by issuing legisla-tion declaring lands on which taxes were in arrears were to be forfeited to the state and sold at public auction. Yet successive legislatures, composed largely of wealthy landowners, left loop-holes in the law. It was not until 1831 and 1837 that laws made wide-scale seizure and sale of delinquent lands possible.[20] In the five years prior to 1832, only eight parcels totaling 714 acres of government land in Barbour County were acquired through patent sales. In the five years that followed, 18 claims were taken out on over 5,000 acres. In the decades after 1837, when the 1831 law was further strengthened, both the total acreage and the number of claimants steadily increased. Between 1847 and 1856, after the Staunton-Parkersburg Turnpike and the B&O Railroad fur-ther opened the county to settlers and markets, 205 claims were filed on over 52,000 acres. The great majority of the claimants were residents of the county. Of 231 applicants between 1827 and 1861, only 21 were non-residents, all of whom lived in neigh-boring Harrison, Randolph and Upshur Counties. A large num-ber of the claimants were landowning farmers who acquired parcels ranging from two-and-a-half to several hundred acres. The larg-est acquisitions, however, were by wealthy citizens of Barbour and neighboring counties. The 15 largest claimants, ten of whom were residents of Barbour, together patented claims on a total of 34,430 acres in the county.[21]

The new land rush completely altered the pattern of land ownership in the county. In 1843, when the county was formed, tax records show that half of Barbour's surface area was owned by non-residents. Significantly, over 20,000 acres were held by persons whose residence was not even known to local tax officials, without doubt tracts on which taxes were not being paid. The vast majority of absentee-owned land was held by Virginians residing in Winchester and Richmond, and by non-Virginians in New York, Pennsylvania, and Maryland. Seven years later, while the number of absentee owners rose in number, the total amount of land they owned fell from 118,000 to 81,000 acres. The trend continued over the next decade. Between 1850 and 1860, residents of Barbour and surrounding counties acquired substantial holdings largely at the expense of proprietors residing in Eastern Virginia, whose total landholdings further declined by 23,000 acres.[22]

The shift in land ownership in large part accrued to the benefit of local investors, who enlarged farms and increased the size of their cattle herds. The case of Lair D. Morrall, the largest land purchaser in this period, is illustrative. According to the 1850 land tax list, he owned 1,425 acres within Barbour's current borders but he farmed only 100 acres and possessed but three head of cattle. In 1860 Morrall paid taxes on 3,736 acres, farmed 230 acres of improved land, and owned 25 head of cattle. Men like Morrall were not only increasing the size of farms they worked directly, but renting out large tracts to tenants and sharecroppers whose numbers grew dramatically. Between 1850 and 1860, the number of tenant farmers increased 25 percent, accounting for over 40 percent of the new farms established during the decade. And like owner-operators, tenants shifted production away from grain and into stock raising. In 1850, about half of the county's 347 tenants owned cattle, for a total of 724 head. In 1860, 84 percent of the 426 tenant farmers owned a total of 1,825 head of cattle, over ten percent of the county's total.

Yet it would be a mistake to assume that agrarian development transformed the everyday life of the entire population of the Northwest. The situation of many, if not most, small farmers differed little from the stark conditions of pioneer days. One widely-traveled commentator claimed that he had seen nothing in the remotest parts of backward Poland or Hungary that compared with conditions in West Virginia.[23] Henry Howe, an artist and writer who traveled throughout Virginia in the 1840s, was struck by the primitive living conditions of the Northwest. He described the home of a "substantial farmer" as consisting of a two-story dwelling with but two windows, the floor devoid of carpets, the family dressed entirely in homespun. Retiring for the night as a guest, Howe had "a fine field . . . for astronomical observation through the chinks of the logs."[24]

Like many urban travelers, Howe was clearly enchanted with the people of Western Virginia and the life they led. The mountaineer, he wrote, "led a manly life, and breathes the pure air of the hills with the contented spirit of the freeman . . . untainted by the knowledge of deceit which those living in densely populated communities are tempted to practice."[25] There is in all of this rather too much of the urban romantic's fondness for the simplicity of rural life. When war brought thousands of Indiana, Illinois, and Ohio troops to West Virginia, most of them farm boys themselves with a more discerning eye, they were dumbstruck by conditions in the region. One soldier wrote to his brother from Philippi that "I have passed through several counties of Virginia, and have come to the conclusion that it is the poorest country I ever saw. I have not seen ten acres of level land in this State, unless it be on the side of a hill."[26] Another noted in his diary that livestock in the area near Barbour County were "the longest, lankiest, boniest animals in creation."[27] An Indiana soldier scouting Confederate positions in Barbour came upon the farm of Conrad Carpenter. According to the 1860 agricultural survey, Carpenter's farm was fairly typical of the county, 44 acres of cropland and 90 of woodland worth $1,200.

> His farm is a specimen of the middle class of Virginia's farms. It is a small opening in the forest, from which the trees have been "deadened," and is secluded from all the world. A few acres of Virginia wheat, a few of corn, and a tobacco patch, are surrounded by a rickety rail-fence, in the corners of which weeds most do flourish . . . Another space is used to pasture two or three old horses;

one or two colts, mane and tail matted with burs; half a dozen sheep, and a cow . . . The cabin of Coon is, like all Virginia cabins, composed of rough logs, sticks, pins, and mud.[28]

Backward too seemed the people, and it was not simply Northern prejudice that made them appear so. During the war, Confederate cavalry swept into the region, most of the troopers natives of Eastern Virginia and the Shenandoah Valley. One of them noted in his diary while traveling through Barbour that, "Of all the paths I ever traveled this was the worst . . . Few or no houses on route and the people who exist in them look as wild as the mountain 'varmints', their only companions."[29] Howe noted that among the people of the Northwest "many cannot read or write, and many that can, know nothing of geography and other branches."[30] Little had changed 20 years later when a captain of Ohio infantry remarked that "These West Virginians are uncultured, uneducated, and rough . . . Many have never seen a railroad, and the telegraph is to them an incomprehensible mystery."[31] Indiana troops occupying Philippi marveled at the ordinary West Virginian's apparent lack of any sense of geography. "Few knew anything of the world at large—many little of their State, and some there were who did not know the county in which they had been born and raised."[32] One local, when asked the name of the county in which he lived, is said to have answered, "Virginny!"[33] Another, who had enlisted in the army and returned home on leave after his initial training, exclaimed, "I'll tell you what . . . If this world is as big the other way as it is towards Wheeling, its a whopper!"[34]

Blame for the lack of education evidenced by these statements can be laid squarely at the feet of the Virginia Assembly which for decades ignored repeated demands by Western leaders for a system of publicly financed schooling. Some of Barbour's better-off families were able to send their children to school in one of three subscription schools in the county. There they received a rudimentary education, as evidenced by the later letters of the graduates, tortuous compositions devoid of punctuation or any discernible rules of spelling. One of Barbour's most famous teachers was William Ferguson, a Pennsylvania-born Dunkard. His fame derived as much from the severity of his teaching methods as from the knowledge he imparted to his students. Cracking heads together and pulling hair, he would scream, "Abomination on your abominated heads! Can't I learn you nothin'!" His former students remembered him to their dying day.[35]

Virtually every contemporary description of Appalachian Virginia depicts its people as isolated and their society as backward. "Rough mountaineer" is a phrase repeated again and again.[36] The images belie the reality. True, Northwest Virginia was economically retarded relative to much of the rest of the country, but its society was far from "rough." Reflecting on the social habits of Barbour's people in the era prior to the war, one resident of the county recalled that, while many farmers may have produced large amounts of whiskey, drunkenness and rowdy behavior were for the most part frowned upon and "good behavior prevailed generally."[37] Though the romantic conclusions Howe drew about what he saw must be taken with a hefty grain of salt, the observations themselves are noteworthy and largely confirm the description.[38] Court records attest to the generally peaceable nature of Barbour society. In the seven years preceding the war, the county's grand jury issued only 47 indictments for assault and battery, an average of just seven a year. Of the 22 cases where the accused pleaded not guilty, half ended in acquittal. During the same period only one man was charged with murder and two others with felony assault. Juries reduced the murder charge to manslaughter and found one of the other defendants not guilty by reason of insanity. The war intervened before the third defendant could be tried.[39]

Indeed, the possession of firearms didn't seem to have been particularly widespread. The popular image of Appalachian mountaineers raised from the cradle with a firm knowledge of firearms is in large part a myth. Most families in Barbour appear to have had but limited experience with weapons. Of 135 estates probated between 1843 and 1861, only 41—fewer than a third—

included weapons of any kind. Most of these were hunting rifles, but there were also shotguns and the odd pistol.[40] When tempers flared and violence broke out, arguments were usually settled with fists rather than guns. When war came in 1861, those who responded to the first call to arms looked desperately to their respective governments for weapons, because they had none of their own.

The picture of Barbour presented by public records and the observations of contemporaries is that of an agrarian society of remarkable homogeneity just awakening to the possibilities offered by an emerging market economy. The county's small elite possessed sufficient wealth to guarantee them a prominence in public life, but not enough to enable them to wield untrammeled economic power in the county. Yet this apparent homogeneity masks important differences between large segments of Barbour's population, differences that probably would not have made themselves felt were it not for the coming of the war. These differences were rooted, not in distinctions of wealth, but rather in the divergent backgrounds of the families who settled in the county. The divisions that would turn neighbors into enemies cannot be fully understood without a careful examination of precisely who settled the county.

Northwest Virginia was not a border region simply in the geographic sense. Sandwiched between Eastern Virginia, Maryland, Pennsylvania, Ohio, and Kentucky, it lay astride some of the principal routes over which the westward migration of America took place. The diverse origins of the Northwest's population came to be one of its defining characteristics. They came from New Jersey, Maryland, and Pennsylvania; from Tidewater Virginia, the Shenandoah Valley, and the South Branch of the Potomac. A significant number came from New England. Several families migrated directly from Europe, mainly from the British Isles but also from Germany, France, and Italy. Nor was the movement into Barbour entirely from the North and East. A fair number came from Kentucky, Ohio, Indiana, and Illinois, many of them former West Virginians who had pushed westward only to find conditions on America's frontier more harsh than they had

expected. "Border state" in reality meant not a demarcation between North and South, but rather one of the few places where
people of the two sections of the country intermingled on a massive scale.

By 1790, some forty families were living in what is roughly
Barbour County today.[41] When Barbour was formed in 1843, its
population was estimated at about 5,000. When the first census
of the new county was taken in 1850, it put the county's population at 9,005. By comparison, the 1860 census counted 8,958
people.

In all, some 600 families made their way to Barbour between 1780 and 1860. It is possible to reconstruct the pattern of
migration into the county by utilizing a variety of sources. Biographies and family histories often provide fairly reliable information on when individual families arrived. Of particular value are
county marriage records. Beginning in 1853 these noted the age
and birthplace of each bride and groom and the names of their
parents. Comparing these to Federal census lists gives a fair ap-
proximation of when a family came to Barbour and where they
came from. From these sources we can determine the period during which 506 families settled in Barbour and the areas from
which they migrated (see Table 1).

A number of trends are evident, the most significant of which
is that the rate and direction of migration into Barbour were by
no means uniform. A considerable percentage of Barbour's residents in 1860 were relative newcomers to the county. Half of the
county's families had settled there during the two decades before
the war. Equally important is the fact that the homelands of most
of these new families differed markedly from those who had preceded them. Whereas nearly half the families who arrived during
the late eighteenth and early nineteenth century came from Maryland or Northern states rather than from Eastern Virginia, the
pattern during the 1840s and 1850s was exactly the opposite.
During these decades, the majority of settlers migrated from Eastern Virginia.

Several factors contributed to these patterns. While Virginia's
land policy favored large-scale land speculators, vast numbers of

-Table 1-
Immigration into Barbour County
1780 -1860

Emigrated from	Up to 1800	1800- 1819	1820- 1839	1840 and after	Total
Eastern Virginia	19	26	30	98	172
Potomac's So. Branch	19	8	14	46	87
Northwest Virginia	4	2	8	35	49
Northern States	32	49	31	43	155
Europe	3	6	4	29	42
Totals	77	91	87	251	506

young men, many of them veterans of the Revolution, were nonetheless eager to take up land in Western Virginia. Where claims had already been established, the original patent holders were in many cases willing to sell portions to new settlers.[42] The territory west of the Alleghenies attracted not only Virginians, but large numbers from Pennsylvania, Maryland, New Jersey, Delaware, and even New England. This pattern continued with only minor variation through the 1820s. Beginning in the late 1830s, however, the expansion of the network of state roads completely altered the nature of migration into Barbour County. Improved roads served to increase the attractiveness of farmland in West Virginia—still cheap relative to prices in the East—while at the same time making travel easier for those seeking a better life in the West. Immigration from the South Branch increased with the opening of the Northwest Turnpike from Winchester to Clarksburg in the 1830s, from an average of four or five families a decade through the 1820s to over a dozen made between 1830 and 1840. Construction of the Staunton-Parkersburg Turnpike in the 1840s similarly sparked migration from the Shenandoah Valley and the Piedmont regions, with over 70 families arriving in the 20 years before the war, after a previous pattern of perhaps a dozen per decade.

It is safe to say that the varying patterns of migration were probably not apparent to those living in the county at the time. Newcomers simply took up their holdings alongside those of families who had lived in Barbour for two and three generations. Like the sons and daughters of the earlier settlers, they were for the most part Virginia-born and bred, differing little either in their lifestyles or manners. Yet the infusion of large numbers of immigrants from Eastern Virginia in the decades prior to the war altered the social characteristics of Barbour society in one significant way. Coming as they did from Eastern Virginia, the extent to which they shared traditional western animosities and distrust of the East is open to question. Furthermore, they arrived at precisely that point in the nation's history when agitation over slavery was beginning to create deep divisions throughout the country. Had it not been for the coming of the war, it is inconceivable that these two elements within Barbour would not have ultimately blended together. Both groups simply shared too many common social and economic traits for divisions to have endured. What was needed for this blending to occur was time, but time was not something the course of national events would allow.

- 2 -

WELLSPRINGS OF
LOYALTY

On the eve of the Civil War, the people of Barbour County pretty much spoke and acted alike, living fairly harmonious lives according to a shared rural tradition. In a very short time the war would divide the county into two bitterly opposed camps of roughly equal size, a division that would last for many years after the war. The demarcation between the two was clear—one side supporting secession and the other remaining loyal to the Union. But what specific characteristics distinguished the two sides, and to what extent have historians accurately described the influences which determined the loyalties of West Virginians?

Previous studies have largely concluded that the core of Union loyalty in Western Virginia was essentially political in nature, its members drawn predominantly from the prewar Whig Party.[1] Yet from the time of Barbour County's formation in 1843—and for many years before—Whigs never managed to win more than a quarter of the county's vote in local, state, or national elections. Unfortunately, available sources identify only 11 party members from the county, a statistically meaningless sample. On the other hand, these 11 were the party's leaders, men who ran for office and served as county electors or as delegates to state party conventions. The ten of these men whose stand on secession are known divided equally. Three held public office under the government of West Virginia, one served in the Union armed forces, and another organized one of many pro-Union meetings held in the county. Of the other five, one served in the Confederate army and four others actively supported the Confederate cause.[2]

While it cannot be assumed that rank and file Whig voters were as equally divided in their loyalties, the fact that their local leadership split on the issue of secession is an indication that, in Barbour County at least, the party may not have served as the foundation of Unionist sentiment, as it has so often been depicted. Far more important is the fact that, at the outset of the war, the vast majority of Barbour's electorate were Democratic voters who overwhelmingly cast ballots for states' rights candidate in 1860. In short, it would be difficult to argue that party affiliation significantly influenced wartime loyalties in Barbour.

No study has yet examined the question of whether Union and Confederate sympathizers in West Virginia divided along class lines. Of all the writers on the subject, only Theodore Lang described the war in terms of a clash between social classes. According to Lang, most Confederates were drawn from the wealthiest and poorest segments of society, while the middle class of well-to-do farmers, merchants, and artisans supported the Union. Citing no evidence, Lang's seems to have based his conclusions entirely on his own impressions.[3] Given Barbour's rather compressed social structure, it would be surprising if marked class distinctions existed between Union and Confederate sympathizers. In order to determine this, property values for each individual as reported in the 1860 census are given in Table 2.

The only significant class difference between the two groups seems to have been the slightly higher percentage of Confederates from the wealthier families of the county. Of the ten wealthiest families in the county, seven counted members who sympathized with or fought for the South, including John H. Woodford, Sr., the richest man in the county. There is even evidence of class resentment by Unionists against these well-to-do secessionists, most of whom lived in Philippi. When at the beginning of the war Federal troops drove a scratch rebel army from the town, many leading secessionist families fled with them. "The people of Philippa [as Philippi was originally known] were living like kings," declared one Union-minded woman, "and might have been yet, if they had behaved themselves." Another wrote of his

-Table 2-
Distribution of Property*

Value of Property	Land Owners	Landless	Total	%
Unionists				
Under $500	65	207	272	38.7
$500—2,499	240	2	242	34.5
$2,500- 4,999	98	1	99	14.1
$5,000- 9,999	57	0	57	8.1
Over $10,000	32	0	32	4.6
Totals	492	210	702	100.0
Confederates				
Under $500	26	155	181	36.2
$500—2,499	141	7	148	29.8
$2,500- 4,999	82	0	82	16.5
$5,000- 9,999	46	0	46	9.3
Over $10,000	41	0	41	8.2
Totals	336	162	498	100.0

*The totals for each group do not equal the total number of individuals in-cluded in the study as the 1860 census omitted property values for a number of households.

pleasure at hearing that "The people of Philippa who have been lying on beds of down for so long, are now lying on beds of thorn."[4]

Yet it would be a mistake to characterize the county's wealthy families as being united in their support for Virginia's secession. Numerically, Barbour County's wealthy Unionists—those owning property valued at more than $5,000—almost exactly equaled their Confederate counterparts. Woodford's own son John was wholehearted in his support for the Union while another son, Asa, helped to raise the Tenth West Virginia Infantry for the Union.[5] Andrew Miller, after Woodford the richest man in the county, also counted himself a loyal Union man. Overall, the distribution of property among Barbour's Union and Confederate sympathizers was remarkably similar, and tended to mirror property distribution for the county as a whole. Both sides drew support from all segments of the county's population, from landless day laborer to the richest proprietor, and in roughly equal proportions.

Certainly the primary economic factor propelling the country to war was the institution of slavery. While there is no question that the issues of slavery shaped public opinion in Barbour County, the reality was that slavery was but an incidental element in the county's economy, touching the lives of only a handful of people. The 1860 census listed only 38 slave owners in Barbour, owning 88 slaves. Most of these slaves were females used as domestics by Barbour's wealthier families.[6] The recently widowed Caroline Boner, with 11 slaves the largest slave owner in the county, was the only person to rely on slave labor to any significant degree. Most of her slaves were sold shortly before the war when her late husband's estate was divided among her children.[7]

"Scratch a slave owner anywhere in Virginia," declared Granville Hall, "and you would find a secessionist, so unerring is the instinct of self-interest."[8] In fact, the relationship between slave ownership and secession was by no means as clear-cut as Hall would have it, at least in Barbour County. Isabella Woods, whose husband Samuel was the county's leading proponent of secession, was no less equally steadfast in her allegiance to Virginia and the Confederate cause. Yet she considered slavery to be an inherent evil.[9] David B. Lang, a cousin of Theodore Lang, also opposed slavery. He nonetheless joined the Confederate army in 1862, rose to the rank of lieutenant colonel and died fighting in Eastern Virginia.[10]

Abolitionist sentiment in Barbour was by no means widespread, but it had its adherents and compelled many to oppose secession. The O'Neal family was to a man opposed to the institution. James Proudfoot, one of the county's most prominent citizens, was so moved by the John Brown raid that he freed his slaves outright. Michael Haller, who became captain of the county's Union Home Guard during the war, became an ardent abolitionist after reading the Lincoln-Douglas debates, and was one of the handful in the county to have voted for Lincoln in 1860.[11]

William Wilson and his sons, all of whom would serve in the Federal army or the West Virginia government, were directly engaged in the underground railway, hiding runaway slaves in their cellar.[12] Emmett Pittman's support for the Union was directly shaped by his own experience. As a teenager just before the war he had seen a female slave beaten to death for claiming to be too ill to work. Pittman declared to an incredulous uncle that, "When I grow up, I will be a Lincoln man!"[13]

What is most striking about the role slavery played in Barbour is that it does not seem to have been a factor in determining the direction of wartime loyalties even among those few who actually owned slaves. In fact, Barbour's slave owners were nearly evenly divided between Union loyalists and secessionists. One slave owner and the sons of seven others served in the Confederate army. Five more could be identified as Confederate sympathizers. Four slave owners are known to have sympathized with the Union cause, one serving in the Union armed forces along with the sons of six others. Indeed, some of Barbour's most prominent Union activists were slave owners. Henson Hoff owned slaves, yet he served as chairman of the only pro-Union meeting to have taken place in Barbour prior to the war and was elected to West Virginia's House of Delegates in 1864. One of his sons served as an officer in the Federal army and two others held positions in various offices in local government. John H. Woodford Jr. and Doctor Elam D. Talbott were slave owners and belonged to families whose members largely supported secession. Yet both strongly supported the Union cause, Woodford serving as chairman of the largest pro-Union rally held in Barbour during the war.

Even among the non-slave owning Unionists, there is clear evidence that the issue of slavery had little to do with their support of the Union. Daniel Capito, proprietor of the Philippi Inn, was a staunch supporter of the Union cause yet felt no qualms about hiring slaves from their owners even as late as 1862. When Capito learned that his brothers, who had long before moved to Indiana, had become abolitionists, he reacted with shock and dismay.[14] Nathan Taft was a Philippi lawyer who would become one of the most ardent loyalists in Barbour. In 1861 he was elected county prosecuting attorney, filling a vacancy created after the previous office-holder had "gone South." In that position, he made vigorous efforts to secure the return of runaway slaves who had fled to Ohio. His efforts were supported by David Bryer, another Union man, who wrote to the governor of Ohio on Taft's behalf, urging his help in returning the slaves and pointing out that by doing so he would do much to convince the people of West Virginia that a Federal victory would not mean the eradication of slavery.[15] Even so uncompromising a Unionist as Spencer Dayton, who would become the acknowledged leader of Unionism in the county and whose hatred of secession bordered on the fanatic, did not advocate an end to slavery—at least in the early months of the war. Writing to President Lincoln in June of 1862, he urged that while the war should be vigorously prosecuted, the property rights of slave owners should be maintained. Forfeiture of slaves, he insisted, should be resorted to "just so far as may become a military necessity for the suppression of the rebellion."[16]

If slavery was not a deciding factor shaping sentiment in Barbour, then how influential was the Methodist-Episcopal Church's position on slavery in generating support for the Union? There is little doubt that Episcopal-Methodism was strong in Barbour. Its roots dated back to the beginning of the century when itinerant preachers began visiting pioneer settlements.[17] The 1860 census notes that, of 335 families whose religious affiliations were listed, 201 were members of the Methodist-Episcopal Church.[18]

While individual members of the church vigorously opposed both slavery and secession, the church itself was deeply divided over the slave question and remained so until the very eve of the war. The church's schism of 1844 centered on the question of slave ownership by church bishops, not by individual members, who had been free to own slaves since 1808.[19] After the split into Northern and Southern branches agitation over slavery in the Northern segment continued throughout the 1850s, as abolitionist sentiment in the Northern and New England Conferences exerted pressure to extend the ban on slave ownership to all members.[20] This agitation had the effect of increasing membership in the Southern Methodist Church in border areas like Western Virginia.[21] Fearful of further encroachments on membership, the leadership of the Northern church resisted any move to alter existing rules governing slave ownership. The culmination of the struggle came in 1861, only a few weeks before the war erupted, when the General Conference adopted a new rule declaring slavery to be "inconsistent with the Golden Rule" and admonished "all preachers and people to keep themselves pure from this great evil." This was as far as the church ever came to an outright ban on slave ownership, but it was sufficient to cause massive desertions to the Southern Methodists.[22]

The West Virginia Conference of the church was caught between the growing abolitionist tendencies within the parent body and the increasing strength of the Methodist-Episcopal Church, South. The Conference sought to preserve membership by treading a careful middle ground. Making no effort to alter the 1861 rule condemning slavery, the Conference at the same time refused to concur with it.[23] The result was that on the eve of Virginia's secession a significant number of Methodist-Episcopalians were held to the fold by only the most tenuous of ties.

The degree to which membership in the Methodist-Episcopal Church influenced Union sentiment in Barbour can be determined by comparing the number of Union and Confederate sympathizers who were known to have been members of the church. Biographies and extant church records, in addition to the 1860 census, yield the identities of 278 individuals who could be confirmed as belonging to the church. Although the majority—some 166—were Union sympathizers, 112—40 percent—were Confederate sympathizers, including one of the only two Methodist ministers in the county.[24]

While these figures reveal considerable support for the Union among those belonging to the church, the fact that so significant a portion supported secession and fought for the South indicates that the influence of the church was by no means decisive in shaping sentiment within the county. Indeed, half a dozen members of the church were listed as owning slaves in 1860. In the end, the war had the effect of splitting the church in two. After 1861, control of local churches and meeting houses passed entirely into the hands of Unionists, who barred ministers with secessionist views from preaching and expelled Southern sympathizers.[25] After the war Confederate veterans established the first Southern Methodist churches in Barbour.[26]

While Methodist-Episcopalianism was the largest single denomination in the county, other churches also had heritages dating back to the pioneer era. Indeed, during the early decades of the century, Western Virginia in particular and America in general gave every appearance of being one great religious debate, as Methodists competed with Baptists, Presbyterians, and other evangelical faiths for the souls of Americans. The contest was especially acute in backwater frontier communities like Barbour, where itinerant preachers traveled tirelessly to spread the faith. By mid-century, several denominations in Barbour had long-established churches with sizeable congregations.

The Baptist Church claimed the second largest membership in the county and the distinction of having established the first church in Barbour in 1795.[27] Close to Baptists in terms of membership was the Methodist-Protestant Church. Breaking away from the parent Methodist-Episcopal Church in the late 1820s over the issue of the authority wielded by bishops, Methodist-Protestant preachers found fertile ground for converts in Barbour County. George Nestor, one of the founding fathers of Methodist-Protestantism in West Virginia, was born and raised in the county.[28] Beyond these, Barbour's faithful included German Baptists (popularly referred to as Dunkers by non-members) and United Brethren, as well as small groups of Campbellites, Presbyterians, and Lutherans.

And just as Methodist-Episcopalianism was not the only church in Barbour, neither was it the only denomination to have grappled with the issue of slavery. At one time or another in its early history, each denomination had been opposed to the institution to some degree. And as with the Methodists, most early church leaders in the South had been forced to accommodate themselves to the reality that many thousands of their members were economically and socially welded to slavery. Soon Southern church leaders worked out theological justifications for slavery's existence, creating schisms that divided churches into Northern and Southern branches.[29]

The 1840s were a period of intense ferment for Baptists as abolitionist sentiment grew in Northern congregations. Unlike Methodists, Baptists had no national governing body, individual congregations being considered independent bodies free to make their own decisions on matters including slavery. However, two Baptist institutions dear to the hearts of all members, the Foreign and Home Mission Societies, split into Northern and Southern branches.[30] The slavery issue also created bitter antagonisms within the Methodist-Protestant Church. Despite attempts by its General Conference to avoid an outright break, the Northern and Western Conferences severed ties with the Southern Conference in 1858, revised their church constitutions to include clauses condemning slavery, and barred members from owning or trading in slaves. Although many leading members of the church in Western Virginia were sympathetic to the position adopted by the Northern conferences, the West Virginia Conference remained tied to the Southern branch.[31]

Only the United Brethren and German Baptists avoided disruptions over the slavery issue. From their beginnings, both had vigorously opposed slavery. Existing members were forbidden to own slaves and new members were expected to dispose of any they owned as a condition of joining. The leadership of the United Brethren Church in West Virginia was unalterably opposed not only to slavery, but to secession as well.[32] Unlike the United Brethren, the German Baptists took no position on secession. As one of the historic pacifist churches, the German Baptist Church not only opposed military service, but sought to limit contact with government as much as possible. Its members were expected to remain neutral in any conflict.[33]

In order to determine the extent to which the positions on slavery of these various denominations influenced the political allegiance of individual members, the religious affiliations of 346 Union and 249 Confederate sympathizers were obtained from census lists, biographies, and church records.[34] The results, shown in Table 3, reveal a number of interesting trends. The sympathies of Baptists were almost the exact opposite of Methodists, with the majority supporting the Confederate cause and a sizable minority remaining loyal to the Union. In fact, Federal soldiers stationed in Barbour County perceived the Baptist church in Philippi to be a secessionist stronghold and burned it to the ground.[35] By contrast, the distribution for members of the Methodist-Protestant Church, despite its adherence in West Virginia to the Southern wing of the church with its constitution condoning slavery, almost exactly paralleled the Methodist-Episcopal Church. During the war, control over Methodist-Protestant churches passed into the hands of Union sympathizers; secessionist-minded members simply stopped attending services.[36] In short, neither church's position on slavery appears to have significantly influenced sentiment among the church's members.

-Table 3-
Religious Affiliation

Denomination	Unionists	Confederates	Total
Methodist-Episcopal	166 (61.0%)	112 (39.0%)	278
Baptist	62 (44.9%)	76 (55.1%)	138
Methodist-Protestant	53 (60.0%)	34 (40.0%)	87
United Brethren	41 (89.1%)	5 (10.9%)	46
German Baptist	9 (40.9%)	13 (59.1%)	22
Presbyterian	3	8	11
Lutheran	7	1	8
Catholic	2	1	3
Campbellite	3	0	3
Totals	**346**	**250**	**596**

Perhaps the most surprising fact revealed by these figures is the active participation in the war by members of the German Baptist Church, six of whose members enlisted in the Union army and five in the Confederate. The leader of the congregation in Barbour County, Reverend Henry Wilson, was an ardent secessionist shot to death during the war. Three of Wilson's sons served in the Confederate army, and two were killed in action. Certainly the proscriptions against military service so fundamental to the German Baptist faith failed to overcome more secular demands generated by the war.

The only major denomination whose position on slavery seems to have significantly influenced its members was the United Brethren, whose members overwhelmingly supported the Union. Otherwise there is only slight evidence that affiliation with a particular church measurably influenced sentiment in Barbour County. While most Methodists supported the Union and most Baptists the Confederacy, significant numbers within each church took opposite positions, evidence that one's position on the political questions of the time were more a function of individual conviction than of precepts handed down by church leaders.

In a society only a generation or so removed from pioneer conditions, church affiliation was far more fluid than is often realized. Most churches in Barbour were established in the 1840s and 1850s, some only a few years before the outbreak of the war.[37] Settlers whose families had belonged to a particular church for generations often found no ministers of their faith within miles of their new home. This was especially true for Lutherans who came to Barbour in the first decades of the century and for Irish Catholics who began settling in the county in large numbers in the 1840s and 1850s.[38] Itinerant Methodist, Presbyterian, and German Baptist ministers continued to visit communities in the county up to the outbreak of the war, preaching to congregations outside their own denominations and seeking to convert listeners to their fold. "The spirit of church rivalry," said John R. Philips, "was more competitive than today in the average community."[39] How strong conversions to existing churches among such people may have been is certainly open to question. The willingness of so many German Baptists to renounce pacifism is clearly an indication that the precepts of their church were but superficially accepted.

Far more important in shaping sentiment were influences of a decidedly secular nature, the most important being the degree to which people in Barbour felt bound by ties of loyalty to the state of Virginia. Virginia's secession demanded that the people of the Western counties decide whether their ultimate allegiance was with their state or with the United States.

Table 4, showing the birthplaces of Barbour's Union and Confederate sympathizers, shows that while a number of Unionists were born in Northern and border states, the Civil War in Barbour County was a struggle fought mainly between native-born Virginians.

-Table 4-
Birthplaces of Barbour County's
Unionists and Confederates

Region of Birth	Unionists		Confederates	
Virginia	621	(86.5%)	499	(98.0%)
Georgia	1	(0.1%)		
Border States (Maryland and Kentucky)	37	(5.2%)	2	(0.4%)
Northern States (Pennsylvania, Ohio, Illinois, Connecticut, New York, Maine and New Jersey)	51	(7.3%)	4	(0.8%)
Europe	8	(1.1%)	5	(1.0%)
Totals	718	(100.0%)	509	(100.0%)

It is not surprising that many of the most prominent Unionists in Barbour were men who had only recently settled in Virginia. Spencer Dayton was born and raised in Connecticut, Nathan Taft in New York. Martin Myers, at whose store Dayton and others drew up resolutions opposing secession at the beginning of the war, was born in Pennsylvania. While many of the leading Union men in Barbour County were Northerners who had settled in Virginia, the same cannot be said of the rank and file Unionists of the county.

Yet sectional differences between the two groups begin to emerge when one examines the family backgrounds of those born in Virginia. The birthplaces for the fathers of 621 Virginia-born

Unionists and 499 Confederates could be established from census lists, county records, and biographical material. Among Unionists' fathers, 153 (a quarter) were not native Virginians. Sixty-five were born in Pennsylvania, 51 in Maryland, and 26 in New York, New Jersey, New England, Ohio, and Illinois. Ten others had emigrated from Europe. By contrast, 463 fathers of Virginia-born Confederates, over 90 percent, were also born in Virginia. Of the rest, five were born in Europe and the others in Pennsylvania, Maryland, and Kentucky.

This divergence becomes even greater the farther back the families of each group are traced. The same source material reveals the birthplace of the grandfathers of 422 Virginia-born Unionists and 435 Confederates whose fathers were native Virginians. Combining these with data on non-native Virginians of both groups, we can determine how long—that is, for how many generations—the families of Barbour's Unionists and Confederates had resided in Virginia (See Table 5.)

The differences between Unionists and Confederates are readily apparent. Seventy percent of Barbour's Confederates were descended from families that had lived in the state for at least three generations, compared to only 27 percent for Unionists. Yet even these figures do not reveal the full extent of the sectional differences. Of 133 first and second generation Virginia

-Table 5-
Sectional Heritages of Barbour County Unionists and Confederates

Heritage	Unionists	Confederates
Non-native Virginian	97 (14.4%)	10 (2.1%)
1st generation Virginian	153 (22.8%)	35 (7.3%)
2nd generation Virginian	241 (35.9%)	98 (20.4%)
3rd generation or more	181 (26.9%)	337 (70.2)%
Totals	672(100.0%)	480 (100.0%)

Confederates, 33 (a quarter) were descended from European immigrants who had settled in Virginia. Of 394 Unionists of the same category, only 66, less than 15 percent, were sons or grandsons of European immigrants. The rest were descendants of men born in the North.

For Barbour's Confederates this heritage was almost exclusively Virginian. Their families had for the most part come from Eastern Virginia and had been Virginians for generations. Their primary allegiance was to the state that had been the birthplace of their fathers and grandfathers. As one Confederate explained when recalling why he had enlisted in the rebel army, "I was a Virginian as were my people, and when my state went to war, I saw no other course open but to follow the fortunes of the Old Dominion."[40] A Federal officer was struck by such attitudes. South of Philippi his men arrested a woman for concealing weapons intended for rebels troops. "The woman of the house was very indignant, and spoke in disrespectful terms of the Union men of the neighborhood . . . she said she had 'come from a higher sphere than they, and would not lay down with dogs.' She was an eastern Virginian... poor as a church mouse."[41]

So deep-rooted was this allegiance to Virginia that Confederates actually viewed their state as a nation unto itself. The war diary of James Hall of Barbour County is strewn with references to Virginia as "our country" and "our nation."[42] David Lang wrote in similar terms, telling his wife that if the war dragged on long enough for their sons to reach military age, she should "inspire such patriotism in each of them that they should shoulder their muskets in defense of their country."[43] John R. Philips waxed eloquent when explaining his reasons for joining the Confederacy:

> I prided in being a Virginian. I had seen no other land
> or state save that comprised within her borders. Her blue
> eternal hills claimed all my allegiance and simple and
> ignorant, I gave her all she demanded, my soul, my

manhood were wrapped up in my patriotism for the dear old state . . . She was to me—my country, all of it.[44]

Loyalty to Virginia among those who were not born in the state was almost non-existent, and in this context Samuel Woods was a distinct and prominent exception. Born in Canada near the Maine border, Woods had been raised in Pennsylvania before coming to Barbour County in 1849. His support for states' rights in general and Virginia's secession in particular were positions Unionists in Barbour could neither understand nor forgive. Otherwise, nearly all Yankees in Barbour remained loyal to the Union, their attitudes about Virginia perhaps best expressed by Dayton in a letter to Governor Pierpont in the early months of the war in which he declared Virginia to be "the meanest state in (or out of) the Union . . . ."[45]

Native-born Virginians likely had the most difficulty in deciding whether their allegiance would remain with the national government or with their native-state. At least 18 men from Barbour County are known to have enlisted in one army only to desert and enlist in the other. Most of these desertions took place at the very outset of the war, a confused period when many in the county had yet to throw in their lot with either side. These men generally remained in one army for only a few weeks before switching allegiances. For some, the change of loyalties occurred well after the war had begun and after they had spent a considerable time in one army.

The seeds of sectional conflict in Barbour County were sown decades before the actual outbreak of hostilities. For every family that had crossed the Allegheny Mountains from Eastern Virginia, there was another that had pushed up the tributaries of the Monongahela River from Pennsylvania or had followed wagon trails into Western Virginia from Maryland or New Jersey. A fair number had come from as far away as New England, settling first on French Creek in Upshur County, their descendants spreading across the countryside and into Barbour. All came in search of cheap land, but they brought with them attitudes and traditions which shaped political loyalties for future generations.

When war came, both sides would claim their cause to be a struggle for liberty and against tyranny. Where they clashed was in the concept of how best to preserve the one and defeat the other. Those who fought for the Confederacy did so because they considered themselves above all Virginians, regardless of their personal views on slavery, and they held to the belief that their state rightfully demanded their loyalty, as it had the loyalties of generations who had preceded them. That sense of obligation was far less entrenched among the descendants of those who had come to Virginia from the North. Given the long-standing pre-war grievances over taxation, representation and internal improvements, their allegiance to Virginia, what Theodore Lang dismissed as "that fatal deity of the Virginians," could only have been luke-warm at best. When the degree of that allegiance was tested by the secession crisis, they refused to join themselves to the perceived Eastern oligarchy, which had so grudgingly conceded the political gains of the previous decade. As we shall see, however, opposition to secession did not immediately translate into whole-hearted support of the Union cause. Only when directly threatened by the war did large numbers of those who had opposed secession come to actively participate in the war to preserve the Union.

- 3 -

DARK CLOUDS GATHER

A great deal of what we know about Barbour County on the eve of the Civil War is based on the 1860 Federal census. The enumerator for Barbour that year was Henry Sturm, a member of one of the county's prominent families. His job as enumerator was the latest in a succession of public offices he'd held, including militia officer, justice of the peace, sheriff, and state representative. Required to visit every farm and house in the county, Sturm had not only to count the number of people in every household, but also their farm animals, their crops, and their acreage. He also had to estimate the cash value of each type of property. Beginning in July, Sturm's work took up most of the summer and fall before the final rolls could be copied and mailed.

That same summer saw the first rumblings, for 1860 was also an election year and it was clear that this election was likely to decide if there was even going to be a United States of America. Already the Republican Party had nominated Abraham Lincoln, a candidate who in the eyes of many Southerners threatened the existence of their way of life. The Democratic Party had been split, die-hard delegates from the Deep South refusing to agree to the nomination of Stephen Douglas and choosing as their own candidate John C. Breckenridge. As the crisis deepened, John Bell emerged as a fourth candidate, promising a compromise course to those who believed that the election of Lincoln, Douglas, or Breckenridge would inevitably lead to secession and war. It would be interesting to know what Sturm was thinking as he roamed the countryside that summer, for his job placed him in the unique position of being able to take an unofficial poll of political sentiment in the county. Whatever conclusions he may have arrived at will never be known. Within a few months he would again be listing the names of many of the same young men he had entered on the census schedules, but this time on a muster roll of a volunteer company he raised and placed at the disposal of the governor of a seceded Virginia.

As the presidential campaign unfolded, the great national crisis was mirrored in backwater communities such as Barbour County. Twenty-one year old John R. Philips, who would become a captain in the Confederate army, was then thinking about his future. His parents, moderately well-to-do farmers of Valley Furnace, had been able to send him to school under the tutelage of William Ferguson. Philips was considering a law career, and spending much of his spare time observing activities at the county court house. He recalled the winter of 1860-1861 as a "stormy period. The dark clouds gathered over the land. Discussions were angry and presaged the outbreak of strife." Heated arguments had in fact brought the court to a standstill, its ordinary business pushed aside by debates of local lawyers such as Spencer Dayton, Nathan Taft, Samuel Woods, Albert Reger, and Thomas Bradford.[1] All would later play leading roles in the coming war, and would soon constitute a new hierarchy of leadership in Barbour County.

Of this new group, none would gain as much prominence as Dayton and Woods, Dayton as leader of the county's Union loyalists, Woods as Barbour's pre-eminent secessionist. The two had much in common. Both were lawyers who came to Philippi at the end of the 1840s with little more than the clothes on their backs and a determination to excel in their profession. As Northerners, they had to overcome deep-seated Southern prejudices. When Dayton began submitting his applications to practice law in the various county courts of the area, one local judge insisted Dayton would first have to establish a one-year residency in the state. Dayton promptly made his way—on foot—to Pennsylvania, a state with which Virginia had a standing agreement to admit each other's lawyers to their courts. There he presented the license he had secured in one Virginia circuit, got one for Pennsylvania, marched back with it to the court whose judge had rejected him and demanded he be admitted. The judge, "in evident impatience and ill-humor," reluctantly agreed, but admonished all who would listen, "If any of you have any dealings with this young lawyer, I would advise you to look out for yourselves. He played a genuine Yankee trick on me and I cannot help myself."[2]

The story reveals as much about Dayton's tenacity as it does about the limits of Southern hospitality. If any took the judge's caution to heart, their misgivings were quickly dispelled by the obvious dedication Dayton gave to his work. The same respect was soon earned by Woods, and the two came to be recognized as the leading lawyers of Barbour County and the area. Dayton and Woods formed a law partnership with John S. Carlisle, then a resident of Philippi who would later become one of the foremost leaders of the statehood movement. The economic boom of the 1850s enabled Dayton and Woods to amass considerable fortunes. By 1860 they were without question not only the wealthiest lawyers in Barbour, but also among the largest landowners in the county.[3] Their common backgrounds and a shared love of literature naturally drew them together, and the two soon became close friends. When the war came, they chose opposite sides and the two never spoke to one another again. The destroyed friendship came to personify the divisions suffered by all of Barbour County's people.[4]

The break between Dayton and Woods would not come until the spring of 1861, many months after the presidential election. Officially, Barbour County voted 910 for Breckenridge, 422 for Bell, and 39 for Douglas.[5] It's known that votes were cast for Lincoln, yet the very idea that Virginians would vote for the "Black Republican" was considered so scandalous that these votes were not included in the published returns.[6] At first glance, it would appear Barbour's voters exhibited an overwhelming solidarity with the Cotton States. Yet the widespread support for Breckenridge should not be equated with support for secession. The Northwest of the state in general had long been a stronghold of the Democratic Party, and the 1860 result replicated long-standing voting patterns.[7] Many of the votes for Breckenridge reflected secessionist sentiment in the county, while other votes for him were almost certainly cast for precisely the opposite reason. Breckenridge's campaign downplayed his pro-secessionist statements, urging voters to support him as a means of preserving the Union. Lincoln's victory, so it was argued, would lead inevitably to the secession of the Deep South. At the beginning of 1860, Barbour's Democratic caucus had instructed their representatives to the party's convention to switch their support from Douglas to Breckenridge for this very reason.[8]

In holding to traditional party allegiances, Barbour's electorate behaved no differently than voters across the border-state region.[9] Nonetheless, the 1860 election masked growing divisions within Barbour, divisions based on two radically different visions of how best to preserve political liberties. Years after the war, Woods addressed a convention of the Daughters of the Confederacy and used the occasion to explain why he and so many others like him had felt compelled to fight for the Confederacy. Woods emphatically denied that slavery was the fundamental cause of the war, reminding his audience that in the entire Confederacy, with a population of over eleven million, there were but 450,000 slave owners. "How is it possible . . . that eight and one half millions of people consecrated their lives and fortunes, and gave the best they had, for the service of 450,000 of their number, whose pecuniary interests . . . ran counter to the interest of all the other millions?" The answer, he declared, was that the war was a struggle for liberty. "The people believed they were engaged in a life and death struggle for the independent government of themselves by the states, which they set above all price, and worthy of any sacrifice."[10]

Woods's definition of the Southern cause was echoed by others in Barbour. Well into the war, during one of many bone-wearying marches that Stonewall Jackson demanded of his men, John R. Philips paused to reflect upon just what it was he and his compatriots were struggling for. "If you had seen what I had seen, no doubt would ever cross your mind in regard to the earnestness of our people. All they ask is independence and this they will have or this nation will bleed away its noblest blood. . . . May God give us liberty!"[11]

Those in Barbour who came to support secession did so because they were convinced that only by leaving the Union could liberty be preserved. In their view the Federal Union was formed by independent, sovereign states for the express purpose of securing personal liberties. When that compact was broken, each state had the right and duty to withdraw. Thomas Bradford made the point clear when seeking election to the Richmond Convention in January, 1861. "The Constitution was ratified by the individual States, each acting for itself as an independent sovereignty, and when the powers delegated by that constitution are perverted to the injury and oppression of any or either of the States, they have the indisputable right to resume them. . . . I am for Virginia's resuming the powers she delegated to the General Government, and forming such other government as may best secure the liberty, safety, and happiness of her people."[12]

Barbour's Union loyalists likewise saw the conflict as a struggle for liberty, and for them secession and its supporters were the very instruments of tyranny. Early in the war, Dayton denounced the "abhorred league of slave holders whose guilty agents are warring against their country, and the liberties of mankind."[13] For men like Dayton these liberties, threatened by a Southern oligarchy bent on preserving its exclusive control of the organs of government, could only be guaranteed by the Federal Union.

Later in the war, Barbour's Unionist citizens would hold mass meetings in support of the war effort, each time proclaiming in resolutions that the Southern Confederacy "sought to suppress human liberty and free institutions upon this continent." They swore they would do whatever they could to defeat "our brothers of eastern Virginia who strove to sever our allegiance from the best of governments and attach us with themselves in a border serfdom to a miserable oligarchy of felons and traitors."[14]

Unionists like these were the direct heirs of the earlier struggle for Western rights that had left in its wake a deep-seated distrust of the Eastern section of the state. When secession came, Eastern leaders from the governor on down would call upon the people of the Western counties to remember that they were above all else Virginians, and that any wrongs left unsatisfied would surely be put right. This was one of the great miscalculations of the war, for Western Unionists had become heirs to something else as well. They had come to consider themselves not so much citizens of Virginia as citizens of a single nation. Secessionists failed to understand how deeply the idea of national unity had taken root in the region and how much any attempt to destroy that unity would be considered not only morally wrong, but treason.

To be sure, one of the principal rights that Barbour's secessionists sought to preserve was that of slave ownership. The refusal of abolitionists to allow the extension of slavery into the territories, the refuge provided runaway slaves by Northern states, and the widespread sympathy with which John Brown's raid on Harper's Ferry had been greeted in the North were all perceived as direct attacks on Southerners' constitutional rights. Bradford's campaign statement began as a studied analysis of the legality of secession. But he almost trembled with indignation when reciting the perceived wrongs which the South had suffered at the hands of their Northern countrymen over the issue of slavery.

All the evils which now threaten the very existence of our Government have been produced by the lawless and unconstitutional aggressions of the non-slave holding states . . . . They have traduced and slandered us before the nations of the earth. They have sent their hired mercenaries among us for the express purpose of inciting our slaves to insurrection. . . . They have sent their Myrmidons among us to murder our people and steal and destroy our property, and when these infamous malefactors escape into those States they are protected by their executives from the just penalties which our laws denounce against them.[15]

Bradford castigated Northern abolitionists who had elected Lincoln, whom he declared to be "openly pledged to the miserable dogma that the negro is the equal of the white man."[16] Thompson Surghnor, the fiery editor of Barbour County's only newspaper, repeatedly lashed out against "Union shriekers who are attempting to Abolitionize Virginia."[17] Statements like these inflamed fears that a Union victory would mean the immediate freedom of all slaves, and propelled many into the Confederate ranks when war finally came. After Confederate forces were driven from Barbour County and surrounding counties at the beginning of the war, a Union army officer noted that many of the rebel prisoners, a number of whom were from Barbour, had told him that "they were deceived and entered the service because they were led to believe that the Northern army would confiscate their property, liberate their slaves, and play the devil generally."[18]

While attitudes about slavery, especially among Union loyalists, would soon be transformed by the war that slavery had brought about, the immediate concerns of Barbour's citizenry just before the war centered on the rights and wrongs of secession, and in that context support for the Union among slave owners was no more a contradiction than support for the secession among those opposed to slavery. "Some threats were made," recalled Philips of this period. "The strong arm of the national government was pointed to by the one party and the other retorted by reminding their opponents that there was a possibility of treason against Virginia."[19] Advocates and opponents of secession were forcing people to choose between two irreconcilable concepts of political liberty, the structure of government and the very definition of what it meant to be an American.

Precisely when the growing national crisis first began to be felt in Barbour County is somewhat less clear, and traditional historical sources do not provide an answer. Historian Hu Maxwell stated that Barbour had been divided into two camps well before the outbreak of the war. John R. Philips claimed that as late as early 1861 "people were reluctant to leave the Union and hugged the idea of compromise and peace."[20] There is, however, persuasive evidence of increasing tensions in Barbour as early as 1858. This evidence comes from an examination of marriage patterns in Barbour in the decade prior to the war. Traditionally, marriages in most rural societies represent far more than the union of two people who share affection for one another. It constitutes a kind of quasi-alliance between families, each of which is expected to provide the bride and groom with a portion of the family patrimony. The importance of such considerations was widespread enough to have provoked comment by travelers. Noting an apparent absence of affection between husbands and wives, one writer of the time reported that "marriages are made to unite contiguous tracts of land or to keep desirable possessions in the same family."[21] One elderly Barbour County farmer in 1861, sensing that a visiting Indiana soldier was somewhat taken aback by the haggard appearance of his wife, explained that he had married the woman, "not for looks, but for service."[22]

In search of evidence that national issues were affecting the lives of Barbour Countians, marriages of known Union and Confederate soldiers and sympathizers and members of their immediate families were selected from county marriage records for the years 1853 to 1865.[23] These were then grouped into three categories: marriages in which both bride and groom were either themselves Union sympathizers or were members of a family that included Union sympathizers; marriages between two Confederate sympathizers or persons belonging to families that included Confederate sympathizers; and finally, marriages in which the bride and groom or members of their families took opposite sides during the war. Table 6 shows the marriage patterns revealed in this analysis.

The results are striking. Fully half the marriages in Barbour between 1853 and 1857 involved persons who chose as their partners people who would later hold opposing views during the war, or married into families which would include persons of opposing loyalties. Beginning in 1858, however, there was an increasing tendency for Barbour County's newlyweds to select partners from families whose members would share similar sentiments during the war. This tendency became more pronounced during

-Table 6-

Marriage Patterns in Barbour: 1853-1865

Years	Unionist to Unionist	Confederate to Confed.	Unionist to Confederate	Number
1853-1855	30.4%	17.4%	52.2%	69
1856-1857	23.2%	24.4%	52.4%	82
1858-1859	40.5%	17.5%	41.9%	74
1860-1861	39.2%	33.3%	27.5%	51
1862-1863	64.4%	15.1%	20.8%	53
1864-1865	52.0%	26.6%	21.4%	94

the war years, until by the last years of the conflict the proportion of individuals marrying into families of opposing views dropped to one in five.

Marriage patterns in Barbour County not only reveal the extent to which everyday life had become infused with politics, but they also shed light on when the divisions became most pronounced. While the proportion of marriages between members of Unionist and Secessionist families began to drop as early as 1858-1859, the most dramatic decline occurred in the years 1860-1861. That divisions crystallized during this period and not earlier is further evidence that the paramount concern of Barbour's citizenry was not so much the issue of slavery, which had existed in the region almost since the arrival of the first settlers, but the question of secession. For it was precisely during the years 1860 and 1861 that secession first became not only a possibility to be debated, but a reality to be faced.

Within a month of the 1860 presidential election, South Carolina withdrew from the Union, followed soon after by the rest of the Cotton States. In February, 1861, Governor Letcher called for a state convention to decide on the course Virginia should take. The two candidates who stood for election to the seat designated for Barbour were Woods and Bradford. Like Woods, Bradford was a lawyer who had come to Barbour several years before the war. Unlike Woods, he came from deep in

Eastern Virginia. Although both candidates acknowledged the right of Virginia or any other state to secede from the Union, Bradford campaigned on a platform demanding Virginia's immediate secession. Woods, on the other hand, hoped that some formula could be worked out that would avoid so irrevocable a step. At the conclusion of his published campaign statement, he reminded his readers that the Federal Union had secured peace and prosperity for all Americans and declared that, "Every effort and sacrifice, not inconsistent with the sovereign rights and honor of Virginia, should be made to preserve the same from destruction." Conditioning the Union's preservation on Virginia's own sovereignty should have alerted those in Barbour who opposed secession that Woods's Unionism was by no means absolute. Yet throughout the campaign he passionately urged his listeners to "stand by the Union . . . and not disturb the sisterhood of the states."[24] Largely because his platform combined elements satisfactory to both sides of the issue, Woods defeated Bradford by a 301-vote majority.[25]

However conditional Woods's Unionism may have been, the fact that he prevailed over an outright Secessionist indicates that most people in Barbour at that time were not prepared to see Virginia follow the Deep South states out of the Union. That sentiment was shared across the state. The majority of the delegates elected to the Convention had declared themselves at least nominally pro-Union. In fact, this Unionist majority was more apparent than real. Most of those who counted themselves in the group were men who, like Woods, already accepted the validity of the doctrine of secession, but opposed Virginia joining the Confederacy so long as the Federal government made no attempt to force the seceded states back into the Union. Solid Unionists—those opposed to secession under any circumstances—were limited to members elected from the Northwest and certain sections of the Shenandoah Valley.[26]

The Convention opened on February 13, and for several weeks its members exchanged positions on the rights and wrongs of secession and the conditions under which they would or would not support it. Moderates—those opposing both secession and

Federal coercion—and unconditional Unionists maintained an uneasy majority throughout this period. Within two weeks of the opening session, Woods presented a series of resolutions declaring that the allegiance of citizens to their states superseded that owed to the Federal government; and resolving that if the Union used force against the Deep South states, Virginia should join them and "her citizens would be in duty bound to render allegiance and obedience to her alone." Pointedly, no mention was made of any desire to avert such an outcome. His resolutions provoked heated debate in the Convention and gave clear notice that Woods was beginning to distance himself from the Unionist majority within the body.[27]

As Secessionists in the Convention increased their agitation, their political kindred in Barbour County were at their most active. Despite the existence of widespread Unionism in the county, Secessionists were better organized and had the advantage of the participation of most of the county's elected officials. As a result, Barbour early on earned a reputation as a hotbed of secession in a region where Unionist sentiment prevailed. While pro-Union rallies were being held in neighboring Preston, Taylor, and Harrison counties, Barbour's most influential citizens were organizing pro-secessionist meetings. As early as January, a self-proclaimed States' Rights meeting on Hackers Creek issued resolutions declaring that "The cause of South Carolina is our cause, and we shall see her righted to the bitter end, and when she falls, Virginia must fall with her." Further rallies took place in February and March, each drawing up resolutions of similar tone and content.[28]

Newspaperman Thompson Surghnor did much to inflame public opinion toward the growing Secessionist camp. Decrying the "Union shriekers" then dominating the Richmond convention, he declared to his readers that "We have no faith in the Convention. . . . It was never the intention of a majority of that convention to do anything but to further their designs against the Democratic party of Virginia. . . . Men who continue to talk of the Union and of saving the Union, are either knaves or fools."[29] By March virtually all of Barbour's elected officials had declared themselves in favor of immediate secession. Even Isaac Strickler, the Federal postmaster at Philippi, saw fit to intercept "abolitionist" literature and ceremoniously burn it in the street. During all this time not a single public meeting in favor of preserving the Union was even attempted.

On March 7 the largest mass meeting ever held in Barbour County took place at the county courthouse. There Secessionists issued resolutions declaring their support for Woods' stand at the Convention, and demanded that "the State of Virginia should lose no time in making common cause with her sister States of the South." Only one man, Spencer Dayton, rose to condemn these sentiments, but before he could finish speaking, one of those in attendance pointed a rifle at his chest and Dayton was forced to flee for his life. From that point on until Federal troops occupied the county in June, the Palmetto flag flew unhindered from the courthouse.[30]

A month after the courthouse meeting, Confederate troops in South Carolina opened fire on Fort Sumter. The next day Lincoln called upon the states to furnish men and arms to suppress the rebellion. Governor Letcher promptly and sternly refused. Faced with the reality of armed Federal intervention, the Unionist majority in the Convention quickly evaporated. Woods, now solidly aligned with the Secessionist camp, placed his name at the head of a list of delegates calling upon mobs in the city to come down to the Convention hall and add their voices to those demanding Virginia secede at once.[31] When an ordinance of secession was presented and put to a vote on April 17, only 55 of the Convention's 155 members voted against it. Of these, 31 represented counties that would later be incorporated into West Virginia. Only five delegates from the Northwest, including Woods, voted for secession.[32]

Unionists in Barbour County were shocked by Woods' apparent about face, and none more so than Dayton. For him, Woods had not only betrayed his country people, but their friendship as well. Some now declared Woods' prior campaign statement and speeches to have been nothing more than "covert disunion masked in the livery of heaven," others that Woods had now shown "the cloven foot."[33] The fact was that Woods had not fundamentally altered his position on secession. A careful reading of his campaign statement in January and the resolutions he presented to the Convention the following month reveal nothing contradictory in his views on either states' rights or secession. His argument was that the Federal government could never be the guarantor of individual liberties, and that each state possessed the right and duty to withdraw from the Union when those liberties were challenged. This duty applied even to those who, like Woods, had transferred the obligations of citizenry from one state to another.

Woods's perceived about-face was actually a reaction to changed circumstances. At the beginning of the year, efforts were being undertaken at the national level to work out a compromise to the secession crisis. John Crittenden of Kentucky had issued his proposals for a settlement in December, representatives of the border states had drawn up another plan in January, and an ad-hoc congressional committee had begun hammering out yet another. All three quickly failed, and by the time the election for delegates to the Richmond Convention took place on February 4, the last hope for a solution rested with the Peace Conference scheduled to convene in Washington on the same day. Whatever hopes it held out for success were quickly dashed when none of the seceded states agreed to participate. By the time Woods gave his maiden speech on February 18, it was clear to all that the Conference was similarly doomed to failure.[34] Woods had consistently opposed any act by the Federal government to coerce the seceded states back into the Union and, with the possibility of compromise all but dead, his resolutions emphasized his conviction that Virginia must also oppose coercion. With Lincoln's call to arms, Woods's break was complete.

Without question, Woods's vote was applauded by Barbour's Secessionists, who now embraced him as their own spokesman. For Union loyalists who had sent him to Richmond, his perceived betrayal of the faith they had placed in him was based primarily on their own delusion about Woods. But perceptions are everything and Unionists would never forget or forgive Woods for his treachery. From that moment on, he was singled out for retribution.

A popular vote was required to ratify the Convention's decision, but in reality Virginia had already seceded. The day prior to the Convention vote, state troops took possession of the Federal arsenal at Harper's Ferry and seized the U.S. Navy yard at Norfolk. Within days Letcher called out the state militia to repel an expected Federal invasion. When the election finally took place on May 24, it passed by an overwhelming majority of the state's voters. Yet voters in the Northwest rejected secession by a ratio of three to one.[35] Barbour is officially said to have returned a majority of 231 votes in favor of secession. That vote, together with the widespread secessionist agitation preceding it and the leading role played by so many of the county's prominent citizens in the movement, earned for Barbour County a reputation as a secessionist maverick in a Unionist region.

But there is considerable doubt as to whether the majority of Barbour's voters actually favored secession. While one count reported a 231 majority in favor of secession, another claimed a majority of 350 against the ordinance.[36] The returns for the county have been lost, making it impossible to resolve the question, but it is certainly possible that votes against the ordinance may simply have been tossed out by secessionist-minded county officials. Further, by the time the election took place, Secessionists in the county had already organized three companies of volunteers, who were soon reinforced by companies from other counties. Certainly a good deal of intimidation must have taken place at polling places, particularly as voting was by open declaration rather than by secret ballot. At least one local Union man claimed that soldiers who occupied Philippi were allowed to vote despite the fact that they weren't residents of the county.[37]

Even before the elections took place, a counter movement to secession had gained momentum in the Northwest. A few days after the secession ordinance passed the Convention, delegates from the region left Richmond to begin organizing resistance. Among them was the former law partner of Dayton and Woods, John S. Carlisle, now a resident of Clarksburg. On April 22 he led a public meeting there at which he presented the "Clarksburg Resolutions" denouncing the Convention vote and calling for a general convention at Wheeling on May 13 to determine what course the people of the Northwest should take. These resolutions were disseminated throughout the territory, and when the First Wheeling Convention met, some 400 delegates representing 26 counties took the first step on the path that led to West Virginia's statehood.[38]

Unionists in Barbour County, intimidated by the Secessionists' show of force, were hard pressed to respond to Carlisle's summons. Already Secessionists had begun to arrest those they deemed traitors to Virginia, and many Unionists had gone into hiding or had fled the county altogether. A handful who remained organized a secret meeting at the shop of Martin Myers in Philippi, a gathering later dubbed by locals as the "Shoe Shop Convention." There they drew up resolutions repudiating secession, and chose four of their number to represent Barbour at the first Union convention at Wheeling. But with all roads out of Philippi closely guarded, three of the delegates excused themselves from attempting the journey. Only Spencer Dayton had the courage to match his convictions with action. Quietly saddling his horse at midnight, he galloped past the pickets at a dead run and made his way to Wheeling.[39]

Immediately upon passage of the ordinance of secession, Virginia began organizing for war. Colonel George Porterfield was ordered by Richmond to gather together volunteer and militia companies from nineteen counties in the Northwest, organize them into five regiments, and defend both that section of the state and the all-important Baltimore and Ohio railroad. To his dismay, not a single man was there to greet him when he reached the rendezvous point at Grafton on May 14.[40] Realizing the extent of anti-secessionist sentiment in the region, he wired Richmond that he would assemble whatever troops he could get his hands on at Philippi, 15 miles to the south, and from there march back to Grafton and hold the railroad. Philippi was as good a place as any to start, particularly as Barbour County had raised three companies for the state. But over the next two weeks, only four additional companies from neighboring Taylor, Harrison, Marion, and Upshur counties joined Porterfield. He begged Richmond for reinforcements, but his pleas were largely unheeded in the hard-pressed Confederate capital. Only a few additional infantry and cavalry companies from the Shenandoah Valley were sent, bringing the Confederate force at Philippi to about 775 men.[41]

To Philippi's citizenry, the troops camped about them seemed a formidable host. John R. Philips, now a lieutenant in one of Barbour's companies, remembered that "People saw what appeared to them a multitude. . . . The exaggerated idea went forth that an army was in their midst."[42] Porterfield, a veteran of the War with Mexico, had no illusions about what this paltry force could do. Holding a single town would be difficult enough, much less defending the entire Northwest. Even those who had responded to the governor's call would be of little use in a fight— they were untrained, undisciplined, and for the most part unarmed. Some weapons seized the month before from Harpers Ferry were sent to Philippi, but not enough to arm all of the men. Those that were distributed were almost useless. Philips described them as "old, heavy rifles, rusted and out of order." The Barbour Greys got none and were forced to arm themselves with shotguns they'd brought with them. The 75 men of the Barbour Lighthorse entered the field with 40 sabres, a pistol and one knife. Another company, according to one of its members, possessed only "squirrel rifles with a few rounds of ammunition, some old Dirk knives and . . . revolvers. These guns were not dangerous unless they were thrown at a man." A militia company commanded by James Dilworth of Barbour County armed themselves with scythes, corncutters, and pitchforks. Even with these crude implements, they were better armed than the company from Upshur County which arrived at Philippi without one weapon of any kind.[43]

Porterfield was nonetheless determined to make some kind of stand, and marched his little army out of Philippi on May 23, bound for Grafton. They left amid a great deal of fanfare. "Bouquets were thrown at us by *fairy* hands," recalled James Hall, a member of the Barbour Greys, "and aged citizens came out to welcome us."[44] When Porterfield reached Grafton the next day, he learned that 23,000 United States troops under General George McClelland had crossed the Ohio the day before. Sent by Washington to secure the all-important B & O railway and to support Unionists in the Northwest, McClelland's army was headed straight for Porterfield. Ignoring orders and not even bothering to notify Richmond, the Confederate commander beat a hasty retreat back to Philippi.

The holiday atmosphere that had surrounded their departure from the town quickly dissipated with their inglorious return. According to Philips, "Philippi was a pandemonium." With actual fighting now imminent, many of the men began to reassess the prospect of plunging into battle. "No order, our drill foolishness," explained Philips. "No system about anything." The conduct of their officers gave the men little reason for encouragement. "Our officers knew nothing of war. They obeyed but little, expected but little, and helped increase the general disorder. . . The colonel that was commanding us sat in the Courthouse, a polished Virginia gentleman, but as ignorant of war as much as of the ten commandments."[45]

Porterfield had intended to continue on to more defensible positions in Randolph County, where further reinforcements awaited him. However, McClelland drove his own troops with a zeal he would never again exhibit in the war, reached Grafton on the May 30, and by June had two columns of 3,000 men each marching hard on Philippi from the west and the northeast. In the morning of June 3, both began to take up positions in the heights above town; not a single man in Porterfield's army had an inkling of their presence. Although Porterfield had sent out pickets the night before to guard all approaches to town, it had rained hard all night and the pickets reasoned that no Yankee would venture out on such a night and certainly neither should they. The Confederates were thus completely taken by surprise when the first cannon shot smashed into their camp.

Just before the firing began, the ill-starred Porterfield was blessed with one stroke of good fortune—the only one, it seems, of his brief campaign. The two Federal columns had aimed at reaching Philippi at 4 a.m. The 3,000 men who came in from the west reached Philippi at about 3:30 a.m., manhandled two field-pieces up a hill across the river and waited for the signal—a pistol shot—that would alert them that the other jaw of the trap was in position. Meanwhile the troops of that other column had been slogging their way towards Philippi in the downpour, across backcountry roads in ankle-deep mud, and they reached their position at about 4:00 a.m. Just above Philippi, the soldiers awakened Mrs. Matilda Humphreys, whose husband and older sons were camped with Porterfield's Confederates. She sent her youngest son to warn the unwary troops. He didn't get far before soldiers grabbed his horse and pulled him from his saddle, at which point his enraged mother drew a pistol from her skirt and fired at his attackers.[46]

The Federals across the river heard the shot and, assuming it to be the signal they'd been waiting for, opened fire. In fact, the troops struggling with Mrs. Humphreys—she'd continued the battle with rocks and sticks before finally retreating into her house—weren't quite into position when the first artillery rounds crashed into town. Porterfield's cavalry immediately galloped out of town, followed quickly by his infantry. Some few wanted to at least make a show of a fight, but, as one of them later put it, "Cooler heads realized the folly of the undertaking."[47]

The near bloodless battle—only ten men are known to have been wounded—was over in a matter of minutes. It is safe to say that the United States troops, who had themselves enlisted only a few weeks before, were as much astonished at the outcome as were the Confederates. Estimating Porterfield's force at perhaps 2,500 men, they expected a hard fight and were totally unprepared for what happened when they opened fire. "They scattered like rats from a burning barn," one eyewitness reported gleefully. "They didn't even retreat at all—they ran, fled most ingloriously—ran like sheep in every direction that promised safety." Another Union soldier recalled with evident relief that "What promised at first to be a tragedy ended in a farce."[48] Ironically, while the Federal troops were all well-armed, the rain through which they had marched all night rendered most of the weapons useless. If few of Porterfield's men had rifles, few of the Federals had rifles that would fire. "It was well for us that the rebels retreated," recalled one Indiana soldier after it was all over, "as I don't believe ten guns in either company of our regiment could have been fired." Noting that Porterfield's men were still sleeping when the attack came and were, quite literally, caught with their pants down, some dubbed the affair "The Shirt-Tail Retreat." The name that finally stuck was "The Philippi Races."[49]

Many leading secessionists fled with Porterfield, leaving their families to deal with the Yankees. Dozens of women grabbed their children and fled to the woods, emerging with white handkerchiefs fluttering at the first approach of Union troops. Samuel Woods, who had returned to Philippi only a few days before, quickly saddled his horse. His wife Isabella, who had listened with concern to the speeches he had given the townsfolk describing the rapaciousness of the Yankees, asked him what she was to do. Pausing to reflect for a moment, he told her, "Oh, I guess they won't molest you," and with those words of encouragement rode off.[50]

The general conclusion among Porterfield's men was that he was, at best, thoroughly incompetent or, at worst, had sold them out.[51] The hapless colonel would later be court martialed for the fiasco and never again saw active service. Most of the Barbour men under his command that day would eventually be organized into the Thirty-First Virginia Infantry. Those who remained behind in Barbour County, Confederate and Unionist alike, would live under Federal control for the rest of the war, though none of them could foresee any of this at the time. All they knew then was that the war had begun in earnest, and on their very doorstep. Whatever position they would take in the conflict, it would become the focal point of their lives for the next four years.

- 4 -

PATTERNS OF
ENLISTMENT

Virginia's ordinance of secession was passed by the Richmond Convention on April 17, 1861. With ratification by voters a foregone conclusion, Governor Letcher immediately called out the state militia to repel an inevitable Federal invasion. Throughout Eastern Virginia the call was greeted with widespread—almost delirious—enthusiasm, as tens of thousands of men flocked to recruiting posts. The response in the Northwest could not have been more different. In most counties the call was ignored entirely, while in others only a handful of men signed up. Barbour County was almost alone in the region in rallying to the support of the Old Dominion.[1] Within days of Letcher's call Henry Sturm, Albert Reger, and William Jenkins each began recruiting volunteer companies for the state, and by the end of the month had enrolled over 200 men. Colonel Daniel Auvil, commander of the county's militia, brought out another 400 men, most of whom were soon sent home for want of arms. This was by far the largest number of troops contributed by any county in the Northwest that spring.

According to popular image, the defeat of the Confederates in 1861 liberated the Northwest from rebel control and gave Union authorities a free hand to recruit loyal West Virginians into the United States Army. In reality, between 10,000 and 15,000 Western Virginians would enlist in the Confederate army, most of them after 1861. In Barbour County, the men who signed up early amounted to a little over half of the total who would eventually join the Confederate army. Federal victories during that summer of 1861, far from producing a groundswell of support for the Union cause in Barbour County, generated but a handful of recruits. In the six months following Porterfield's defeat at Philippi, only 60 men from Barbour enlisted in Federal regiments. It was only in August, 1862—fourteen months after the war began—that Barbour's Union men began to join the army in significant numbers.

If enlisting in the army was the ultimate proof of one's loyalty to the Northern or Southern causes, then the pace of enlistment in Barbour indicates that for most Unionists and a large percentage of Confederates, the decision was shaped largely by developments long after the war had begun. Ultimately, a total of 908 men from Barbour served in the armed forces—47 percent of all males of military age then living in the county. This truly staggering figure must have placed enormous strains not only on Barbour's economy, but on each family that sent men off to war. What is even more remarkable is that very few were drafted, the vast majority joining voluntarily. The volunteering spirit, especially among Unionists, was first fanned by the war's repeated intrusions into the lives of the people, bringing the realization that an end to the war would require personal sacrifices. The enlistment patterns were thus shaped by the progress of the war and the degree to which people were willing and able to meet its challenges.

While Barbour County's Secessionists were busily organizing their volunteer companies in May, Daniel Wilson and five others slipped across the county line and made their way to Grafton, where they joined a Union company being organized by George R. Latham. These were the first of 445 men from the county to enlist in the United States Army. A few days after Wilson enlisted, he gained the dubious distinction of being involved in an incident that resulted in the death of the first soldier of the war.[2] A Confederate company was at that time being organized at nearby Fetterman, and Latham sent Wilson and one Bailey Brown over to investigate. Challenged by rebel sentries, Brown fired his pistol and shot off the ear of one of the guards. The guard promptly fired back, killing Brown instantly. An amazed Wilson stared down at the body of his companion, exclaimed, "Why, I believe you are dead," and hurried back to Grafton.

The following month, 20 more Barbour County men traveled to Clarksburg and enrolled in what would become the Third West Virginia Infantry. By that time Confederate forces had been cleared from Barbour County. Yet even after subsequent Federal victories at Rich Mountain and Laurel Hill in July, the reluctance of Barbour's Union men to join the army is striking. Between July and December only forty men signed up in Federal regiments, most of them traveling to Grafton to enlist in the Sixth and Seventh West Virginia Infantry. In part, this meager response can be explained by the absence of any Federal recruiters. Although dozens of volunteer companies had been formed in Northwestern counties at the outbreak of the war, no effort was made to organize any in Barbour County. It wasn't until August that the War Department authorized Governor Pierpont to raise ten regiments in West Virginia. Even then, none of these actively recruited in Barbour but set up recruiting posts in neighboring counties where their ranks were quickly filled by local volunteers. It wasn't until early 1862 that Federal recruiters finally appeared in Barbour County.

The previous fall, Thomas Harris of Gilmer County had been appointed colonel of the Tenth West Virginia Infantry and had set about issuing commissions for men to begin raising companies. Marshall Coburn of Barbour County received his commission in January, but found the task of recruiting soldiers for the Union more difficult than he had anticipated. By June he had been able to enroll but 50 men, 47 of them from Barbour County. So meager was the response that Nathan Taft, the adjutant of the county's militia, proposed drafting known Confederate sympathizers into the army to fill up the quota.

If the task of securing recruits was proving difficult for Union authorities, the problem was even more desperate for their Confederate counterparts. The Richmond government still considered the Northwestern counties to be legally part of Virginia. While it was clear that the majority of the people who lived there had thrown their support to the Union cause, it was also recognized that a significant portion remained loyal to Virginia and represented a pool of manpower the hard-pressed army could ill afford to ignore. The problem was in tapping it. At the beginning of 1862 only two regiments of the Confederate army—the Twenty-fifth and Thirty-first Virginian Infantry—included men drawn from Northwestern counties above the Kanawha River. Even in these regiments, only 12 of 20 companies had been recruited west of the Alleghenies.[3] Both companies had already seen heavy fighting and had suffered considerable losses. Although reinforced to some extent by enlisted men from Eastern Virginia, army recruiters tended to adhere to a policy of making up losses by recruiting in the counties in which units had originally been raised. Unless efforts were made to recruit in West Virginia, these regiments would continue to decline in strength. "If they keep our Regt. here," complained James Hall while stationed in Monterey, "they will never get another West Virginia volunteer."[4]

So long as Federal troops controlled West Virginia, the only means by which men could be enlisted into the Confederate army was to either wait for them to make their way to Confederate lines or send officers into West Virginia to bring them out. Both were extremely dangerous undertakings. The Federal army was constantly on the lookout for anyone trying to pass into Eastern Virginia. Confederate recruiters sent into Western Virginia had to be known to the people among whom they worked, which meant they would also be known to local Unionists. Those officers who volunteered for the job usually carried a list of "safe houses," homes of Confederate sympathizers who could be counted on to harbor the recruiters and their enlistees. Traveling at night on little-used trails to avoid detection, recruiters were forced to contact only small parties of a dozen or so at a time, returning again and again until their companies were brought up to strength.[5]

One of the earliest attempts to draw upon the potential Confederate manpower of West Virginia met with immediate disaster. In April, 1862, seven men sent into Marion County were informed upon almost as soon as they reached the county. Three were killed and the rest fled back to Eastern Virginia.[6] More successful was Thomas Armesy of Barbour County. From the summer of 1862 to the spring of 1863, he ranged throughout Harrison and neighboring counties, bringing in scores of recruits for the Seventeenth Virginia Cavalry. His efforts were abruptly halted when he was taken prisoner in April, 1863, and sentenced as a spy to hard labor.[7] By far the most active Confederate recruiter in the Northwest was John D. Imboden. A native of Staunton and a prominent politician prior to the war, Imboden had distinguished himself at First Bull Run while in command of a battery. In April, 1862, he obtained a special commission to organize a corps of rangers, to be recruited mainly from the Northwestern counties under Federal control. His rangers were intended to act as an irregular mounted force operating behind enemy lines, harassing Federal outposts, waylaying wagon trains, and generally, as Imboden himself put it, "To make the country too hot to permit a Yankee to show his head outside of his camp."[8]

Although most of Imboden's men were ultimately recruited in Confederate-held Highland, Pendleton and Pocahontas counties, a large number were drawn from behind Union lines, mainly in Randolph, Tucker, Braxton, Lewis, and Barbour counties. The first recruits from Barbour joined Imboden in June, 1862. That month Granville Carlin and Mortimer Johnson, both Barbour men who had joined the army the previous spring, slipped into the county where they secretly gathered about a dozen recruits which became the nucleus of Company F, First Partisan Rangers.[9] Like Armesy, Carlin's recruiting career ended soon after it had started when he was captured the following September. When the troops guarding Carlin and those taken with him were ambushed, they began shooting down the prisoners, wounding Carlin before he was able to escape.[10]

The pace of both Union and Confederate recruitment in Barbour increased dramatically in August, 1862, propelled by events both within and beyond the county's borders. On August

4, Lincoln issued a call to the states to contribute another 300,000 men for the army. If state quotas could not be met with volunteers, the balance was to be made up with a draft. As if to impress Barbour's Unionists with the necessity of contributing more men, two Confederate columns descended upon the Northwest, bringing with them the realization that Western Virginia could not expect to remain immune from the war. On August 14, Imboden led his small command of 300 men into neighboring Tucker County, intending to destroy the Cheat River bridge at Rowlesburg. A week later, Brigadier General Albert Jenkins left his camp at Salt Sulphur Springs with 500 cavalrymen and embarked on a raid that would carry him right though Western Virginia and across the Ohio River.

Although Imboden was soon forced back across the mountains, Jenkins achieved considerable success, destroying large quantities of military supplies and generally creating havoc with United States commanders trying to stop him. Beyond the purely military gains of the raids was the equally important psychological boost given Confederate loyalists in the Northwest. Moreover, the presence of Confederate columns in the region offered an excellent opportunity for sympathizers to make their way to Confederate lines without fear of being apprehended. A Union man in Beverly reported that "the rebellious portion are fleeing in consternation from the draft. I have pretty reliable information that not less than four hundred rebels have left the counties of Harrison, Lewis, Upshur, Barbour, and Randolph, taking with them all the goods and horses they could lay their hands on."[11] As soon as Jenkins appeared in Upshur County, 89 men from Barbour and a dozen others from neighboring counties slipped across the mountains to Imboden's camp in Pocahontas County. Led by Hannibal Hill of Barbour, the men promptly joined Imboden's little army as Company C, First Partisan Rangers. "This company," Imboden noted on its muster roll, "is organized out of a band of political refugees from Barbour County who made their way through the woods and mountains to join my corps in the weeks preceding their organization."[12]

The effects of the raids on Union sentiment were equally significant. Since the previous summer, those who had opposed secession had been shielded from the war by Federal regiments occupying the mountain passes to the east. The two raids that August revealed just how weak this shield actually was. Complaints from prominent Unionists flooded Governor Pierpont's office. "I think it is a burning shame," wrote Arthur Boreman, the future governor, "that Imboden is permitted to stalk through the country without even being annoyed by our men." "I think there is a screw lose someplace," complained an exasperated William Farnsworth, whose store in Buckhannon had been picked clean by Jenkins, "and I think it is in the head of the commander of this region. . . . Unless some plan is adopted soon. . . this whole region will be completely overrun." Similar sentiments were expressed by Judge William Harrison of Clarksburg, who feared that "the people will lose their confidence in the ability of the Government, either state or Federal, to protect them and will yield up to the South as the Secesh now urge them."[13]

But far from demoralizing the anti-secessionists of the Northwest, these Confederate raids energized the loyalists by bringing home the danger of their situation. This resulted in an outpouring of support for the Union cause and a flood of enlistments into Federal regiments. Mass meetings were held throughout Western Virginia in support of the war effort, the new state movement, and the call to arms. In Barbour County, a mass meeting was organized by John H. Woodford, Jr., Nathan Taft, Spencer Dayton, and other Union leaders at Philippi on August 20, 1862, only days after raids on nearby Saint George and Buckhannon. This rally is said to have been the largest mass meeting ever held in the county, and one observer wrote that, "The conviction seemed expressed on every man's face that . . . if we would maintain our beneficent Government and secure protection and peace for ourselves and our families, we must fight for the one and defend the other." Resolutions were passed decrying secession and its supporters, who were invited to "go where they can find friends to please and work to do." Committees formed to enlist Barbour's draft quota, and a resolution passed calling for the county's magistrates to levy a special tax to support bounty payments of $25 for each volunteer.[14]

Taft himself worked tirelessly to recruit men, and within a week raised a company for the newly organized Fifteenth West Virginia Infantry.[15] Marshall Coburn, who had been unable to recruit a single man since May, was able to bring his company up to full strength. Dozens of other Barbour Countians traveled to other counties to enlist. In all, a total of 144 men from Barbour County joined the United States Army in the two months following the raids, more than in any other single period of the war. Not a single man had to be drafted to complete the county's quota.

The raids in August 1862 thus did as much to galvanize Union support for the war effort in Barbour County as they did to provide Secessionists the means of escaping to join the Confederate army. The same pattern would be repeated the following spring, when Confederates launched the largest raid of the war into West Virginia. In April, 1863, two brigades of cavalry, one under the command of General William Jones and the other led by Imboden, swept across the Northwest and for the nearly a month destroyed bridges, rolling stock, and military supplies valued at over one million dollars.

One of Imboden's stated aims was that these raids would produce thousands of new recruits for the Confederate army. Towards this end he persuaded Lee to temporarily attach the Twenty-fifth and Thirty-first Virginia Infantry regiments to his command. "These two old regiments are from the Northwest," he reminded Lee when first proposing the raid, "and would fight like tigers the vandals who have so long domineered over their helpless families." He promised that upon his return they would be returned to their former brigades "with their exhausted ranks filled from their own section of the country."[16] If the commanders of the two regiments shared Imboden's optimism, they were sadly disappointed. Instead of the 2,000 new recruits Imboden predicted, fewer than 500 joined his column, and only a handful of these were sent to the Thirty-first Infantry. Virtually all of those who joined Imboden were instead incorporated into the newly formed cavalry brigade of General William Jackson, a commandeer nicknamed "Mudwall" by his men, in mocking comparison to his more competent cousin "Stonewall." Among them were 40 men from Barbour who, under Captain Edward Corder, formed the nucleus of Company D, Twentieth Virginia Cavalry. Corder had been commissioned to organize a company for Jackson's cavalry and accompanied Imboden on the raid. When Imboden captured the town of Beverly at the beginning of the raid, the Federal commander in the region ordered all units in the vicinity to withdraw to Clarksburg. Once Union forces abandoned Barbour County, Corder was able to bring his company to full strength.[17]

The men who joined Corder that spring represented the last significant wave of Confederate volunteers from Barbour County. By the end of the year, Federal attacks were carrying the war into the strongholds of the Confederate army in the Greenbrier and the South Branch, and by 1864 into the Shenandoah Valley. With the tide of the war turning against them, the ability of Confederates to recruit in West Virginia was crippled. Although small detachments would continue to slip across the mountains, most met with disaster. Such was the case in March, 1864, when a group of Imboden's cavalry who had robbed stores in Harrison and Tucker Counties was cornered in Randolph by local Home Guardsmen. Attacked while sleeping, most were shot dead and the rest fled in every direction, making their way back to their lines as best they could.[18] It was during this raid that thirteen men from Barbour County made their way over the mountains to Confederate lines to enlist in Corder's company.[19] They were the last men from Barbour to join the Confederate army. Clearly, the willingness of Secessionists in the county to risk their lives for the Southern cause had reached the point of exhaustion.

Just as the raids of August, 1862, had served to swell Union ranks, so too did the Jones-Imboden raid. Following the wave of enlistments in the months after the Jenkins and Imboden raids, the number of men from Barbour who joined the Union army fell off dramatically, only 15 volunteering for Federal regiments between December and April. After the Jones-Imboden raids the pace of enlistments rose again, over 20 men volunteering in two months. But the Jones-Imboden attacks had demonstrated that the Union army was incapable of protecting local Unionists from Confederate marauders. In the weeks following the raid, the newly established state government of Arthur Boreman set about creating a permanent force of state guard companies in those counties most frequented by rebel raiders. The Home Guard companies, as they came to be called, were to supplement Federal regiments by patrolling the counties in which they were raised. Barbour County's company was organized in July and soon numbered some 50 men.[20]

Yet there is clear evidence that Barbour's Unionists eventually succumbed to the same war-weariness that infected the Secessionists. In January, 1864, Lincoln issued a call for another 600,000. Barbour County's quota was set at 78.[21] Recruiters struggled to meet it, but by the end of March only 34 men had enlisted, most of them re-enlisting veterans. In desperation county officials offered bounties of $200 as an inducement for men to volunteer, and by April Barbour's quota was finally completed.[22] Yet 50 of the men credited to the county were in fact nonresidents who came into the county and enlisted in order to collect the bounty.[23]

Occupation of the Northwest gave the United States government a decided advantage over Confederate recruiters. Only one man from Barbour County joined the Confederate army after April, 1864, while some 102 men—a quarter of all those who served—joined the Union army during the last year of the war. The last draft call was issued in February of 1865 with Barbour's quota set at a staggering 222 men.[24] There was no possibility of meeting this number with volunteers, and for the first time in the war the draft had to be enforced in Barbour. The names of those subject to the draft were chosen by lottery, and included many ex-Confederates who had deserted and returned home.[25] The war ended before most of those drafted were actually mustered into the army. Many of those who were drafted, either because they sympathized with the South or because they simply didn't want to take a chance at being among the last casualties of the war, hired substitutes for themselves, often employing veterans whose terms of service had expired.[26]

The 1860 census for Barbour County listed 1,885 males who would be of military age during the war, i.e., 18 to 45 years old. Of these, nearly half served at one time or another in either the Union or Confederate army. Though this extreme rate of military service must have had a huge impact on the county's social and economic institutions, the patterns of enlistment served to somewhat lessen the blow. Most of those who joined the army did not serve for the entire war. As we've seen, the vast majority enlisted well after the war had begun, and many of the early volunteers were discharged before the war ended. Large numbers of Confederate soldiers deserted the army, secured paroles for themselves, and returned home. Sixty-two men who served in the state Home Guard or militia never really left home at all.

Still, the question remains of how the people of the county managed to send to the army as many men as they did. In an agrarian society such as Barbour County's, the absence of an able-bodied man could mean much more than simply an emotional loss for his family. The lost labor was difficult or impossible to replace, and the death or disability of a farming man would be a disaster. Forty-three Barbour County women were widowed by the war. The devastation to the families was minimized by what appears to be a conscious strategy aimed at balancing the demands of the war with those of the family. Of the 1,600 or so families listed in the 1860 census, 1,098 included men of military age. Of these, 571 had husbands, fathers, or sons who would serve in the army. Examining the structures of the families which did or did not send men to the war reveals a distinct pattern. The vast majority of men who joined either army came from families with two or more males of military age. Moreover, there appears to have been a concerted effort by families to avoid having all of their men leave for the army. Only 26 of the families with three or more males allowed all of their men to enlist. And while most families with two males of military age sent men into the army, only 19 percent sent both. In short, the typical volunteer from Barbour left behind a brother, a father, or an older son to work the family farm.

Given these facts, it is surprising that a quarter of those families with a single adult male allowed the man to enlist. Of these men, though, ten families joined Barbour's Home Guard and two were drafted. Still, fully half the men from this group—66 to be exact—were the primary breadwinners, husbands who joined regular army units and left behind them wives and children. Perhaps the explanation for this can be found in the fact that most of the men from these families enlisted during the first six months of the war. Most then thought the conflict would last months at the most. Adam Bowman remembered that when the Barbour Greys were first organized, he and his comrades were "deluded with the idea that to meet the enemy was to vanquish him at sight."[27] His close friend John R. Philips shared the same delusions. "I told our friends we would be with them within the year, and promised the girls their beaux back at the coming of Christmas." [28] As the realization grew that the war would be protracted and costly, men became less willing to leave their families without an adult male at home.

By the first months of 1864, local authorities were able to meet recruitment quotas only with some difficulty and a good deal of bookkeeping subterfuge. By 1865, quotas could be met only by implementing the draft outright, clear evidence that the war's demands for men had outstripped the willingness of people in Barbour County to furnish them.

- 5 -

WAR IN THE
MOUNTAINS

Soon after Confederate forces were swept from Barbour County, Spencer Dayton wrote to Governor Pierpont a letter that was at once fretful and insistent, expressing his fears that Federal troops occupying the county would be sent east in pursuit of the retreating rebels. He demanded assurances that any soldiers withdrawn from the county would be immediately replaced, preferably by arming local Unionists. "If we do not, there will be rebellion among ourselves. . . .. I tell you Sir, that once let these active and influential minions of treason . . . get back among us . . . the scepter will vanish from our grasp." There was, for Dayton, only one way to answer the threat. "Nothing Sir, but the gaping muzzles of Death . . . will hold these traitors to their good behavior."[1] Dayton's prediction that the security of Unionists in his county would be won only at the point of a gun was more accurate than even he may have wished. For while the much-heralded Battle of Phillippi—proudly labeled by locals to this day as the first land battle of the war—was to be the only engagement fought within the county, Barbour would nonetheless be targeted by the Confederate army for much of the war. And just as Dayton feared, the raids to which Union loyalists would be subjected were for the most part launched by the very same men who had fled with Porterfield.

When Porterfield's little army was driven from Philippi, it retreated east into Randolph County and regrouped at Huttonsville. There Porterfield, although desperately short of men, summarily dismissed Captain Jenkins's entire company, it is said because its ranks included too many "abolitionists" for Porterfield's liking. A more likely reason was the company had been on picket duty the night before the attack, making it a logical target for Porterfield's blame. A handful of Jenkins's men stayed on and joined up with Sturm's Mountain Guards and Bradford's Barbour Greys. The rest had had just about enough of war and, with Jenkins, returned home. Many would later enlist in the Confederate army, while others joined Federal regiments. Porterfield had been right about some of them after all.

The force at Huttonsville was soon reinforced by militia and three regiments of infantry, the entire force now under the command of General Robert S. Garnett. The motley collection of militia and volunteer companies that had fought with Porterfield were organized into regiments, the two Barbour companies incorporated into the Thirty-first Virginia Infantry. Yet Garnett's army was still heavily outnumbered by the Federals under McClelland, who in July struck at Rich Mountain and forced the rebels into a desperate rush north and then east over little-used mountain passes. At Corrick's Ford an attempt to beat back the Federals failed miserably, Garnett himself being killed. From then on the retreat degenerated into a complete rout.[2]

It was only by a combination of sheer luck and a good deal of blundering by Federal commanders that the remnants of Garnett's army were able to escape into Eastern Virginia, eventually making their way to Monterey. Scores had been left behind, some later to make their way back to Confederate lines, most deserting the army for good. Of the Barbour men in Sturm's and Bradford's companies, 29 deserted during the retreat.[3] Those who stuck with the army were thoroughly demoralized. One soldier of the Thirty-first recalled that "It would be impossible to describe the condition of the men . . . footsore, weary, half-starved, ragged, dirty, discouraged, and many of them sick." "I have never been more discouraged than I have since I've been in the army," wrote James Hall of Barbour County while at Monterey. "I have the blues terribly."[4]

Federal success in Western Virginia gave the North its most important victory of the first year of the war. A third of Virginia had been won to the Union, territory from which its armies could be launched deep into the Confederacy. In the spring of 1862, the United States high command launched a two-pronged attack into the Shenandoah Valley from Western Virginia. The campaign, timed to support General George McClelland's assault on Richmond, succeeded despite being badly mauled by Confederates troops under Thomas "Stonewall" Jackson. After McClelland's defeat before Richmond, the war moved to northern Virginia, where a Confederate victory at Second Bull Run in August was followed by an invasion of the North that ended at Antietam the next month.

Both armies that year included regiments of West Virginians who had enlisted the previous spring, and the battles in which they fought held significance beyond their strategic outcomes. In more than one fight, West Virginians faced each other, their units often so close that they were able to call out across the battle line during brief lulls in the fighting. The soldiers knew full well that they were firing at men from their own section of the country, including former friends, neighbors, and relatives. The "gaping muzzles of Death" demanded by Dayton were embraced, transforming the war into an unyielding struggle of unforgiving violence.

Those battles were significant in yet another aspect. By drawing the war eastward, the campaigns of 1862 freed Western Virginia from the immediate threat of the Confederate army. A kind of complacency appears to have settled in among Barbour's Unionists, their indifference to the war evidenced by the difficulties Federal recruiters experienced in generating enlistments that spring. After Bull Run the Western Virginia theater became a kind of sideshow to the more dramatic events unfolding in the East. Federal plans to use Western Virginia as a base of operations against the East were shelved, due largely to the difficulties of maintaining supply lines over hundreds of miles of sparsely populated, almost trackless mountains. Until the winter of 1863-1864, the role designated for Federal forces in West Virginia was largely that of "strategic defense," using the Alleghenies as a barrier protecting Union loyalists in the Northwest and, above all, the Baltimore and Ohio railroad. Guarding this mountain expanse required large numbers of men and material. By 1863 some 40 regiments—over 35,000 men—were on duty in West Virginia and the lower Shenandoah Valley. Half these regiments were raised in West Virginia, most during the spring and summer of 1862. Indeed, with the exception of the Fourth and Seventh West Virginia Infantry, virtually all the regiments raised in West Virginia were used to garrison the new state.

Holding and guarding so vast a territory precluded the concentration of troops at any given place. Instead, individual companies were strung out across the Northwest, each guarding some strategic town, bridge, mountain pass, or section of railroad. It was often the case that as soon as a company was recruited, it would be immediately assigned to some isolated post where it would remain for months or even years. The companies of the Sixth, Tenth, and Fifteenth West Virginia Infantry, regiments in which the vast majority of Barbour County's men served, spent at least a year in the field in this kind of duty before they ever operated together as a single regiment. In fact, the Sixth spent the entire war in this kind of service. Organized specifically for the purpose of patrolling the line of the B & O, its companies were scattered along 400 miles of track between Oakland, Maryland and Parkersburg, West Virginia, on the Ohio River.[5]

This kind of service virtually guaranteed a deterioration in morale, as boredom set in among the troops. Yet for many of Barbour's Union soldiers the tedium of military life was alleviated by the fact that they were stationed for long periods within their home county. Marshall Coburn's company remained at Philippi for three months, then transferred to nearby Beverly for the next two years. George Latham's company of the Second West Virginia Infantry was posted to Belington after it was organized. When it returned from the Bull Run campaign it again took up its former camp in Barbour County. Company K of the Sixth Infantry, which included a dozen Barbour men in its ranks, spent the summer of 1862 at Philippi. Captain Fenelon Howe's company of the Fifteenth Infantry was detached from the regiment to spend the winter of 1863 in Barbour.[6] At least a dozen of Barbour's

Union soldiers took advantage of being stationed near home to marry their sweethearts.[7] The proximity of family and familiar surroundings probably explains why so few of Barbour's Federal soldiers deserted during the war.

Confederate soldiers from Barbour could well envy their Union counterparts. Any attempt by rebel soldiers to get home on furlough meant a dangerous crossing of enemy lines, and even if they succeeded they were constantly threatened with capture. Even so, many took the chance. Henry Shaffer was the first. Taking an unauthorized furlough soon after the Battle of Philippi, he was immediately captured and spent three weeks in prison before he was released on oath.[8] Henry Barron of Philippi was taken at his home in 1862, as was James Golden a year later.[9] When Amos Ridgeway came home on leave he narrowly escaped capture by Haller's Home Guards by dashing out the back door, jumping a stream, and hiding himself in some bushes. When Haller's men gave up the chase, the elated Ridgeway whistled Yankee Doodle and danced a jig to celebrate his good fortune.[10] Ridgeway was indeed fortunate. Over the course of the war some 40 Confederates from Barbour County were taken prisoner as they tried to visit their homes.

Occasionally, raids into West Virginia afforded Confederates opportunities to make the attempt. The Jones-Imboden raid in 1863 brought virtually all of Barbour County's rebel soldiers to within a few miles of their homes. Many took advantage of the raid to see their families, some, like David Lang, for the last time.[11] Federal forces had temporarily left the county, and for the first time since the beginning of the war Confederate soldiers were free to openly visit their families. Captain Philips of the Thirty-first Virginia spent over a week at his parent's home, attending Sunday services, participating in log rolls, and "seeing the girls."[12] More often, small groups of Confederates would make their way into Barbour, ostensibly to raid on Union outposts or gather recruits, but in reality simply to get home for a few days.

For those Barbour County families with sons in opposing armies, furloughs could be occasions for violent confrontations. The Hall family, one son supporting the Union and another in the Confederate army, was forced to hide one whenever the other came home.[13] Barton Cross, with four sons in the Confederate army, devised a system of alarms to alert the boys to the presence of their brother Levi, serving with the Fifteenth West Virginia. If any of them made their way to the family farm they were to first alert their father by beating on a hollow tree near the house in order to prevent the brothers from crossing paths.[14]

The ability of so many of Barbour's Confederate soldiers to get home is explained by the fact that, with the exception of those in the Thirty-first Virginia, attached to the Army of Northern Virginia, most joined up with regiments stationed fairly close to the county. Confederate regiments raised in West Virginia during 1862 and 1863 played a role not unlike that of Union regiments raised at the same time. Just as Washington viewed the Alleghenies as a barrier between Confederate Virginia and the loyal Northwest, Richmond saw the mountains as a natural barrier against invasion from the West. Indeed, if the level of manpower devoted to guarding the western flank of Virginia is any indication, the Confederate high command was even less concerned for the region than was the Federal.

In April, 1862, John D. Imboden was appointed to raise a brigade of rangers to guard the western frontier of Confederate Virginia and, as much as possible, carry the war into Federal-held Western Virginia. Over the summer his brigade swelled to over 1,500 men, comprised almost entirely of West Virginians. Except for cavalry brigade in the Shenandoah Valley, Imboden's rangers—joined in 1863 by another brigade of West Virginians recruited by General William Jackson—for a good while represented the only real Confederate military force in the northern Alleghenies. They were, moreover, frankly viewed by senior commanders as second rank soldiers of dubious reliability. John Breckenridge, once a presidential candidate and now a Confederate general, complained at one crucial moment in the war that Imboden's men were "doing next to nothing." Jubal Early earned Imboden's permanent ire when he characterized Imboden's troops as "inefficient, disorganized, undisciplined, and unreliable."[15]

Robert E. Lee was able to mollify Imboden to some extent, but clearly shared Early's views about the capabilities not only of Imboden's troops, but those of Jackson as well. Writing to Jefferson Davis in early 1864, he recommended against allowing any further augmentation of their forces since, "the men who go into them will be to a great extent lost to the general service. . . . My own opportunities of observation have not impressed me favorably with regard to the discipline and efficiency of General Imboden's troops, and the accounts I receive represent the others [Jackson's command] with few exceptions to be no better."[16]

Another and more important reason that Lee made this recommendation to Davis was the fact that a large number of Imboden's and Jackson's "recruits" were actually deserters from the Army of Northern Virginia. "There is a strong disposition manifested by the men to enlist in commands serving near their home. . . . I refer particularly to Western Virginia. I am informed that this disposition is encouraged by the officers, who are naturally desirous to increase their forces."[17] The problem of desertions was especially acute in regiments like the Thirty-first Virginia, raised entirely from counties in the Northwest. No fewer than 136 men from the regiment, including 18 from Barbour County, made their way to Imboden's and Jackson's brigades, some few transferring formally, but most simply deserting. Colonel John Hoffman of the Thirty-first waged a largely unsuccessful campaign to get these men back to his regiment which was being bled dry by desertions.[18] Manpower was in short supply throughout the Confederate army and few commanders were willing to part with a single recruit no matter what his background. When one company commander wrote to the commander of one of Jackson's regiments demanding that he return a deserter, the colonel replied that, "Yes, he is here and if you send for him you would best send as much as a brigade of soldiers if you expect to take him back."[19]

It is easy to understand why so many men of Thirty-first Virginia, especially, deserted to Imboden and Jackson. Few regiments in Lee's army had seen as much fighting or had

undertaken so many forced marches. James Hall of Barbour
County noted in his diary, "I dread the hell fired marches we will
have to undergo. I am in a dismal scrape now, and if I ever get
out, I will be more careful what part of the service I will enter
again."[20] Serving with Imboden or Jackson's cavalry not only
meant they would be closer to home, but they would be riding
instead of marching.

Yet the large-scale desertions from Lee's army should not
be seen as evidence of a desire to avoid hard service. The men
who abandoned units in Eastern Virginia were to a man Western Virginians who had joined the army in 1861. In their minds
they were not forsaking the Confederate cause, but rather getting into that part of the Confederate army that represented the
best chance of carrying the war back into Western Virginia.
However Lee may have felt about them, they were all he had and
he was forced to rely heavily upon them. They could at least ride
and shoot, and their very existence enabled him to withdraw
more trustworthy regiments to the East.

And in fact these meager forces were able to carry the war
into West Virginia in a series of raids that confounded Union
commanders and shook Union loyalists from their lethargy. Im-
patient to strike at Federal authority in the Northwest, Imboden
began launching raids across the mountains. The mountainous,
heavily forested, and sparsely populated geography of the region
was ideally suited to this kind of warfare. Thoroughly familiar
with the territory and aided by locals sympathetic to their cause,
they could pinpoint their targets with relative ease.

By the winter of 1862, Imboden felt strong enough to
launch larger-scale attacks. In November he led 300 of his men
into Tucker County, just east of Barbour. His aim was the destruction of the Cheat River bridge at Rowlesburg. An earlier
attempt to destroy the same bridge in August had ended in failure when his force had been detected almost a soon as it left
camp. This time Imboden got no closer to his goal. Reaching
Saint George on the morning of November 9, he captured a
small Federal garrison only to learn that his presence had once

again been detected. Paroling his prisoners, Imboden retreated back over the mountains.

In order to carry out the role envisioned for them, the rangers had to be mounted. Yet securing horses was a perennial problem, particularly as available mounts in the Shenandoah Valley had been depleted by cavalry regiments organized in the early months on the war. As a result, many of Imboden's men resorted to the time-honored practice of stealing horses. If the owners were known to be Union sympathizers, so much the better. During his first raid into Tucker County, just east of Barbour, Imboden had personally ransacked the store of Solomon Parsons, one of the most prominent Union men in the county.[21]

Horse stealing by Imboden's men reached near-epidemic proportions during the winter of 1862-1863. Michael Haller complained that "The loyal citizens have suffered much by the frequent depredations committed by the horse-thieving murderers. The county is completely stripped of all valuable property."[22] Another citizen from neighboring Harrison County, noting that "Lewis, Upshur, Barbour, etc., seem to be exclusively visited by this kind of marauding, thieving gentry," complained that local army commanders were simply incapable of protecting people's property because their troops were largely infantry. "When will it be thumpt into the craniums of the powers that be that it is all folly to think of putting down guerrillas during this generation unless our infantry are mounted?"[23]

So rampant had horse stealing become that some transformed it into a regular and lucrative trade, stealing mounts from farmers and then selling them to the Confederate army. Ned Lynch of Barbour, who had deserted from the Thirty-first Virginia, became one of the most notorious horse thieves in the region, declaring to one listener that he could "make more money in the horse business than at anything else." When Lynch was finally captured he was found to be carrying several thousand dollars in Confederate bonds, profits of a lucrative trade that the officer who ran him down earnestly hoped Lynch would never get a chance to spend. "Hold him fast," implored the lieutenant, "If you can't do it any other way, tie a rope around his neck and hang him from the third story window."[24]

The money to be had in trading stolen horses was even too great for some Federal soldiers to ignore. Following the campaign in Eastern Virginia, George Latham's company of the Second West Virginia was posted to Barbour County. Now commanded by Daniel Wilson, the men spent most of the next year and a half chasing down horse thieves and rebel recruiters, among them Peyton Booth, Wilson's own cousin.[25] Wilson's efforts were greatly appreciated by local citizens, one of whom declared that "his untiring energy and devotion to the cause . . . are a barrier and prevent depredations which otherwise would be frequent."[26] A week after the compliments were published in the *Wheeling Intelligencer* three of Wilson's men were arrested for plotting to steal local horses which they intended to sell to the enemy.[27]

If the United States infantry was largely unsuccessful in thwarting Confederate raiders, at least one commander hit upon a scheme he hoped would put a stop to the practice. General Robert Milroy's zeal for the Union cause was matched only by his determination to impose swift retaliation on civilians rendering aid to Confederate guerrillas. "It once occurred to me," he explained, "that a great advance towards the preservation of order and public safety would be accomplished if I could make the policy of citizens of rebel sentiments to discourage, instead of encourage, these outrages. I therefore avowed my intention of compelling rebel citizens aiding in their perpetration to compensate the Union citizens for their losses."[28]

Imboden's November raid into Tucker County provided Milroy with the first opportunity to test the policy. On November 27, Milroy ordered Confederate sympathizers in Tucker to be assessed fines to compensate those whose horses and other property had been seized during the raid. Milroy made it clear he intended his orders to be obeyed. "Upon failure of anyone to do so their homes will be burned and the men shot." A company of Ohio infantry was sent to Tucker to ensure the orders were carried out.[29] Word of the assessments was carried to Imboden by refugees on December 7, and he immediately notified President

Davis, adding that "This is only one of a thousand barbarities practiced here in these distant mountains of which I have almost daily heard for the last few months. Oh, for a day of retribution."[30] Davis in turn informed Lee of Milroy's orders and instructed him to notify his Federal counterpart that "unless he promptly and satisfactorily responds, say within five days, measures will be taken by retaliation to suppress the indulgences of such brutal passions as are indicated in the order of General R.H. Milroy."[31]

Lee was as appalled as Imboden and Davis. On January 10 he sent a dispatch across the lines to General Henry Halleck, the Federal commander-in-chief, demanding to know if Milroy's orders "have received the sanctions of any soldier" and whether "your government will tolerate the execution of an order so barbarous and so revolting to every principle of justice and humanity." Lee concluded by assuring Halleck that unless a satisfactory response was received, "this government will be compelled to protect its citizens by the immediate adoption of retaliatory measures."[32] Halleck received Lee's letter four days later. Although completely unaware of Milroy's orders, he certainly comprehended the consequences which would follow if these orders were carried out. Replying to Lee the same day, he assured him that "Measures will be immediately taken to ascertain whether the papers are genuine, and, if so, General Milroy will be notified that his conduct in issuing them is disapproved." Never one to circumvent established channels of communication, Halleck simply passed a copy of Lee's dispatch down the chain of command, commenting in the margin that "Brigadier Milroy had no authority to issue these orders, which are deemed in violation of the laws of war. If such orders were actually issued, they must be revoked."[33]

Halleck's instructions did not reach Milroy until three weeks later. By then fines totaling over $6,000 had been extracted from a dozen or so citizens in Tucker County, including one who was said to have been forced to sell his pants in order to raise the money.[34] While the order was finally revoked and the collected money returned, events had already sparked Confederate retaliation. The same day that Lee wrote Halleck, he sent another dispatch to Imboden urging him to complete the organization of his rangers into a brigade to be incorporated into the regular army. Although he had given Halleck ten days to reply, he told Imboden that, "with regard to the orders of Milroy, you must endeavor to repress his cruelties as much as possible." Lee went on to suggest that it might be a good idea to apprehend officials elected under the Pierpont government, specifically mentioning that the office of sheriff should be rendered "as dangerous a position as possible."[35]

Imboden jumped at the opportunity. The unlucky official upon whose head fell the wrath of the Confederate high command was James Trayhern, sheriff of Barbour County. On Sunday evening, January 4, he and district magistrate James Harvey were in Trayhern's home, examining tax lists and accounting for about $2,000 in taxes collected by Trayhern. Suddenly there came a determined pounding at the door with shouts threatening to break it down. Through the window Trayhern and Harvey saw 20 or 30 mounted rebels. Quickly Harvey and Trayhern's son scampered up into the attic. Trayhern was just able to pass about half the tax money up to them when the door burst open and the house filled with soldiers. Captain Hannibal Hill and his men had been watching Trayhern for days and now wanted the tax money he had collected. When Trayhern handed over the $1,000 he had been unable to hide, one of Hill's men insisted there was more. When a quick search of the house failed to uncover the rest of the money, Hill's men ransacked Trayhern's store, carrying off some $500 worth of goods. They then led half a dozen horses out of the stable and ordered Trayhern onto one of them. He was under arrest and was to be taken to Richmond to be tried for treason. The raiders moved on to the home of John Shroyer, another magistrate, where they got three more horses. They were less successful at the home of Henry Martin. When Martin saw them surround his house, he called out to imaginary soldiers to "shoot the scoundrels!" The ruse worked and Hill's men fled.[36]

When word of Trayhern's abduction reached Philippi the next morning, troops immediately began covering the roads in search of Hill and his men. Near the home of Henry Bowman a squad from a company of the Sixth West Virginia Infantry came upon Bowman and his neighbor Henry Wilson. The soldiers, men from Marion County who had been stationed at Philippi since the previous summer, were well-known for dealing harshly with rebels. Before coming to Barbour they had apprehended two Confederate recruiters near Fairmont and summarily executed both of them. [37] Their posting to Barbour had created much consternation among secessionists in the county. Sarah Jane Holt, the widowed sister of Samuel Woods, had several run-ins with them. They were, she complained, "all low and mean." [38] Both Bowman and Wilson were well known to the soldiers as "mischievous and influential secessionists" with sons in the rebel army. Within a few minutes they had been shot dead. The soldiers reported that the two had ignored orders to halt and were killed when they attempted to flee. The men's families claimed otherwise, accusing the soldiers of outright murder.

In a war imbued with as much romanticism as the American Civil War, kidnapping and killings such as these are a stark reminder that the war in border regions like West Virginia was carried out with as much hatred and violence that people could inflict on their enemies. Almost every county in West Virginia includes in its history some account of atrocities committed by one side or the other, from burnings and bushwhacking to murder. While Bowman and Wilson were not the first civilians to be killed in Barbour, their deaths sent shock waves throughout the county's Secessionist community since both were unarmed farmers in their fifties who, it was alleged, had nothing to do with Trayhern's abduction. Indeed, Wilson was a German Baptist preacher whose religious tenets prohibited him from taking up arms. Isabella Woods, by then a refugee in Waynesboro, detected a distinct change in the attitudes of friends still in the county with whom she remained in contact. Writing to her husband on February 7, she related that the recent events there had "made their hatred and ill feelings more intense." [39]

Word of the tragedy spread quickly to the rebel army. When John R. Philips, now a captain in the Thirty-first Virginia, learned of the deaths, he wrote to his close friend Adam Coleman Bowman to both express his sorrow over his father's death and to relate how news of the killings had affected him. "I have brewed my hands in the blood of my foes until I was tired of the butchery, but now again my anger comes with all its fierceness, and now woe to the accursed cut-throats that fall in my path. Oh! Heaven avenge us!"[40] His father's killing radically transformed Coleman's attitude about the war. "My nature changed," he would later explain, "and revenge took the place of the common soldier." He immediately wrote to Governor Letcher, pleading for a command of his own. Bowman got his commission, but never really got over the bitterness left by his father's death. Years after the war he claimed that he would carry to his grave "the fires of the furies over a crime as dark as hell."[41]

The people who were fighting the war were changing, because the war itself had changed. The campaigns of 1862, in which men from Barbour and other counties in West Virginia had participated, had proven that men from the region were perfectly willing to kill former friends and even close kin who wore the uniform of the enemy. The kidnapping of Trayhern and the killing of Bowman and Wilson destroyed any illusions about a limited war restricted to armed combatants. And the abduction of Trayhern and the killing of Bowman and Coleman set in motion a chain of events which contributed to the mounting of the largest and most famous Confederate raid into West Virginia.

The reaction in West Virginia to Trayhern's kidnapping was immediate. The *Wheeling Intelligencer* promptly called for the arrest of "certain noted conniving and winking and influential Secessionists in Barbour, men who are justly suspicioned of being the procurers of the abduction of the sheriff. Whether they are not the procurers, they should be arrested, for only by their arrest can an innocent and unoffending Union man be released." The editorial went on to demand laws authorizing the arrest of "distinguished Secessionists," to be held hostage for the return of any Union men kidnapped by Confederate raiders. Although Governor Pierpont submitted a bill for such a law at the end of January, he didn't wait for the legislature to act on it. Within days of the kidnapping he ordered the arrest of eight men in Barbour County to be held until Trayhern was released.[42] The arrests were clearly welcomed by Barbour's Unionists. Even the deaths of Wilson and Bowman were acceptable so long as they contributed to putting an end to the horse stealing and kidnapping to which the people of the county had been subjected. "It is melancholy indeed," wrote Spencer Dayton, "to reflect that two men, in view of the necessity to adopt measures of a stern character, for the procurement of our citizens, should have thus expiated their zeal in the rebellion, but the results portend future good."[43]

Dayton could not have been more mistaken. News of the arrests and killings quickly reached Confederate authorities. As expected, Imboden was the first to act. On January 20 he wrote directly to Milroy (apparently without authorization) declaring his intention to "arrest and imprison as dangerous enemies of my state and country every man I can lay my hands upon, who holds any office under the usurped State of West Virginia." Furthermore, if he found that those responsible for the deaths of Wilson and Bowman were members of Milroy's command, he would execute two prisoners "of the highest rank" as retribution. If any of the hostages were executed, he would hang two prisoners for each one killed.[44]

Milroy sent a copy of Imboden's letter to Pierpont, suggesting it be laid before the legislature so that appropriate measures could be taken in retaliation if Imboden carried out his threats. He also replied directly to Imboden, denying that any of his troops had been involved in the affair (true enough—the Sixth West Virginia was not part of his brigade) or that he had any knowledge of the killings. He went on to point out the obvious: If any prisoners of war in Imboden's hands were executed, for whatever reason, then the Federal government would have little choice but to reply in kind. Noting that authorities in Richmond were considering a $100,000 reward for his own capture, Milroy closed with the taunt, "Hadn't you better come down and make the speculation?"[45]

Just as the actions of Imboden and Milroy threatened to escalate into a series of retaliatory executions that could only discredit both governments, cooler heads began to prevail. In Barbour

County, Secessionist sympathizers passed resolutions demanding an end to Confederate marauding and kidnapping.[46] Pierpont, at first prepared to arrest another 50 civilians if Trayhern was not released, decided instead to secure his return by exchanging him for two Secessionist-minded county officials arrested the previous year. Accordingly one of the Barbour hostages, Dr. Abraham Hershman, was released on condition that he persuade two influential men of the county to travel to Richmond to open negotiations.[47]

The two who volunteered, John R. Williamson and William Elliot, a brother of one of the hostages, interceded with Governor Letcher and secured Trayhern's parole. The unfortunate sheriff was allowed the freedom of Richmond until a decision was made as to what was to be done with him. For his part, Trayhern swore that he would never serve as sheriff again.[48] Further negotiations stalled when the Confederate agent for exchange refused to consider releasing Trayhern until the Barbour hostages were set free.[49] Meanwhile, General Lee, having gotten word of Imboden's threats to hang prisoners of war, instructed him that anyone accused of murder must be turned over to civil authorities for a proper trial. Lee added that, "I do not think retaliation upon the Union people of the northwest would help our cause in that region."[50]

The efforts to work out a peaceable solution for Trayhern's release were of little consolation to the families of the hostages, and certainly did nothing to assuage the grief of Wilson's and Bowman's families. Indeed, Wilson's wife is said to have died from grief a short time after her husband's death.[51] Nor did the negotiations relieve the fears of other Secessionist sympathizers in Barbour, a number of whom lived in constant fear of further arrests and killings.[52] One of the few people to see any possible benefit from the entire affair was John D. Imboden. For him, growing resentment in the Northwest offered an opportunity to strike a major blow at the Union cause. Having failed twice to destroy the Cheat River bridge, on March 2 he submitted to Lee a far more ambitious plan for a large-scale raid into West Virginia. This time the aim would not be simply to destroy bridges but, "If possible, to hold that section of the country long enough to overthrow the government," which he likened to an oriental despotism exercising control by terror over three-fourths of the population. Even if he was able to occupy the region for only a short time, Imboden expected to raise several Confederate regiments from a population disaffected by the recent actions of Federal authorities. "These expectations may seem wild, but I assure you, general, that at no period since the war commenced has the opportunity ever been so good to gain a foothold in the northwest."[53]

There is no evidence that Lee ever expected Imboden to realize these aims, but he nonetheless approved the plan, even adding a brigade of cavalry and two infantry regiments—the Twenty-fifth and Thirty-first, both raised in West Virginia—to the strike force. With an attack by the Army of the Potomac expected that spring, a large-scale raid on Federal lines of communication with the West held the prospect of diverting Federal troops or preventing reinforcement of the Eastern front. The timing of the raid had political advantages as well, since it would coincide with the first elections to be held in the newly created state of West Virginia. Finally, Lee was as outraged as anyone else by the atrocities being committed in Western Virginia, where he had personally met with defeat during the first year of the war. Occupation of the Northwest, for however brief a period, would at least bring some comfort to those in the region still loyal to Virginia.

The Jones-Imboden raid that began in April 1863 was thus as much a product of the previous winter's marauding, killings, and arrests as it was a product of military considerations. Overall command of the operation was given to General William Jones, commander of a brigade of battle-hardened cavalrymen then stationed in the lower Shenandoah Valley. His brigade and the column commanded by Imboden were to operate separately at first, with Imboden seizing Beverly and then joining with Jones, who would strike out along the line of the Baltimore and Ohio railroad. The task of destroying the rail bridge and viaduct at Rowlesburg was given to Jones, Lee apparently being reluctant to assign so important an objective to someone who had already failed twice to reach the town.

Imboden quickly secured his first objective, routing a Federal force from Beverly on April 24. Much to the consternation of Jones, Imboden then decided that rather than link up with Jones he would instead use his column to keep open an escape route for both brigades. Turning southwest he brushed aside a company of Federal troops at Buckhannon, where he remained for eight days awaiting word from Jones.[54] Jones meanwhile was having an equally difficult time adhering to the original plan of the raid. When his brigade reached the outskirts of Rowlesburg on the 29th, Jones accepted at face value the claim of a local civilian that the town was defended by over 1,500 men (the actual number was a mere 250). After a halfhearted feint at the town's defenses, the Confederates moved on, leaving the primary objective of the raid unscathed. Exhibiting more aggressiveness at Fairmont, Jones captured the town after a brisk fight and then blew the railroad bridge there into the water.[55]

The two columns finally joined at Buckhannon on May 2. From there they proceeded to raid through a dozen counties over the next two weeks, destroying bridges, rolling stock, and supply depots. Thousands of head of cattle and several hundred horses were seized. On paper, at least, the military gains seemed impressive. In reality, the raid was a failure both militarily and politically. The destroyed bridges were rebuilt in a matter of weeks, no troops were diverted from the Army of the Potomac, and the elections were hardly disrupted.

Perhaps the most significant result of the raid was the realization by Confederate commanders of just how much they had overestimated the strength of Confederate sympathy in the Northwest. Instead of the 2,000 new recruits Imboden expected, fewer than 500 joined his ranks. Even this modest increase in Confederate manpower was offset by the desertion of over 200 of his own men during the raid. Imboden was forced to admit that he had completely miscalculated sentiment in the region. "The people now remaining in the Northwest are, to all extents and purposes, a conquered people. Their spirit is broken by tyranny where they are loyal to our cause, and those who are against us are the blackest-hearted, most despicable villains upon the continent."[56]

For Confederate sympathizers in Barbour County, the raid offered only the briefest respite from Unionist oppression. Rumors of the pending invasion had been circulating for weeks, and those aware of them had anxiously awaited Imboden's arrival.[57] When Imboden occupied Buckhannon, those loyal to Virginia paraded in the streets, waving Confederate flags and taunting their Union neighbors.[58] But when Confederate troops finally arrived in Barbour at the beginning of May, it proved to be a financial disaster for Secessionists and Unionists alike. Imboden had issued strict orders to his men prohibiting the seizure of personal property. However, the men of Jones's command, none of whom were from the Northwest, generally acted as though they were invading enemy territory and treated all civilians as disloyal. When his brigade occupied Philippi on May 1, his men "requisitioned" cattle and horses without regard to the professed loyalties of their owners.

Several Secessionist merchants and cattlemen lost all they had. John R. Williamson, who had worked to resolve the hostage crisis resulting from Trayhern's kidnapping, lost thousands of dollars worth of livestock and other property. William McClaskey's Secessionist sympathies had led him to resign his position as deputy sheriff after 1861; Jones's men freely took what they wanted from his store, paying him in worthless Confederate script and at pre-war prices to boot. McClaskey was fortunate in getting paid at all. When the rebels took off with cattle and horses belonging to Thomas Hite, whose two sons were serving in the Confederate army, his demands for payment were met with curses.[59] A few resisted and managed to save at least some of their property. James Corder, whose brother Edward was at that very moment recruiting men for his company, saw all his cattle driven off by Jones's men. He pursued the troopers and, though they threatened to shoot him, pleaded for their return. The Confederates relented and Corder was able to secure one yoke of oxen.[60] His other brother Joshua did great service to the community by saving the bridge spanning the Tygart River at Philippi when Jones ordered it burned down. Kneeling on the span and praying, Corder refused to move until the exasperated troopers finally gave up and left. It is one of the few covered bridges in West Virginia to have survived the war.[61]

Hearing of all this, Isabell Woods wrote to her husband that "Jones's company of cavalry has done our cause great harm in the N.W. . . . Great outrages have been committed upon Union and 'Secech' alike, so I hear."[62] The raid certainly did nothing to improve the lot of the Barbour hostages. If anything their situation was made worse when they were transferred from prison in Wheeling to Camp Chase in Ohio, to prevent their liberation should Jones attack the city. The Ohio prison was notorious for its horrendous conditions, with hundreds of inmates succumbing to disease. The hostages soon petitioned to be returned to West Virginia. Pierpont agreed, but not before one of them, Samuel Elliot, died of disease.[63]

Though the Jones-Imboden raid was largely a failure, the commanders continued their incursions into West Virginia. Raids continued throughout the summer of 1863, including full-scale attacks on towns throughout the region. As confounding as the raids were to Union loyalists, they were also marked by a certain poignancy. The Confederates who carried them out were by and large West Virginians. Most of the Federal troops guarding the territory were likewise recruited there and it was inevitable that in these fights former friends, neighbors and relatives—even brothers—would face one another in battle. A case in point was General William Jackson's attack on Bulltown in September, 1863. The town was defended by companies of the Sixth, Eleventh, and Fourteenth West Virginia Infantry and included men from Barbour serving in the Sixth. Among Jackson's troops were Captain Edward Corder's company, raised in Barbour only a few months before, along with other units raised in counties where the Bulltown defenders had joined up with the Union army.

Jackson's forces surrounded Bulltown, and Jackson twice called on the Federal commander, Captain William Mattingly, to surrender. Mattingly refused both offers, declaring he would, "fight 'til Hell froze over, and if he had to retreat, he would retreat on ice!"[64] The battle lasted for the better part of the afternoon, Mattingly's men beating back repeated assaults by Jackson's troopers. At one point a truce was called so that both sides could bring in their wounded. A Union soldier wrote at the time that his comrades mingled freely with the rebels during the two-hour truce, "laughing and talking just as if we were the best of friends. . . . A great many had friends and relations among them, and it was good for curious reflection to see them meet and talk. As soon as the flag of truce had expired they would be shooting at each other again."[65] Unable to dislodge the defenders, Jackson finally gave up and withdrew.

The turning point in the war in West Virginia came that same summer, largely the result of the appointment of two men to Federal command: Generals Benjamin F. Kelley and William Averell. Kelley had organized the first regiment of Union troops in West Virginia and led them against Porterfield at Philippi, where he had been seriously wounded. For most of the war he commanded units directly responsible for guarding the B & O. Although his troops never fought a major engagement, they were kept constantly busy in countless small skirmishes up and down the line. When promoted to the command of all Federal troops in West Virginia in 1863, he embarked upon a complete reorganization of his command, aimed at rooting the Confederates from their strongholds in the Alleghenies. In this he was ably assisted by Averell. A cavalryman by training and experience, Averell quickly determined that the infantry under his command could do little to stop the repeated raids carried out by the swifter-moving Confederate cavalrymen. Under Kelley's direction, he transformed the Second, Third and Eighth West Virginia Infantry into cavalry regiments, a task that proved relatively easy as most of the men were fairly good horsemen.

The reorganization of Averell's command was completed by the fall, and he immediately embarked on a series of raids into Confederate-held territory. Much to his credit, Averell was able to solve a problem that had confounded both armies since the beginning of the war: the Appalachian Mountains. Consisting of a series of high ridges separated by narrow valleys, these mountains often defeated commanders before the enemy was engaged. Averell hit upon a new tactic, using the mountain geography to his advantage. Instead of crossing west-to-east, he marched up and down the valleys themselves, traveling quickly and striking deep into Confederate territory. When confronted with an enemy force trying to block his path, he simply sidestepped them by crossing over one ridge and continuing his march along the next valley. Perennially short of manpower, the Confederates charged with defending the territory found themselves repeatedly out-maneuvered, and when Averell chose to fight, it was usually on his own terms.

Averell's first raid aimed at destroying William Jackson's brigade in Pocahontas County.[66] Jackson established a defensive line on Droop Mountain and was soon joined by a brigade of infantry under General John Echols, who had pushed his men 56 miles in just over 40 hours. As with the Confederate raids of the previous summer, Barbour County men fought on opposite sides. Scattered among the various companies of the two regiments were not only former neighbors from Barbour, but close relatives as well. William Cade and Henry Carter of the Tenth West Virginia each had brothers serving with the Jackson's Twentieth Cavalry. Wesley and John Bean of the Twentieth also had relatives in the Tenth, their three cousins John, James and Thomas. James Paugh, a private in the Tenth, would be so severely wounded that day that he was mistakenly listed as having been killed in action. Across the lines was his cousin Wilson who had grown up on the farm next to his.

Eventually the pressure on the Confederate positions became too much for the hard-pressed troopers, and Echols ordered a general withdrawal that soon degenerated into a complete rout, the rebels fleeing 20 miles to Lewisburg before their officers could halt them. Averell pursued them for a day or so with his cavalry, but broke off the chase when it was reported that reinforcements had reached Echols in Lewisburg. His cavalry was then ordered to make its way to Hightown and from there to Petersburg. Meanwhile the Tenth West Virginia remained at Droop Mountain, guarding prisoners, caring for the wounded, and burying the dead before returning to Beverly. Among the Confederates taken that day was James McNeil, a captain in the Twenty-second Virginia Infantry. While sitting by the roadside, his brother Moore, who would become captain of Barbour's Home Guard towards the end of the war, happened upon him and extended his hand. James coldly refused. "We are not shaking hands today."[67]

Averell continued to hammer at the Confederates throughout the winter, launching raids deep into the mountains at rebel depots at Salem and then at Dublin. While the Confederate army in the Alleghenies was not broken, it would never again pose a serious threat to West Virginia. Meanwhile, negotiations for Trayhern's release continued to drag on. Finally, almost exactly a year to the day after his abduction, he was released and returned home. Pierpont ordered the release of the Barbour hostages two weeks later.[68] Yet the consequences of Trayhern's kidnapping and the killings that followed did not end with the freeing of the prisoners. In the summer of 1863, Governor Boreman had organized a force of Home Guardsmen to protect local Unionists from Confederate raiders. Confederates themselves almost universally viewed them as nothing less than bushwhackers and thieves. One rebel soldier characterized them as "meek and coward in the extreme, [seeking] every opportunity to abuse women and children and helpless and crippled men." Even loyal Union men at times complained of their activities.[69]

The Barbour Home Guards were organized in July and August, 1863, led by Michael Haller. An outspoken abolitionist, Haller had been one of a handful of men in Barbour to have voted for Lincoln in 1860. His uncompromising attitude toward Secessionists was expressed succinctly in a letter written to Boreman soon after receiving his commission. "No permanent peace can accrue to our county until . . . the leading rebels are shot or confined to military prison."[70] Haller's men kept themselves busy keeping a close watch on local Secessionists and apprehending the occasional Confederate soldier caught trying to slip home on a furlough. At least one of the prisoners who fell into their hands, a Lieutenant Raleigh Stewart, appears to have been summarily executed. Perhaps for this reason it came to be assumed by Confederates that Haller and the Home Guardsmen under his command were responsible for the killing of Bowman and Wilson, and several attempts were made by Confederate soldiers to avenge the deaths by ambushing the Guardsmen.[71] However, it was only in the weeks after Lee's surrender at Appomattox that they finally succeeded. On April 24, 1865, a group of Captain Hill's men slipped into the county and ransacked the home of Sanford Nestor, a private in Haller's company. Haller and several of his men tracked the rebels to the farm of Nicolas Holsberry on Teter's Creek, where Hill's men lay in ambush. In the brief fight that followed, Haller was wounded and taken prisoner along with two of his men. All were summarily executed, it is said after being made to kneel and pray for the Confederacy.[72]

- 6 -

KEEP THE HOME FIRES BURNING

Isabella Woods's children were fast asleep when the horsemen approached their house. They didn't hear the hoof beats in the farmyard, the thump of the lighted torches thrown onto the roof and against the walls, and didn't smell the smoke as the flames began to consume the tinder-dry wood. It was only when the house was nearly engulfed in flames that the roar of the fire finally awakened them. They had just enough time to scramble to safety in their bedclothes before the clapboard farmhouse was completely ablaze. By morning it had been reduced to pile of smoldering ashes.

The war was not a year old when the arsonists struck. The farmhouse was actually the home of Andrew and Barbara Trimble, tenant farmers of the Woodses. Isabella had moved her family and their possessions into the house after she could no longer bear the taunts, harassment, and silent stares of former friends and neighbors at Philippi. Then, the day before the fire, she had been warned—ironically by a black freeman—that her husband's Unionist enemies would try to destroy his notes, deeds, and other evidence of debts owed to him. Isabella left with the papers that evening. She had no inkling that the attempt to destroy them would nearly cost the lives of her children. In fact it's unlikely the arsonists themselves intended to harm anyone. Trimble and his wife were away that night, and the men probably assumed the house was empty.[1]

Although the Woods family lost virtually all their possessions in the fire, they were in fact quite fortunate. In 1863, the home of Henry Andrick, whose eldest son was serving in the Confederate army, was set afire. Two of his children, nine-year-old Jacob and ten-year-old Mary, perished in the flames.[2] By then arson seemed to have become an almost commonplace occurrence in Barbour County as Union men avenged themselves against their Secessionist neighbors. Jacob Shank's tannery was burned to the ground that year. Braxton Durrett, arrested for Secessionist activity, found his home burned when he was released. The home of Joshua Corder was occupied by Federal troops at the beginning of the war. When the soldiers left they set it ablaze. In all almost a dozen families in Barbour, all perceived as Confederate sympathizers, saw their homes, barns, or stables burned during the war.[3]

Such acts were only the most pronounced examples of an increasing level of violence among neighbors whom the war had turned into enemies. Hu Maxwell, the foremost historian of the county, gave only cursory service to this aspect of Barbour's history. Writing while many of the war's participants were still living, he decided that "Upon this phase of the county's history the curtain will not be drawn."[4] The fact is that the hatred and animosity generated by the war were not simply the result of the fighting between the two sides. The Civil War is said to have been America's first modern war because it drew into the conflict not only the armies of the contending parties, but the civilian populations of both sides. Nowhere was this more true than in places like Barbour County, where the two sides lived within the same community. Civilians actively supported the war effort not simply because the men fighting it were their fathers, husbands and sons, but because the aims of the war touched the lives of each of them.

It started even before the war itself. As early as April, 1861, persons traveling through Philippi were accosted by mobs of Secessionists led by John Payne, the cashier of the local bank. If their interrogations revealed the least hint of opposition to Virginia's secession, they were run out of town.[5] When Porterfield occupied the town at the end of May, one of his first acts was to order the arrest of all known Union loyalists. Some two dozen men were apprehended and taken to Monterey, where Governor Letcher personally swore he would hang the lot of them.[6]

The occupation of Philippi by Federal troops did nothing to alleviate the threat to Barbour County's civilians. The soldiers generally considered themselves to be occupying enemy territory and at first treated all civilians as Secessionist traitors. Daniel Capito and Dr. Elam Talbott, both Union men who greeted the Federals as saviors, were arrested as soon as they stepped out of their homes. The two were released only after relatives of Capito from Indiana vouched for their loyalty.[7] The first resident of Barbour to die in the war—ironically a slave—was killed by an Indiana soldier the very day the troops occupied Philippi. The soldier, himself black, challenged the man to deny he was a "rebel." The slave, who clearly had no idea what a "rebel" was, failed to answer quickly enough and was shot down.[8]

As Unionists who had been persecuted by the Confederates returned to town, they demanded retribution. One local Union man urged "a little vigorous action in this quarter. . . . The judicious hanging of half a dozen of these Copperheads would be better today, than a couple of additional regiments at Philippi."[9] No lynchings took place, but several politically active Secessionists who had remained in the county were arrested, while those who had fled with Porterfield were indicted for treason.[10] The combination of the fighting at Philippi and the arrests turned the county seat into a virtual ghost town as its population fled to the countryside or Eastern Virginia. The abandoned homes of known Secessionists quickly became targets of plunder for the Ohio and Indiana troops occupying the town. The home of Elisabeth Jarvis, whose son had fled with Porterfield, was ransacked, the soldiers pulling off doors and weatherboards for firewood. Local Unionists joined in ransacking the homes of Samuel Woods, Albert Reger, and Isaac Strickler.[11] Thompson Surgnor's newspaper office was destroyed, his printing press thrown down a well, and his typeset "scattered to the four winds so that no more treason should be brought to light through their agency."[12] By the end of June, one regiment of Ohio troops had some 96 men in the guardhouse on charges of breaking into houses.[13]

As a semblance of order returned to the county, local Unionists organized a special election to fill those offices vacated by Secessionists who had either fled the county or refused to serve under the Pierpont administration. Nathan Taft became prosecuting attorney and Lewis Wilson head of the county court. Both had ample reasons for harboring deep personal resentment against Confederates. Wilson had recently returned to Philippi from Wirt County, where he'd been forced to abandon thousands of dollars worth of oil-drilling equipment to bands of marauding Confederate guerrillas.[14] Taft had been one of the first men Porterfield imprisoned, and was saved only when his captors were chased out of Philippi. From then on he carried out a vendetta against those he held responsible for his arrest, among them his own mother-in-law.[15]

With the judicial system now reconstituted under their control, Union loyalists began striking back at Secessionists. Lawsuits for past debts were filed against Confederate soldiers and sympathizers who had fled the county, the plaintiffs confident of prevailing since the defendants could not possibly appear in court. Wilson ordered seizures of furniture, household belongings, and other personal property to pay for the judgments.[16] In the course of one week in January, 1862, Isabella Woods was served with ten separate summonses for her husband to appear in court, all filed by local Union men. Unable to find a lawyer to handle the cases, she wrote to her husband that she had no idea what she could do. "Secessionists don't attend the court or observe their laws at all." Spencer Dayton, she complained bitterly, was particularly vigorous in pressing suits against them, including some $3,000 in claims he had purchased from other creditors of Woods. "He is determined to beggar you if possible."[17]

Other forms of harassment were often just as costly. Elisabeth Jarvis, whose home had been ransacked at the beginning of the war, was forcibly evicted in 1863 to make way for Union officers and their families.[18] An officer of the Sixth West Virginia

Infantry, boarding at the house of Sarah Jane Holt, Woods's sister, refused to pay his rent on the grounds that she was "Secesh." "I wish Imboden would come," Holt complained to her sister-in-law. "I would have his duds thrown out pretty quick."[19] Typical was an incident that took place in 1864 when several companies of the Twelfth West Virginia on their way to the front were searching for a place to bed down near Belington. The post commander there suggested they would do well to camp on a particular farm nearby. "That is the very place you should go into camp," he assured the colonel. "You can't punish them half enough, they are the meanest damned rebels in the state." Taking him at his word, the troops pulled down the hapless farmer's hayricks for their bedding and pulled up his fence posts for their campfires. Then they broke into the smokehouse and made off with the family's entire meat supply, along with every chicken on the farm. When the exasperated owner complained, the colonel ordered a search of his camp, but no stolen provisions were found. Satisfied, the colonel and his staff sat down to a "very fine roast of ham" and assured their host they had not the slightest idea how it had gotten into their mess.[20]

Unionists by no means held a monopoly on harassment, even after the rout of Porterfield and his men. William Price, a county magistrate and colonel of the county's militia, was arrested by some of Jackson's men during Jackson's attack on Beverly in 1863 and held in prison at Richmond for eight months before he was released.[21] Adomiron McDonald had fled to Barbour County in 1863 to escape threats made on his life by Secessionists in Calhoun County, only to find himself taken prisoner during the same raid.[22] The kidnapping of Sheriff Trayhern was by far the most notorious "arrest" by Confederates in Barbour. So bloodthirsty was the raiders' reputations that local Unionists accepted without question the rumors that Hill's men had lynched Trayhern.[23]

Confederate troopers constantly raided into Barbour County, stealing horses and robbing stores at every opportunity. Sometimes the raids could take a lighthearted turn. Early in 1864,

Confederate Bert Gall of Barbour and a small party from the Twentieth Virginia Cavalry slipped into the county on a recruiting expedition. Devault Wilson, who had served as a Union scout at the beginning of the war, tried unsuccessfully to alert Federal troops to Gall's presence. Learning that one of Wilson's sons had deserted the Union army and was then at home, they slipped into the house and, posing as Federals, ordered the young man to turn himself in to Colonel Latham. When Wilson and his son reported to Latham as ordered, the colonel chuckled that Wilson had been right after all, and that there indeed "had been some Johnnies out there."[24] Most raids were far more serious—deadly serious. During one in 1865, John Shroyer, a county magistrate, was shot to death when he attempted to stop some of Hill's men from stealing his horses.[25] In July, 1863, a group of Confederates led by John Booth entered Barbour to settle a personal score with Jacob Lunenbarger, a neighbor of Booth's before the war. Barging into Lunenbarger's home, Booth leveled a pistol at Lunenbarger's chest and swore he would kill him then and there. Lunenbarger was saved when his quick-thinking wife grabbed an axe and sank it into Booth's skull.[26]

Nor were Secessionists who remained in Barbour silent victims of Unionist oppression. While many could do little except hope for the return of the Confederate army, others actively defied Union authority at every opportunity. A newspaper reporter arriving at Philippi only a few weeks after Porterfield's defeat was startled to see "a couple of pretty and plucky Secessionist girls" brazenly parading in the street wearing rebel rosettes and Secessionist aprons.[27] When Company K of the Sixth West Virginia arrived in town in the summer of 1862, Helen Capito and Elisabeth McClaskey wrested the company flag from an astonished standard bearer and tore it to shreds. The two young women were arrested and made to sew a new flag and formally apologize for their behavior. Their parents were required to post bonds to insure their future good behavior.[28]

While the antics of young women may have been irksome, of far greater concern to local military commanders was the widespread guerrilla activity. The heavily forested and sparsely populated regions of eastern Barbour, Tucker, and Randolph counties were used to advantage by local Secessionists, who would ambush small patrols or individual soldiers and then melt back into the civilian population. Within three weeks of the Federal rout of Porterfield, Barbour County Unionists complained that "Secessionists here are active and determined. They embrace every opportunity to convey information to the rebel forces," while others "with rifle in hand, fire at straggling parties of our men."[29]

The first casualty of the guerrilla war occurred within a month of the Confederate defeat at Philippi when one of Captain Latham's men was ambushed. The following October, four others were ambushed by guerrillas near Belington. One soldier was killed and the others pinned down for an entire night. Finally, one of the party managed to escape and make it back to camp, returning with 20 men who tracked the guerrillas down to Mike Crim's farm. Crim, on suspicion of helping the ambushers escape, was shot down, his home burned to the ground, and his farm "generally cleaned out."[30] The campaign continued throughout the winter with only mixed results. By the spring of 1862, Latham had killed or captured over a dozen guerrillas, including their leader, Bill Harper of Tucker County. Any relief Latham may have felt, though, was short-lived, as the guerillas reorganized under Bill's brother Zeke. "Can there be nothing done," Latham complained to Governor Pierpont, "in the way of militia organization to suppress these bands of marauders without taking the troops regularly in the U.S. service for that purpose?"[31]

Loosely organized guerrilla bands were not the only means by which secessionists in Barbour County resisted Union occupation. When Imboden mounted his first attempt to destroy the Cheat River bridge at Rowlesburg in 1862, local sympathizers Sam Elliott and Garrett Johnson guided his small force through the mountains.[32] Elliott was notorious for this kind of activity, which ended only when he was taken prisoner as a hostage for Trayhern. Others soon took his place. Among them was Enoch

Johnson, who guided a squad of Imboden's men to within a few miles of Philippi, where they destroyed a supply train.[33]

Women, too, provided valuable service for the Confederacy and in much the same manner as their men folk—hiding wounded soldiers, and spying on Union troops and relaying information on their movements. Annie Murphy and Louisa Ellyson, both of whom had brothers in the Confederate army, were arrested in 1864 on charges of cutting telegraph wires, spying and "doing a great many other things which they ought not to do."[34] Twenty-year old Margaret Reed was arrested shortly after the Jones-Imboden raid for having carried information on Union troop strength to Imboden. Her incarceration did little to dampen her zeal for the Southern cause. Held in a local hotel, Reed made life miserable for her captors by spitting on any Union soldier passing under her window. Her captors transferred her to Wheeling as quickly as possible. There she continued to confound authorities, at one point assaulting her jailor. Reed's antics gained her a certain notoriety in the city, prompting a reporter to visit her in jail to get a first-hand look at this Secessionist Amazon. He found her to be "a very intelligent young woman and is rather prepossessing. . . . She looks as if she could take care of herself."[35]

Secessionist activity and open avowals of support for the Confederacy served to further provoke Union repression. Local constables and Home Guardsmen kept a careful watch on known Southern sympathizers. John Montgomery, despite having a son in the Union army, was arrested because a Union man had been bushwhacked near his home. Francis May was turned in by his own brother for uttering "treasonable language." Thomas Moran found himself in prison on the amorphous charge of "disloyalty."[36] Anything perceived as giving aid and comfort to the enemy was grounds for arrest. Merely writing to or receiving letters from friends or relatives in Confederate-held territory could result in imprisonment, as Elisabeth Morrall learned to her dismay when she was arrested for passing letters across the lines.[37]

In all, over 50 civilians were arrested in Barbour County. The number increased each year as the war on the home front intensified: seven in 1861, sixteen in 1862, 21 in 1863. While only six civilians were arrested in 1864 and none the next year, the decline was by no means due any relaxation of the war effort. Rather, most Confederate activists had by then already been apprehended or had fled the county. Some had been arrested more than once, and the repeated release of Secessionists prompted some local Union men to take matters into their own hands by burning the farms and homes of their enemies. At least one man, Thomas Ice, was abducted from his home and nearly lynched before friends rescued him.[38] As Unionist oppression intensified, Secessionists who remained in Barbour became increasingly isolated. Isabella Woods lamented to her husband that "Friends and relations have been afraid to assist each other in this neighborhood lest their houses be burned by the Abolitionist party. A good friend is hard to find."[39]

The internecine violence and harassment in Barbour is all the more striking because the society in which it took place was not a fundamentally violent one. Those who participated in such activity were respectable farmers, merchants, and even professionals who in ordinary times tried to live within the bounds of law and scripture. Indeed, there were some in Barbour whose compassion led them to place friendship above politics. Hamilton Bartlett and Francis Payne, both described as "good Union men," intervened to secure the release of friends and neighbors arrested for alleged Secessionist activities.[40] Even so stalwart a Union man as Spencer Dayton could be moved to intervene on behalf of erstwhile friends turned traitor. Thomas Bradford was as die-hard a rebel as any in Barbour, yet when a Federal officer confiscated his law library, Dayton immediately retrieved the books, kept them safe throughout the war and returned them to their owner afterward.[41] Such magnanimity seems to have been the exception rather than the rule. When one Barbour Unionist wrote an open letter to the *Wheeling Intelligencer* decrying "the farce" of releasing rebel sympathizers who had taken the oath of allegiance, he probably reflected the opinion of most other Union men in the county.[42] People on both sides felt fully justified in attacking opponents because they saw the war as a struggle against tyranny.

John R. Philips declared that "He who would coerce Virginia was to me a Vandal. The foe that should set a hostile foot upon her shore was, in my judgment, worthy of death."[43] James Hall felt the same. "May the young men . . . in the North think of their responsibilities of making war upon an innocent people who never did them harm. Is conscience dead? Is reason dumb?"[44]

By the same token, Unionists in Barbour sought to eradicate any vestige of secession or its adherents, declaring that anyone "unwilling to actively sustain . . . national unity and perpetuate law and liberty had better leave us and go where they can find friends to please and work to do." As if to emphasize their determination, they demanded that any Secessionists who remained "in our midst . . . ought to be regarded as traitors, and if caught within Union lines, dealt with as spies."[45] Joseph Shoemaker, a private in Captain Coburn's company, was arrested for the murder of Jacob Philips, a civilian prisoner under his charge. Shoemaker denied his guilt, claiming he was merely escorting his prisoner across the Philippi bridge when a shot rang out and Philips dropped dead. A number of local Unionists, including his jailor, urged his immediate release. It was not so much that they believed his story, but they simply couldn't understand why he had been jailed in the first place "simply for killing a rebel." Shoemaker nonetheless remained in jail until the end of the war, when he was tried and acquitted of the charges.[46]

Barbour's Unionists saw the war not only as a struggle for liberty, but as a means of breaking the stranglehold on local politics that had been maintained by the county's wealthy families. In their view, Secessionists sought to reinstate a government "in which offices, civil authority, public employment and emoluments . . . should be limited, exercised and transmitted among a hereditary and privileged class of citizens and rulers."[47] The war created just such an opportunity. Virtually all of the principal county officers had either joined the Confederate army or fled to Eastern Virginia. Gone were James Hartman and Lair Morrall, clerks of the county and circuit courts, Daniel M. Auvil, prosecuting attorney, William Daniels, the county sheriff, and William Johnson,

Barbour's delegate to the Virginia legislature. Others who remained in Barbour County, including half the members of the county court, refused to serve out their terms of office. Their support for the Confederacy created a political vacuum that was quickly filled by Union men of lesser wealth and lineage, many of whom had never before held public office.

The new state constitution adopted in 1863 did much to accelerate pre-war trends towards greater democratization of politics, with provisions designed specifically to break the hold of local elites. First and foremost, it instituted the secret ballot. No longer would men have to cast their votes under the watchful eye of some local squire to whom they might be indebted. Secondly, voter qualifications were relaxed by reducing residency requirements from two years to one. Finally, and perhaps most important, county government was completely reorganized. In place of the old county court, the new constitution introduced the township system. Each county was divided into three or more townships headed by supervisors elected from the district, with all business relating to the township conducted at meetings open to all voters. The new organization aimed at increasing direct participation of citizens while circumventing the power of prominent men to place relatives and cronies in official positions.[48]

The extent to which the war transformed local politics in Barbour County can by seen by examining the kind of men who were voted into office between 1861 and 1865. A comparison of the distribution of real and personal property values reported in the 1860 census for officers elected in 1856, 1860, and during the war reveals that the war had indeed drawn into office not only a greater number of the county's less wealthy citizens, but some who could only be described as downright poverty-stricken. Prior to the war, two-thirds of all office holders owned property worth more than $2,500, and over of third of them owned property worth more than $5,000. During the war, more than half of those elected to public office owned property worth less than $2,500, and sixteen had property valued at less than $500. And whereas all pre-war officeholders had been landowners, six magistrates elected during the war were not. Eleven men elected to office in 1856 and 1860 had held prior offices in the county; during the war that number was four.

The new breed of Barbour's political leaders represented a sharp shift of political power away from the Democratic Party to the Republican. In the 1860 presidential election, Lincoln had received only 1,402 votes in the counties later incorporated into West Virginia, with 85 percent of those votes registered in the three counties of the northern panhandle.[49] In Barbour County it is probable that fewer than half a dozen votes were cast for Lincoln. When war came, those West Virginians who remained loyal to the Union formed the Union Constitutional Party. Initially embracing Republicans, Whigs, and Democrats alike, the party's outspoken support of the Lincoln administration's war effort eventually transformed it into the state branch of the national Republican Party.

In Barbour County, hundreds of men who before the war had been loyal voters for Democratic candidates switched their allegiance to the Republicans. Spencer Dayton is but the most prominent example. A one-time Whig, Dayton had a few years before the war become a Democrat and had quickly risen in party ranks to become senatorial elector in 1859. By the middle of the war Dayton had become the acknowledged leader of the Republican Party in Barbour.[50]

His rise to power both mirrored and was made possible by the Republican ascendancy in the county. At the beginning of the war, the party did not even exist in the county. Barbour had for decades been a Democratic stronghold, local Whigs never mounting a significant challenge. The secession crisis split the Democratic party into pro- and anti-secession wings. With Porterfield's defeat, Union Democrats joined with those Whigs who opposed secession, took charge of local affairs, and organized the war effort in the county.

Other political leaders emerged from the war-time strife in Barbour County. The most prominent leader at the war's outset was Nathan Taft. Within a few months after Porterfield's defeat, he was elected both to the House of Delegates and to the all-important post of county prosecutor. As adjutant of Barbour's militia, he took a leading role in organizing recruitment in the county. In that endeavor he was ably assisted by Asa and John Woodford Jr. who, as members of Barbour's most wealthy family, lent considerable legitimacy to the Union cause. Emmett O'Brien, like Taft, Dayton and the Woodfords a Democrat, was considered a man of such exceptional abilities that at he beginning of the war he was offered a general's commission in the Confederate army. He refused and in October 1861 was elected to represent Barbour at the state's constitutional convention.[51]

Whigs in Barbour were also split by the secession crisis. The most important Whig leader to remain loyal to the Union was Lewis Wilson, son of Barbour's first magistrate, on whose land the county seat had been located. In a county so dominated by The Democracy, Wilson was extremely popular with voters. In 1859, when Democrats out-polled Whigs by a two-to-one margin, Wilson lost election to the House of Delegates by a mere 25 votes.[52] In the elections held in September, 1861, to fill county offices vacated by secessionists, Wilson was voted to head Barbour's county court, a position he held throughout the war and for many years after.

Yet beneath this veneer of anti-secession solidarity lurked both political and personal differences that would erupt into bitter conflict. Personal rivalry played a role in fomenting political divisions, most especially that between Taft and Dayton. The two despised each other.[53] The origin of their animosity is unknown, but was early on carried into the political arena. Immediately prior to the war, Taft had chaired the mass meeting held at the courthouse in Philippi. Among the resolutions passed was one drafted by Taft in support of Samuel Woods's declaration that Virginia possessed the legal right to secede if the Federal government used force against the Deep South states. In retrospect, the resolutions were clearly at odds with his later Unionism, but like many others Taft believed that the very threat of Virginia's secession represented the best means of avoiding war and buying enough time to work out a peaceful solution.[54] Dayton's was the lone voice raised against the resolutions, and for his efforts he was forced from the meeting at gunpoint. The incident was not something a man like Dayton would likely forgive or forget. A few weeks later Taft managed to maneuver Dayton out of a seat at the First Wheeling Convention and secure it for himself.[55]

The Taft-Dayton rivalry soon became enmeshed in divisions within Unionist ranks across Western Virginia.[56] While united in opposition to secession, Unionists were by no means in agreement about just how victory was to be achieved. As the war progressed and Union armies met with repeated defeat on the battlefield, many came to embrace a war program aimed at utilizing every means available to secure victory. If radical, even revolutionary, measures were needed to win the war, they should and would be adopted. Army commanders in West Virginia ordered newspapers they deemed injurious to the war effort to cease publication, and arrested many hundreds of suspected Confederate sympathizers. Elimination of press freedom, the suspension of the writ of habeas corpus, and arbitrary arrests clearly struck at basic freedoms. Yet editors who spread doubt about Union victory and civilians who guided guerrillas, hid Confederate soldiers, or even spoke out in favor of the Confederate cause, gave aid and comfort to the enemy and thereby prolonged the war. What mattered to the radicals was victory. And if victory could be won even by attacking the institution that had set the country on the path to war, then they were prepared to see slavery eradicated forever.

Others staunchly opposed the drift toward radicalism, seeing arbitrary arrests and the suppression of the press as hallmarks of political despotism. Rallying around the cry "The Union As It Was!" they sought a victory that preserved constitutional liberties. But like their Secessionist opponents, they cherished a freedom restricted to whites only, and rejected the notion of extending liberties to slaves.

The struggle between these two views of the war's aims was national in character. Within West Virginia the divisions first came to center on the linked issues of slavery and the new state's boundaries. When the Wheeling and State Constitutional Conventions began to hammer out the particulars of the new state, abolition of slavery was not Federal policy. Yet the issue had to be addressed, despite repeated attempts by members of the two bodies to avoid it. Conservatives opposed boundaries limiting the state to largely non-slave counties for fear that slave owners, reduced to a small minority, would be powerless to thwart efforts to abolish the institution. When members of the Second Wheeling Convention sought to limit the new state's borders to just 38 counties of the Northwest, Daniel Lamb, a leading conservative, objected vehemently. "You select precisely that portion of the territory that contains the smallest amount of slaves. . . . This is an abolitionist movement!"[57]

As at the Wheeling Convention, a great deal of the debate in the Constitutional Convention was taken up with the boundary issue, conservatives arguing that preservation of slavery could be guaranteed only by the inclusion of counties with large numbers of slave owners, opponents of a large state countering that incorporation of the slave-owning counties in the Southwest and the Shenandoah Valley demanded by conservatives—counties already dominated by Secessionists—would doom efforts to create the new state. Yet conservatives largely succeeded, and West Virginia entered the Union with at least half its territory under partial or outright Confederate control.

As for slavery, the delegates could only agree on a clause that prohibited importing slaves into the new state.[58] When Congress demanded an emancipation clause as a condition of statehood, conservatives revolted against what they saw as Congressional dictatorship.[59] Even so, the clause providing for gradual emancipation that was finally adopted by the new state would have left the status of most slaves unchanged for decades if the Thirteenth Amendment had not freed them all in 1865.[60]

Nonetheless, conservative success on the boundary issue would have far-reaching consequences for the future of West Virginia. By the time the state was admitted to the Union, radical and conservative factions had begun to coalesce into a Union Constitutional Party dominated by Republicans and a Unionist Democratic opposition. The inclusion of large numbers of Secessionist—i.e., Democratic—counties into West Virginia would initiate a bitter post-war struggle over political control of the state.[61]

Dayton's position in the unfolding political struggle was clear. Although he held no public office, in June, 1862, he managed to get the county justices to pass a resolution demanding the abolition of slavery—three months before Lincoln's Emancipation Proclamation.[62] The resolution was not only a clear declaration of support for the radical program, but also a direct attack on the Woodfords, both of whom were slave owners, and on Taft as well. Taft is said to have "hated slavery." Yet, as the Commonwealth's attorney, he was sworn to uphold the laws of the state and at the time Dayton's resolutions were passed, Virginia—that is, its Reorganized rump—was still a slave state. Taft therefore saw no contradiction in his petitioning the governor of Ohio to return escaped slaves from West Virginia to their owners. Other actions by Taft caused many in Barbour to question the degree of his Unionism. While he had succeeded in securing for himself Dayton's seat at the First Wheeling Convention—largely due to support from conservatives like Lamb—he failed to attend much of the deliberation. He repeatedly secured releases of civilians arrested for Secessionist activities, and was the only lawyer in the county willing to represent Secessionists in lawsuits filed by Unionists.[63]

The summer and fall of 1862 saw the erosion of the political fortunes of Taft and other conservatives in Barbour County. Taft's early support for Woods continued to plague him. When he sought appointment as brigadier-general of militia, influential radicals in the state legislature alleged that he had voted for Breckenridge in 1860 and for the ordinance of secession in 1861. While others from Barbour publicly declared the charges false, declaring Taft to have been a Douglas Democrat and one of the first men in Barbour to be arrested by Porterfield, he failed to secure the commission.[64] That same year Asa Woodford sought the lieutenant-colonelcy of the newly-organized Tenth West Virginia Infantry which he had helped to raise, but he was passed over in favor of the more staunchly Republican Moses Hall.[65]

The support of county magistrates for Dayton's antislavery resolution is evidence that political sentiment was shifting toward the radicals. By the winter of 1862-1863 the shift was all but complete. The sense of security that had existed during the first year of the war had been shattered by Imboden's raids. The continued threat of Confederate invasion, the inability of Federal troops to quell guerrilla bands, and the marauding by rebel raiders persuaded growing numbers in Barbour that only extreme measures would ensure their safety and the defeat of the Confederacy. The result was that more and more voters came to identify the Republican Party with the Union cause. And at their head was Spencer Dayton.

The birth of the party in Barbour County can be traced to May, 1861, when a handful of Union loyalists met secretly at the shop of Martin Myers to organize a counter-offensive to the Secessionist aggression. Those who participated in that meeting— Dayton, Myers, Joseph Teter, Sr., Alpheus Zinn, Henson Hoff, William K. Hall, and Edwin Tutt[66]—would later become the core of the Republican Party in Barbour. Some, like Teter and Zinn, were already men of considerable political influence. Teter was a descendant of one of the earliest settlers in Barbour County, and had served as a county magistrate long before the formation of the county itself. Zinn belonged to a family of considerable wealth whose members had populated county offices for decades and was himself a minor county official at the outbreak of the war. Soon joined by Lewis Wilson, their social and political prominence would no doubt have guaranteed them positions of influence in local politics even without the coming of the war. What distinguished the Republican Party in Barbour was the widespread participation of so many men of more limited means, who had never before publicly exercised political power.

A good example is Myers. His rise to prominence began with the meeting held at his shop. Within a few months he was elected justice of the peace, and in 1863 became chairman of the county Union Party.[67] Like Myers, Hoff had never before held public office. He nonetheless rose quickly in local politics, elected in 1864 to West Virginia's House of Delegates. Their new-found political influence extended to members of their families. One of Myers's sons, Lank, was elected head of Barbour's circuit court while another, Lewis, secured an army commission and later became one of Barbour's representatives at party conventions. One of Hoff's sons also received an officer's commission, while two others served in various local county offices.[68]

By the beginning of 1863, with the new state a reality, Barbour's nascent Republicans set about organizing the faithful for the May elections—the first to be held in the new state and the same ones Jones and Imboden had aimed to disrupt. Committees were formed in each district to get out the vote for the Union Party's slate of candidates—all Republicans.[69] In the midst of the organizing effort came the news of Trayhern's kidnapping, the killings of those thought responsible for it, and the arrest of hostages to be held for Trayhern's release. Coming in the wake of months of Confederate marauding, the events served to create a siege atmosphere in the county. Michael Haller, one of the few men in Barbour to have voted for Lincoln in 1860, had joined the organizing effort that month. "All are for it," he declared of the upcoming elections, "and jubilant over the prospect. Perhaps no people within the limits of West Virginia have a greater right to rejoice than the people of this vicinity and county, for through here is the route which the thieves travel to Dixie."[70]

The May elections resulted in a complete victory for the radical wing of the party. All five supervisors elected were Republicans. With 82 percent of the votes cast, Dayton replaced Taft as county prosecutor; Lewis Wilson was returned to office with all votes cast. Joseph Teter's son and namesake became Barbour's representative in the House of Delegates, while Lank Myers was elected to head the county circuit court.[71] Now in control of local government, the radicals sought to further consolidate their power, in part by working with Arthur Boreman, West Virginia's newly-elected Republican governor.

When friends and relatives petitioned the governor for the release of those arrested for alleged Secessionist activities, it was to Dayton that Boreman turned for advice. More often than not, Dayton recommended against release.[72] Perhaps the most striking example of the relationship between Boreman and Dayton occurred in the summer of 1863, when a controversy arose over Barbour's newly-organized Home Guard company—a pet project of Boreman. George Yeager, commissioned company commander in July, had been a political ally of John Woodford, Jr. and had assisted Woodford and Taft in organizing recruitment drives the previous summer. In August, Dayton and Lewis Wilson wrote Boreman demanding Yeager's removal, accusing him of misusing government supplies and presenting "an undesirable picture for his men to follow." The charges against Yeager may or may not have been true, but Boreman acted swiftly, replacing Yeager with the man recommended by Dayton, Michael Haller.[73]

Yet the Republican ascendancy in Barbour was by no means complete. Although they swept the 1863 elections, not all the candidates who won prevailed by the same wide margins as Dayton and Wilson.[74] The extent of Democratic resilience became evident in the presidential elections of 1864. On the surface it appeared to be another Republican triumph, Barbour casting 593 votes for Lincoln against only 293 for George McClelland, the Democratic candidate.[75] Yet the salient fact of the elections was that over a third of the votes cast were Democratic. Some may have been Secessionist sympathizers at heart, but the evidence is that most were cast by Union men.

That same year Taft and Woodford broke completely with the state Union Party, Taft running for—and losing—election to the state legislature as a Democrat.[76] Other Democrats in Barbour continued to work within the Union Party. At the Constitutional Convention, O'Brien had been among the minority who favored the inclusion of a clause calling for the gradual emancipation of slaves, and had opposed the efforts of conservatives to extend the new state's boundaries into the Upper Shenandoah Valley. After he returned to Barbour County he held various positions in the party's county organization throughout the war, and in 1865 was elected to the House of Delegates.[77] John Keller, another Union Democrat, was elected to the state senate the same year. Both would soon break with the Union Party when the state's Republican-dominated legislature moved to eliminate the civil rights of ex-Confederates, actions they saw as a blatant attempt to ensure Republican control of state and local government into the postwar era.[78] Nonetheless, Democrats in Barbour, whether working within the Union Party or out of it, had been relegated to a distinct minority in the county and would remain so as long as the war lasted.

Concurrent with political changes was an equally dramatic transformation of slavery in Barbour County. First and foremost, the war eradicated slavery in Barbour, and did so long before the gradual emancipation clause of the new state's constitution went into effect. Instead, Barbour's slaves freed themselves *en masse* and began doing so at the very onset of hostilities. The contingents of Ohio and Indiana troops who first occupied Barbour were 90-day volunteers. When their terms of enlistment expired and they returned home, dozens of slaves fled with them, seeking freedom across the Ohio River. Among them was a female slave owned by Alexander Pickens who made her way to Grafton in July, 1861. There she attached herself to an army officer, donned a uniform, and left with him when his unit went west. Two slaves owned by Thomas Holt, the father-in-law of Samuel Woods's sister Sarah Jane Holt, also escaped that month. One of them, Milt, later went to the trouble of sending word to his former master that he had made it to Ohio and was not returning. Milt was, in the words of Isabella Woods, "among the things that were."[79]

The toll on Barbour's slave owners continued. Whenever Federal troops passed through the county, they were followed by slaves, who were harbored by soldiers despite orders not to do so. Northern soldiers weren't alone in helping slaves escape. When in 1862 several companies of the Twelfth West Virginia Infantry marched through Barbour on their way to Grafton, half a dozen slaves attached themselves to the column. When they reached the railhead, Ohio soldiers embarking for home agreed to take the runaways with them—for a price. "In a few moments the money was paid, the Twelfth boys contributing part, and quickly and slyly the fugitives were transferred aboard. . . . They were never heard of afterward." [80] That same year Isabella Woods wrote to her husband that, "If the Federal troops keep possession of this county much longer, there won't be a slave left." Her prediction soon proved true. By the war's end, only a handful of ex-slaves remained in Barbour. The rest, like Milt, had long since become "among the things that were."[81]

While many who would come to support the Union had little real quarrel with slavery in 1861, the exigencies of the war itself forced a re-evaluation of the "peculiar institution." As the war dragged on, slavery came to be viewed more and more as a bulwark of the Southern Confederacy, and its destruction as a means of striking at the ability of the South to wage war. In mid-1962, Spencer Dayton was prepared to support the seizure of slaves of Confederate activists. By August of the same year, two months before the Emancipation Proclamation, Barbour's Union-ists voted to support a resolution that "if the rebels put the insti-tution of African slavery against the American Union, we emphatically say, let slavery perish, if it be necessary to save the Union."[82]

The changing view of slavery was most pronounced among those West Virginians actually fighting, and there is little doubt the trend was directly related to their war-time experience. Soon after the Emancipation Proclamation in October, 1862, a num-ber of army commanders reported that men greeted the news with open hostility. Typical was a letter written by an officer to Governor Pierpont that month. The young lieutenant, command-ing a detachment of the Sixth West Virginia at Grafton, was clearly disturbed by the reaction of his men. "There are many soldiers here who have always been Democrats, all of them loyal men. . . . They seem to think the President is about to violate the Consti-tution, and their old Party feelings seem to be returning again, which cannot help being very troublesome."[83] Civilians too op-posed the new policy, and at times would encourage relatives serving in the army to do the same. The wife of one of Captain

Wilson's men wrote her husband that he should no longer feel bound by his enlistment. "Now as you are merely fighting to free the negroes, I would advise you to desert and come home." The sister of another soldier in the same company urged him "not to go into any battles, but play off sick, for Old Abe has no business to free the negroes. I would prefer desertion to death in the cause you are enlisted in now. Shame on such a cause, if I was a man I would leave and let them that want to fight it out."[84]

Feelings changed as the war dragged on. When the government began recruiting black regiments, a soldier of the Twelfth West Virginia declared in 1863 that, "When I went into the service at first I thought that it would be a humiliation and a disgrace to one if I had to serve in an army where negro soldiers were employed. I have come to the conclusion that they have as good a right to be killed as I."[85] Officers began to see changes in their men's attitudes. "I have noticed," said a lieutenant of the same regiment, "that our boys have never objected to the Emancipation Proclamation since being in battle."[86] Another officer in the First West Virginia noted similar changes in his men. "No one conversant with the enlistments and feelings of the volunteers at the commencement of the war can say that the contest would have been entered into by them had emancipation been the object of the war. It was only after drinking the cup of adversity filled with defeat and disaster that opened the way for its reception by the army."[87]

William Hewitt of the Twelfth West Virginia recalled an incident that to him typified the changing sentiments. Late one night in 1863, the Twelfth found itself marching through Charles Town, the same place where four years before John Brown had been hanged. The troops were tired and the streets deserted. Then someone at the head of the column began singing "John Brown's Body." Soon the chorus was picked up by those following, until the entire regiment joined in with a gusto that roused the townsfolk from their beds. Hewitt figured that before the war, most of the men had probably felt that Brown got what he deserved. But "men saw things differently now. . . . They were fighting to maintain the Union . . . and every step they took was leading to the doom of slavery."[88]

By 1864, these sentiments had congealed into an almost unanimous support among West Virginia's soldiers for Lincoln and his party. In the presidential election that year they were allowed to vote while still in the field. Because their ballots were mailed home to be counted with the vote of the county of their residences, no separate tally of West Virginia's soldier vote exists.[89] However, letters and newspapers reported the votes of several units. The Twelfth West Virginia voted almost to a man for Lincoln, one soldier explaining that "Little Mac [Democratic candidate George McClellan] was a first rate man, but kept blamed bad company." So too did Battery E of the First West Virginia Artillery and Company F of the Sixth West Virginia Infantry.[90] In the Ninth West Virginia only fifteen of 390 men voted for McClellan; all 270 men of the Thirteenth West Virginia voted Republican. The Eighth Corps of the army, which included ten regiments of West Virginians, cast 1,400 votes for Lincoln against 200 for McClellan, most of the Democratic votes being cast by Ohio troops.[91]

This change in attitudes about slavery was nothing less than revolutionary. It had to be so, for only revolutionary means could win the war. Unionists went to war because they saw the conflict in terms of a struggle for liberty against tyranny. Intrinsically bound to both concepts was the idea of freedom, and freedom was not an idea that could be applied in only a limited sense. No matter how much secessionists might proclaim their rebellion to be a struggle for their own concept of liberty, theirs was a society based on the legitimacy of black slavery, and war against such a society inevitably lead to a war against slavery itself.

By implication, embracing slavery's destruction opened the prospect of social and political equality for blacks as well. Whether there were many whites in Barbour prepared to accept such a logical evolution of race relations is questionable. What mattered most to Unionists and Secessionists alike was the war itself, and by the beginning of 1864 neither side could say with any degree of certainty which side would be victorious. However much the two contending parties within Barbour sought—by whatever means were available to them—to further the aims of their causes, the ultimate outcome of the war would be decided by battles yet to be fought near towns and hamlets most of them had not yet heard of.

- 7 -

STRANGERS IN A STRANGE LAND

With the consolidation of radical Republican power in Barbour County came the intensification of anti-secessionist repression. Confederate sympathizers in the county lived in constant fear of arrest or worse. They could expect little or no protection from civil authorities against attacks from Unionist neighbors, since magistrates and constables were often at the forefront of repression. And after the widespread commandeering carried out by Confederate troopers during the Jones-Imboden raid, they could no longer even look to their own army for protection. Their private correspondence was subject to search, their property and persons subject to seizure. Church doors were closed to them. In short, they were living under "Yankee" oppression, all the more onerous by the fact that it was for the most part carried out by their own neighbors.

At least two dozen men and women from Barbour County, many with their families, are known to have moved into seceded Eastern Virginia. Some had already fled with Porterfield's army at the beginning of the war, and others later found life in Unionist Barbour intolerable. Those who fled found that exile presented them with difficulties almost as daunting as the ones they had sought to escape. Leaving behind all they owned, they exchanged a life of fear for one of privation. What was true for civilian refugees was equally true for Barbour's Confederate soldiers. While they endured the same horrors of war experienced by all who fought in the Southern army, their situation differed from that of their comrades in one crucial respect. Their homeland was enemy territory and their families were at the mercy of their enemies. They too were exiles.

Just as Barbour's Unionists sought to recreate political structures and mold their community into a loyalist stronghold, their Secessionist counterparts in Eastern Virginia, soldiers and civilians alike, attempted to sustain some sense of community among themselves and to preserve, as best they could, ties to the community they had left behind. To some extent they succeeded, and by doing so were able to overcome many of the worst hardships of exile. For many others, homesickness, isolation and the ever-present lure of those they had abandoned to the enemy proved to be burdens too great to bear. Against the successive waves of recruits leaving Barbour for the Confederate army and civilians fleeing to Eastern Virginia, there existed an almost equally strong counter-current of the disillusioned who abandoned the cause and returned home. It was a movement that bled the army far more than battlefield casualties. In the end, the hopelessness of exile contributed as much to the defeat of the Confederate cause in West Virginia as did the blows of the Federal army.

Ironically, while Barbour's Unionists encouraged Secessionists to leave the county, Federal authorities had erected barriers to prevent them from doing so. The blockade established at the beginning of the war was by no means limited to the coastline of the seceded states; it extended to all territory outside of Federal control. Forbidding "all commercial intercourse" between the two sections, the blockade essentially forbade all communications, whether by persons, goods, or letter. Passes were rarely granted. The same string of outposts erected in the Alleghenies to deter Confederate raiders from striking into West Virginia was also charged with preventing travel by civilians into Confederate Virginia.[1]

The experience of Isabella Woods typified the problems faced by civilians who sought to escape Union repression. She had considered flight to the East from the moment her husband had left Philippi. Delayed by the illness of her youngest child, it was only after his death that she could begin to give serious consideration to the move. But by then, all roads east were blocked. Friends cautioned her about attempting to secure a pass to travel through the blockade for fear Federal soldiers would seize her horse and wagon, leaving her and her children stranded. By September, 1861, Federal authorities forbade any kind of communication with Confederate Virginia. She was trapped.[2]

Yet she continued to plot her escape. Attempting to use what little influence her husband's pre-war prominence may have retained, she wrote to Governor Pierpont and Senators William G. Brown and Waitman T. Willey pleading for a pass. It was a vain effort, but, she informed her husband in letters smuggled through the lines, "I will keep trying and may succeed yet."[3] When it became clear that no passes would be issued, she decided to attempt the journey without one. Other women, including her sister-in-law, had successfully made brief trips to the East and much to Isabella's surprise, were left undisturbed after their return. "I felt much disappointment that I didn't know Sarah Jane was going over. I could have gone along."[4] After her home was burned to the ground by Union sympathizers, Isabella concentrated virtually all of her energies on getting out. She believed her chance had come when troops guarding the Staunton turnpike at Belington were withdrawn in the early summer of 1862. She began selling off household furnishings and other property to finance the trip. The plan, however, unraveled when the man who had agreed to take her "fizzled out."[5]

Then, quite unexpectedly, her wishes were suddenly granted. In July, 1862, her brother's wife and several other women from Fairmont appeared at her doorstep accompanied by a squad of Federal soldiers. They had been apprehended on their return from illegal visits to their husbands in Eastern Virginia, and local authorities had decided to rid the territory of the women by sending them back for good. Isabella and her children were informed that they were to join the group. In all, some 20 civilians, including six children, were escorted by a full company of infantry beyond Federal lines. Past Beverly the soldiers left the deportees, and the group was soon met by Confederate soldiers who brought them into Monterey.[6] There they joined an ever-growing number of Western Virginians whose support for secession had forced them into exile.

After staying a few weeks with a cousin of Andrew Trimble, the Woodses moved into a house in Waynesboro where they remained for the rest of the war. Yet the escape to Virginia failed to reunite the family. Woods had taken a captain's commission in the army and was posted to Jackson's commissary staff. And so, as before, they were forced to share their hopes and anxieties by letter. While the continued separation was painful, Isabella never regretted her decision to flee. "I don't have the desolate feeling of widowhood I had at home."[7] Her efforts during those years to maintain some semblance of the family's former life were typical of the struggles faced by all refugees from Western Virginia. Neither the Confederate Congress nor the Virginia legislature made significant efforts to alleviate the suffering of refugees from the Northwest. They were essentially forced to rely on whatever scant resources they managed to bring with them or could receive from friends, relatives, or sympathetic civilians.[8]

For a family accustomed to all the comforts provided by Sam Woods's lucrative law practice and land investments, refugee life proved to be something of a jarring experience. "We never lived in a rented house before," Isabella complained to her husband, "and I foolishly thought we would be able to get a house and *pay* for it."[9] The house was all they could afford on Woods's army pay of $200 per month. Former landlords themselves, they were now tenants and quickly developed typical renter attitudes. Isabella described the house as a "rat trap" that leaked whenever it rained, but she still had to endure the owner's harangues that they were allowing the property to "go to rack." When their lease came up for renewal, she was shocked to learn that their landlord, a Mr. Reader, intended to raise the rent to $100 a month. "The sum is more than I'll ever give, unless there is no other to be had. I find the Reader family is very unpopular and, I think, deserve to be. This 'property' seems to make the whole family feel very rich. If he comes around here any more, I shall talk plenty to the old chap."[10]

Woods's army pay was never sufficient to meet the family's living expenses. The winter of 1862-1863 was particularly severe, but Isabella couldn't afford to properly clothe her children. "The boys miss their boots this winter. Sam growls for hours about it and doesn't have dry feet one hour in the day." Although she scrimped and economized as much as possible, war-induced inflation played havoc with her budget. "Everything seems to be growing higher and higher. . . . If prices of necessary articles increase as they have done in the last few months, we will be compelled to forgo all other articles." The children joined in the struggle to make ends meet. Young Frank proudly wrote his father that he had rented out their horse to a neighbor for $5 worth of crushed corn, but "it just lasted a week."[11] Like other refugees, the Woodses were forced to begin selling off what few possessions they had. Isabella suggested they sell their cow, horse, and buggy. She had no use for the latter two anyway. "I would rather sell them," she wrote. "I never want to go any place when you are gone." Her husband consented to letting them go, but not the cow; they might need it. Otherwise Isabella was to "do the best you can."[12]

The penny-pinching, the struggles with their landlord, and the forced sale of their belongings were often too much for Isabella to bear, and she frequently expressed her despair in letters to her husband. For his part, Woods felt obliged to try and shed some perspective on their situation. "I do not intend to chide you for desponding, but it is well to be thankful for the evils we escape. If we have been driven from our home, and our property wasted by the common enemy, so have thousands of others as good as us."[13] His admonitions did little to soothe his wife. "Your moralizing and philosophizing is very good and I can console myself in the same way, but there are times when all fails, even trust in Providence, and I can only see all our hopes and prospects blighted, and a dark and gloomy future. That others have suffered doesn't comfort me any."[14]

Isabella Woods was indeed more fortunate than most of the Confederate wives who had remained in West Virginia. Wives of Union soldiers could at least count on some of their husbands' pay, however meager or infrequent. Soldiers serving as substitutes for draftees could reap substantial payments. When James Moats returned from the United States Army in 1865, a neighbor offered him $1,000 to serve in place of a son who had been drafted. Moats agreed and was preparing to join his regiment when news of Lee's surrender reached him. He kept the money anyway and used it to buy a farm.[15] The wives of Confederate soldiers lacked such resources. Their men, when they were paid at all, received Confederate script of no value in West Virginia. Some women simply gave up trying to maintain their farms and left for Eastern Virginia. Typical was the wife of Isaac Stockwell of the Thirty-First Virginia. She wrote to her husband in 1864 that she was "having a hard time." The family was out of provisions and the crops had failed. She was leaving Barbour for good and would try to meet him in Staunton.[16]

Others were suffering humiliation and rejection by their own compatriots. These were the dozens of officers from West Virginia dismissed from the service in the spring of 1862 when the volunteer Confederate companies of the Twenty-fifth and Thirty-first Infantry were conscripted into the regular army. Although the two regiments had been fighting for a year, Confederate War Department regulations demanded that all officers be elected by their men and as part of their reorganization, ordered that new elections be held.[17] Before the war, most of the officers of the two regiments had been lawyers, merchants, newspapermen, wealthy farmers, and even preachers, prominent members of their communities who had taken a leading role in local Secessionist movements, organized volunteer companies, and led their men into the war. But a year of hard fighting had taught the rank and file that mastery of stump politics did not necessarily translate into combat leadership.

One captain of the Twenty-fifth, a pre-war lawyer who had raised the Pocahontas Rescuers, had before the fighting declared to all who would listen that he could whip 75,000 Yankees with a peach tree switch. One of the first to flee Philippi when the Federals attacked, he was a far more subdued man when he limped into Monterey after Garnett's retreat. "He was not cut out to be a military man," concluded one private.[18] Some of the officers displayed a haughty aristocratic superiority that simply did not sit well with the men they led. William P. Thompson, son of prominent Judge George W. Thompson of Wheeling, was a Fairmont lawyer who had organized the Marion Guards in the spring of 1861. He promptly resigned his commission when he learned a private had been promoted to major over him.[19] Others played the martinet and tried to instill military discipline with disastrous results. James Hall of Barbour chafed at their pettiness. "They have treated me very badly since I have been in the army," he wrote towards the end of 1861. "I remember well every insult. A day will surely come when they will rue everything they have done to me."[20]

That day came on May 1, 1862. In a resounding repudiation of their officers, the men of the Twenty-fifth and Thirty-first threw out most of the politicians who had until then commanded them. Jonathon Heck, a lawyer from Preston County who had served in the Richmond Convention, lost the colonelcy of the Twenty-fifth, as did William Jackson, commander of the Thirty-first and cousin of Stonewall. In the Thirty-first the rejection was wholesale. Not one of the ten company commanders who stood for re-election managed to retain their posts. Thirteen of twenty lieutenants were voted out. Of the new captains elected, five had been lieutenants, one a sergeant, and the other four privates. Officers of the Twenty-fifth fared somewhat better, perhaps because many were graduates of the Virginia Military Institute and other military academies. Even so, only four captains and eight lieutenants managed to win re-election, the rest replaced by men drawn from the ranks.[21]

Most of Barbour's officers were swept away in the elections. In place of Henry Sturm, the men of the Mountain Guards elected John R. Philips, then recovering from wounds in a nearby hospital. The two company lieutenants, Nathaniel Poling and Jacob Hill, both lost out to corporals. Poling swallowed his pride and re-enlisted as a private; Hill returned to Barbour County, where he was chased down and killed by Federal troops. Thomas Bradford, who had lost an election to the Richmond Convention a year earlier, lost another when the Barbour Greys chose George Thompson, a VMI graduate, as their new company commander. Isaac Johnson of the same company was able to retain his lieutenancy, but two other lieutenants were voted out, replaced by men elected from the ranks.

Dropped from the rolls of the regiments, the rejected officers quite suddenly joined the ranks of civilian refugees. Some, like Poling, re-enlisted as privates or joined other regiments. Others set about reconstituting their military careers. Some of these found their way to Imboden's corps where they came to comprise a large proportion of his officers.[22] After serving for several months on the staff of his cousin Stonewall, William Jackson secured a commission to raise his own cavalry regiment. Others returned home, if their homes were in Confederate-held territory. Jacob Hill was not the only rejected officer killed when he tried to return to a home occupied by the Union army. Some, like Bradford, managed to secure positions of one kind or another in the Confederate government. Others, like Sturm, remained refugees for the rest of the war.

Monterey, Virginia, soon became a focal point for exiled West Virginians. Situated on the main road crossing the mountains into Eastern Virginia, it was the first town reached by those fleeing Union-held areas. And so it was to Monterey that Captain Sturm came after being dropped from the rolls of the Thirty-first. Already there was Daniel M. Auvil, Barbour's former prosecuting attorney and militia commander who made his way to the town after his release from prison. So too was Auvil's brother Henry, indicted for treason by Federal authorities. William Johnson, who continued to represent Barbour County in the Virginia legislature, established his residence in the town.[23] They were but a few of dozens of civilians who came to Monterey.

Near Monterey stood Sunnyside, a hotel maintained by Edgar Campbell, a prominent landowner and merchant of Highland County. His establishment quickly became something of a mecca for West Virginia's soldiers and civilian refugees. Virtually every diary and memoir of the war makes mention of time spent there. One trooper from Taylor County recalled that Campbell's "doors were always open for a soldier."[24] John R. Philips's introduction to Sunnyside came in December, 1861, when he was sent there to recuperate from wounds he received at the Battle of Allegheny. He promptly fell in love with the place and returned to it frequently throughout the war. "Mr. Campbell was a Virginian of the true type. His house was elegant and all of his surroundings bespoke of prosperity. . . . There was wealth, ease, refinement, and a species of enjoyable luxury that we had never known before hovering around us in this peaceful valley."[25]

The stream of visitors from West Virginia made Sunnyside both a haven from the war and a rendezvous at which old acquaintances could be renewed and new friendships formed. An army camp had been built nearby, and it was there Imboden established his headquarters when he began recruiting his partisan brigade. Officers and enlisted men alike made their way to Campbell's. Among the principal attractions that drew so many young men to Sunnyside were the several young women who resided there. In addition to Campbell's own daughters—Philips described them as "beautiful, intelligent and well-educated"—there were a number of female refugees from Marion and Taylor Counties, including those who had been forced into exile with Isabella Woods. All of them doted on the soldiers. "We were lionized," recalled Philips, "and oft dozed in the day dreams of a bright future wherein some Highland Mary made home bright and . . . young lieutenants very happy."[26]

Beyond Monterey, Barbour's civilian refugees took up residence in towns in the Shenandoah Valley and along the main road to Richmond. Julia Butcher, the first female refugee of the war from Barbour, took her children to New Market in the summer of 1861. James Hall's uncle and namesake, James D. Hall, had organized pro-secessionist meetings in Barbour during the spring of 1861 and made his way to Staunton in the early months of the war. There he died at the end of the year. Thomas Bradford obtained a post with the Ordinance Board in Staunton. Others, especially those with family and business connections, took up residence further east. Lair Morrall and Isaac Strickler established a mercantile house in Buckingham County. After his discharge from the army, Albert Reger secured an appointment as a tax collector in Fluvanna County. John Payne, clerk for the now de-funct Bank of Philippi, had led mobs in Philippi seeking those delegates returning from the Richmond Convention who had opposed the secession ordinance. He fled with Porterfield's army and found shelter with relatives in Wythe County.[27]

Widely scattered as they were, the refugees established a network by which news and information, carried by letter and word of mouth, were disseminated among themselves. Any sol-dier on furlough or civilian who traveled was sure to call on other West Virginians on their route. While the Thirty-first Virginia was stationed near Monterey in 1863, Philips was delighted by a surprise visit from his father, who spent a week in camp before traveling on to Richmond. Bidding him farewell proved difficult. "Whoever knew the nearness of relations until forced to part with them. I confess the matter unmanned me."[28] Most visits were just as unexpected, but the chance meeting between Philips and his uncle some months later was perhaps more startling than most. Asa Philips, a wagoner for the Union army, had been taken pris-oner during a raid by Imboden's men near Moorefield. Philips saw him only by chance when the prisoners were brought into camp near Monterey.[29]

James Hall was stricken with illness during the Valley cam-paign in 1862 and wound up in a Richmond hospital. When he felt well enough to travel, he headed for Maysville in Buckingham County to spend time with Morrall and with Strickler, who had married his cousin. It had been 15 months since he'd left Barbour County, and being among friends and relations once again was "glorious... I almost fancied I was at home."[30] After his release from prison in 1865, he got his first furlough and immediately set out for home. Federal occupation of the Shenandoah Valley forced him to turn back at Monterey and Hall spent most of his leave with the Woodses in Wayneboro and several more days with Strickler and Morrall afterward.[31]

The many letters of Isabella Woods to her husband recount a continuous stream of visitors, each of whom had some bit of news or rumor about other refugees or those still in Barbour. Their tenant's son Draper Trimble appears to have crossed the mountains frequently before he joined the army in 1863; he was a sure source of information on home.[32] When John R. Williamson left for Richmond to negotiate the terms of Sheriff Trayhern's release, he made sure to stop both at the Woods' house and at Sunnyside, bringing details of the kidnapping and the killings.[33]

The extent to which Barbour's Confederates, both soldiers and civilians, traveled between Western and Eastern Virginia is remarkable given the obstacles and dangers. The fact was that no amount of Federal troops could ever completely cut off traffic. Most journeys were undertaken by soldiers on leave, alone or in small groups. Those who succeeded in getting back were always eagerly awaited. "W. F. Holt returned to our company to pay us a visit yesterday," Hall noted in his diary in 1863. "Having been in the Northwest during his absence, he told us much about our friends in that section of which we never knew before. I would love to have seen some of the things he represented to have seen."[34]

While recuperating from wounds at Sunnyside, Philips learned that his distant cousin Mortimor Johnson had left for Barbour to begin recruiting for Imboden's Rangers. Philips was clearly envious of his kinsman's good fortune. "I suppose my old friend . . . is safe at home . . . seated in his own quiet parlor surrounded by his dear wife and infant family. Perhaps there are others there who are listening to some story that he is telling. How I wish I could step quietly and unnoticed, and take a back seat and watch that happy family."[35] In fact, the reality was far less idyllic than Philips imagined. Johnson's party had struggled through a snow storm for the better part of a day to reach a remote mountain cabin, and now lay exhausted beneath blankets stolen from the Union army—and clearly marked "U.S." Another Confederate scouting party burst into the room and demanded their surrender. Johnson wearily lifted his head and admonished his would-be captors, "What the devil's the matter with you? Do you suppose any but Confederates would be out in such a storm?" Within a few weeks Johnson would be dead, surprised again while on another recruiting expedition into Barbour, but this time by Federal troops who shot first and then demanded the surrender of the survivors.[36]

Furloughs for Confederate soldiers were only rarely granted. While many rectified the infrequent official leaves of absences by taking unofficial ones, they faced certain punishment on their return—if they returned at all. For civilians the problem of communicating with home was compounded by the fact that many moved from one town to another as circumstances dictated. Julia Butcher lived for a time in New Market, later in Waynesboro, and still later in Fisherville. When James Hall, her nephew, got his furlough in 1865, he tried to stop by there to see her, only to learn that she had moved yet again.[37] Isabella Woods completely lost track of Butcher after she left Fisherville. When Elisabeth Morrall fled Barbour in 1863, its was months before she was confirmed as living in Bristol. The constant shuffling from one place to another only increased everyone's sense of isolation and loneliness. Isabella Woods sorely missed Butcher's company after she left town in the spring of 1863. A few weeks later she lost yet another companion when Reverend Abraham Smith of Clarksburg and his wife left Waynesboro. While Isabella had not always gotten along with Mrs. Smith, their common bond of exile had drawn the two women together. "I shall miss her very much."[38]

Given all this, the principal means by which refugees and soldiers maintained contact with one another and with those in Barbour was by letter. Correspondence with others in Confederate Virginia was not without its own peculiar problems. Refugees were homeless, and tended to move as necessity demanded or opportunity allowed. It wasn't always possible for the hard-pressed Confederate postal service to keep up with frequent address changes and many letters never reached their destinations.[39]

Woods's attempt to further his own political career was one casualty of the Confederate postal service. Richmond never relinquished its claimed sovereignty over West Virginia, and the territory continued to be represented in the state legislature. The votes that put Western representatives there were limited to civilian refugees and soldiers from Western counties who, by special law, were allowed to vote in the cities and towns where they resided or in camps wherever their units happened to be stationed. The "elections" usually amounted to a few dozen voters casting ballots, but at least the fiction of a unified Virginia was maintained.[40] Because soldiers from the West outnumbered civilian refugees, their votes usually decided the outcome. The problem for candidates lay in getting notice of their intentions to run for office to civilians scattered across Eastern Virginia and to soldiers constantly on the march. When Woods ran for the state senate, his letter to the men of the Thirty-first Virginia announcing his candidacy got lost in the mail and reached the regiment the day after the poll. Woods lost, much to the consternation of the Barbour men of the Thirty-first, who had already voted for another candidate.[41]

Getting letters to and from Western Virginia presented problems on an entirely different scale. At the beginning of the war, the U. S. Post Office immediately ceased delivery of mail to the seceded states. Any letters addressed to the South were directed to the newly-formed Dead Letter Office. By November of 1862, it had accumulated over 13,000 letters—and several hundred Valentines—which were all ultimately destroyed.[42] By the same token, Confederate authorities undertook measures to intercept mail headed North, fearful that it might contain information beneficial to Federal commanders. The Allegheny border presented a particular area of concern. In April, 1862, Lee instructed General Edward Johnson, whose army at Monterey included large numbers of Western Virginians, to be on the lookout for anyone carrying mail across the mountains and to carefully censor all correspondence. Objectionable letters—and those bearing them— were to be seized.[43]

Faced with such obstacles, Barbour's Secessionists established an ad hoc secret postal service of their own. Soldiers and civilians regularly smuggled mail back and forth across the mountains.

Indeed, anyone known to be traveling between the sections was inundated with pleas to carry letters. Elisabeth Jarvis did so when forced into exile in 1863. When John R. Williamson left for Richmond he also took with him a batch of letters from Barbour and brought back many more with him.[44] Philips's mother Osa made him swear a solemn oath that whenever he came home on leave, he was to bring with him as many letters as he could from others in the army; she would see to it they reached their destination.[45] The homes of Jake Sturm, Enoch Johnson, Sam Elliott, Henry Wilson, and Sam Stalnaker became unofficial post offices for correspondence between Eastern and Western Virginia.[46]

The underground mail service was fraught with dangers for those engaged in it. To be captured with letters from or destined for known traitors opened the bearer to charges of espionage. Jake Sturm was taken prisoner near his home in late 1861. On him were found dozens of letters from soldiers in the East. Although prepared to give an oath of loyalty to get himself out of prison, he continued to linger in jail for years as his repeated petitions for release were denied.[47] One of Elisabeth Morrall's letters to her husband was intercepted before it got out of the county. Morrall was promptly arrested and her letter read in open court. Its contents proved something of an embarrassment to Isabella Woods, for it contained several disparaging remarks about her and her husband. The incident prompted Isabella not only to reconsider their friendship with the Morralls, but to make sure her own husband's letters to her were safely concealed.[48]

By 1863 much of the mail between Eastern and Western Virginia was being carried by troopers specifically detailed for the task. Drawn largely from Imboden's and Jackson's brigades, these men earned renown on both sides of the mountains for their skill and daring. Heavily armed and carrying sufficient rations for several days, they generally traveled alone, bringing with them hundreds of letters. They returned with valuable intelligence on Union troop movements and, as often as not, new recruits for the army. For their comrades, however, their true value was the link they provided to home. One soldier, who had done a bit of this kind of work himself, wrote that, "To him was confided many a tender message for those absent loved ones who were in the Confederacy. . . . On his return . . . there was always a wild rush of soldiers to receive their letters, and get verbal tidings from home."[49]

With husbands, fathers and brothers in the army or in exile, keeping the lines of communication open often fell to women. Amanda Murphy, whose husband was serving in the Twenty-fifth Virginia Infantry, became a regular mail carrier, repeatedly crossing Federal lines on horseback and often pursued by Union troopers. On one occasion, she just managed to conceal her mail bag when they caught up with her. The soldiers decided they'd had enough of chasing Murphy through the hills and figured the only way to disrupt the mail service was simply to shoot her then and there. But when Murphy refused to turn her back to them, they found they couldn't shoot her to her face and instead rode off. The tables were turned during a Confederate raid into Barbour County when a neighbor sought Murphy's help in hiding her son, a Union man. Murphy agreed and put him in her cellar. Soon after she discovered him engrossed in reading letters she'd hidden there and felt she had no choice but to kill the man. She relented only when he told her he himself had a letter he wanted sent across the lines and swore not to reveal what he'd found if she would carry it for him.[50]

Osa Philips came close to being arrested for harboring illegal mail. Haller's Home Guardsmen, who had long suspected her, believed their chance to catch Philips had come when they came across the mother of a soldier in the Thirty-first Infantry making her way on foot to the Philipses' farm. Osa, seeing them ride up, quickly hid the mail in a milk jug. Her choice proved a good one for the soldiers found nothing. Their mission a failure, they demanded some refreshment as compensation. Osa carefully doled cups of milk from the jug. Her son recalled that, "Long afterwards, she would laugh about them drinking the cream off the letters."[51]

The very real dangers involved in carrying illegal mail, coupled with its heavy dependence on the infrequent furloughs of soldiers making their way into and out of the county, rendered the system a haphazard affair at best. Isabella Woods heard nothing from her husband for three months after he fled Philippi. She nonetheless wrote to him religiously, never knowing if any of her own letters would ever reach him. "What has become of you?" she wrote at one point. "I haven't had a letter since the middle of September. In the meantime I have heard you were in Washington County, in Charlottesville, in Monterey, and at Richmond. Amidst all of these conflicting reports I try to comfort myself with the hope you are alive." Often her letters would pile up, awaiting a chance to be sent out. Several times she learned of men leaving Barbour for the army, but time and again none would risk taking her letters for fear of being captured with them.[52]

James Hall, who had retreated to Monterey with the Barbour Greys, waited four months without a letter from home. Detailed as camp postal clerk, he enviously sorted through over 800 letters a day, jealous of the good fortune of those who could so easily write home and get letters in return. From time to time he would begin to write one himself, but always stopped short. "The hopelessness of its ever being received caused me to desist." Finally he got one. Word of its arrival preceded the letter by several days, time which Hall spent "anxiously expecting it." At last, five days later, it arrived. "Today I received the long-expected letter from home. I was truly glad to hear from there, and I never cherished receiving a letter more than I did this one."[53] It was a scene repeated over and over during the war. When two privates in Philips's company made their way to Barbour County in the spring of 1863, their fellow soldiers eagerly awaited their return, for they knew the two would bring back both news and letters from home. They weren't disappointed. "Wilson and Johnson arrived in camp," wrote an elated Philips in his diary, "and brought a number of letters for us. The next day we were busy reading our letters. All are well at home."[54]

Homesickness is, of course, a common experience of soldiers in all wars. What distinguished Barbour's Confederates was that with memories of home came the ever-present knowledge that their friends and loved ones lived under the yoke of their enemy, and that between them stood a barrier manned by over 30,000 Federal soldiers. "I am tired, tired, tired of this life," wrote Hall to himself in 1863. "Anxiety about home and their unprotected condition among the enemy is enough to make the hours glide slowly. Will I ever see my friends around the social board again?"[55] Recuperating from his second wound of the war gave Philips much time to ponder his situation. "Again I am thinking. I miss my home and the mother, father, and my sister and all my friends around Valley Furnace. . . . I turn and think of the loved ones in my dear old Barbour."[56] "Like you," wrote Isabella Woods to her husband, "of late I've been dwelling much upon thoughts of home and wondering at the destiny that has made us strangers in a strange land."[57]

A strange land indeed, for though Barbour's Confederates viewed themselves above all as Virginians, Eastern Virginia itself offered little when compared to their homeland. Travelers to the Western mountains usually viewed the region as a backwater and its inhabitants as little better than rough mountaineers. Yet when Barbour's Confederates compared the two sections, they found there was little in the East to attract them. "The soils of the counties of Louisa, Orange, and Hanover is a white sand and remarkable for its poorness," noted Philips. "It produces nothing in any quantity, but chickapin bushes and the negroes are as thick as skippers in a spoiled ham. The buildings are not anything as fine as they are in Western Virginia. It seems to one that it is almost a land of poverty."[58] Hall felt keenly the social differences between the two sections and pitied his younger brother Jaspar who had left the army and remained in exile, "staying among an aristocratic people, and is a stranger to them all." After a year's campaigning in Virginia, he concluded that, "if they ever retake Western Virginia, I will say goodbye to Dixie forever."[59] Philips put it succinctly: "Oh, what a thing it is to be cut off from home!"[60] It was a reality James Hall returned to again and again. "All my friends are at home—among the Yankees. . . . Truly a home has lost all of its quietude and pleasure when surrounded by a cruel and hostile foe." The occasional letter from friends and family served only to intensify his sense of powerlessness:

> I heard today that the enemy had shamefully treated some of the Citizens of my County, respecting private property and personal violence. May the God of truth and justice curse them with His rod for such infernal treatment. . . . Shall our friends forever be in a land of such oppression? . . . Our country, I fear, is lost, lost forever."[61]

For Isabella Woods, it was not simply that she and her family had been forced into exile, but that their Unionist neighbors had confiscated all they had struggled for over the previous decade. "It seems too hard to have other people living off the fruits of our toil and sacrifice.[62]

For men like Hall and Philips, repression at home only served to rekindle their devotion to the Southern cause, a cause that became for them a war not to protect their homes, but to free them. "May God permit us to be avenged," exclaimed Hall, "even to a small degree, for the insults and mean treatment perpetrated by those cruel vandals of the North."[63] Philips expressed similar sentiments. "I have studied my course of policy for hours and always arrive at the same conclusion, that I would see this conflict through if I was afterwards left to die a beggar."[64] Samuel Woods too felt the pain of homesickness, but remained steadfast in his resolve. Sitting beside a campfire in the winter of 1863, a blanket thrown about his shoulders, he penned his thoughts in a long, somewhat lawyerly letter to his wife:

> Once it was all peace and prosperity, now shaded by the dark and bloody clouds of civil war through which a strong and abiding faith in the goodness and mercy of God . . . are continuously seen breaking through the gloom and darkness—fields of light in which our children, and their children, may in the enjoyment of constitutional liberty, pursue avocations of peace.[65]

Others succumbed to homesickness and war-weariness and simply gave up. Lair Morrall, who had fled to Eastern Virginia at the beginning of the war, sent out feelers to Spencer Dayton about the possibility of his returning, offering a bond of $3,000 as security for his good behavior. Other Unionists in Barbour moved quickly to squelch the prospect, declaring they had no faith whatsoever in any oath he might give.[66] Isabella Woods often considered returning home. When she heard rumors that the blockade was to be lifted, her immediate reaction was to pack up and leave for Barbour. "My imagination is very busy," she wrote excitedly, "I fancy myself ready to go home, that my children have all they want to eat, drink, and wear."[67]

Rumors turned to reality in the spring of 1863, when Imboden launched his raid into the Northwest. From all across Virginia soldiers and civilians flocked to his column, hoping at long last to return home. Soldiers on leave rushed to rejoin their regiments while others, like Philips, simply tagged along.[68] Isabella, hearing that her brother James Neeson had joined Imboden, promptly wrote her husband about the prospects of their going as well. "If he should be successful and hold the country, I am almost determined to go home if I can get through. I can see no hope of an end to this war, and we ought to be able to live off our farm there." By the end of May, all hopes had been dashed. "Our men only made a raid out there." Worse yet, far from enabling any refugees to return home, the raid had served instead to swell the ranks of the exiled. "Many families are coming through," Isabella dejectedly informed her husband, while many others were "anxious for our men to get in that they might get out."[69]

By the beginning of 1864 it was clear to anyone who cared to look at the war realistically that the Confederacy would never be able to wrest Virginia's seceded counties from Federal control. For many who did, it was a realization that turned to demoralization. The result was a new epidemic of desertions, this time not of men leaving one unit to join another closer to home, but of soldiers abandoning the army for good. Between the fall of 1863 and the end of 1864 nearly 200 men abandoned Imboden's Sixty-second Virginia, gave themselves up to Federal authorities in Western Virginia, and took an oath of allegiance to the government.

In Jackson's Twentieth Cavalry the number was nearly the same.[70] One soldier from Harrison County who stayed with the Twentieth to the end of the war acknowledged the problem and its fundamental cause:

> If the loss by desertion had been altogether of the worthless fellows in the army, we could have stood it better but, as a matter of fact, very many excellent soldiers received letters from their homes and reports of suffering and privations of their families until their patriotism became entirely overshadowed by the love they bore their families. A large number of men as these took "French" leave, never returning.[71]

- 8 -

LET MALICE GO

In March of 1864, Ulysses Grant was appointed commander-in-chief of the entire United States Army: half a million men organized into 21 army corps stretching from Texas to Virginia. The nature of the war changed with that appointment. For three years the various armies of the North had fought almost independently of one another, each seeking its own objective with only a limited view of how its movements affected the progress of the war on other fronts. When Grant assumed command, he put into motion a strategy by which all Federal armies would act in concert and with a single objective: the destruction of Confederate military power at all points. No longer would Union armies seek to win and hold territory. Now they would strike the Rebellion until the armies of the Confederacy were ground down and eliminated.

This strategy would also transform the war for West Virginia's soldiers, both Union and Confederate. In Grant's view, the 35,000 troops occupying West Virginia could better protect the new state by invading the Shenandoah Valley. For three years this fertile lowland had served Lee both as a source of supply and as a pathway to outflank any attempt to capture the Confederate capital at Richmond. A Federal army in the Shenandoah would threaten the lifeblood of the Army of Northern Virginia, forcing Lee to withdraw precious manpower from the East and making the destruction of his army so much easier. It was, in effect, the same plan attempted in 1862, but Grant was determined that this time it would not fail. Almost every regiment then stationed in West Virginia would be shifted to the Valley, leaving behind only a few regiments of infantry, a scattering of cavalry, and a few batteries to protect the entire state. Considerable responsibility for protecting loyalists in West Virginia shifted to the Home Guard companies organized in 1863 and expanded in 1864.[1] The relative weakness of these forces was never exploited, for when Grant ordered the invasion of the Shenandoah Valley, every Confederate soldier serving in the Northwest was ordered to the defense.[2]

The Valley campaign was of particular significance for the soldiers of Barbour County. It put into action a larger number of its men than any previous campaign of the war—all told some 220 Union soldiers and 165 Confederates. It would also be the bloodiest five months of the war for them. Between May and November, 1864, 18 men from the county would be killed and another 74 wounded in the Valley. Eight others taken prisoner would die in captivity. Most of these casualties occurred in battles in which Barbour men fought on each side, often with their regiments directly facing one another. Most tragic of all, it pitted a greater number of relatives from Barbour against one another than ever before—some 15 families from the county had sons fighting on opposite sides. Levi Cross, whose parents had struggled so ingeniously to keep him from ever meeting up with his brothers, would now be fighting all three of them. Noah Corley of the Tenth West Virginia had a brother, Allen, and two nephews, John and Samuel Boner, serving in the Confederate army. With Imboden was Jesse Poling of Barbour County. In the Union army was his brother Jacob. With the Tenth West Virginia was Jesse's brother-in-law John Lohr. Levi Kuykendahl and Moses Smith of the Fifteenth West Virginia both had brothers-in-law serving with Imboden's and Jackson's brigades. Johnson Chrislip and John Coontz of the Tenth West Virginia had cousins in the Confederate army. Samuel Welch, Isaac Price, and Isaac's brother William, all serving in West Virginia regiments, had brothers in Virginia regiments, as did Cornelius Hymes, who would be shot dead during the campaign.

During the initial months of the campaign, a succession of Federal commanders suffered defeats at the hands of the Confederate army under General Jubal Early, and by midsummer the Union army was essentially where it had been when it began the campaign in the spring. Grant gave command of the Valley to Philip Sheridan and reinforced his army with two army corps from his own Army of the Potomac. In September Sheridan's army decisively defeated Early at the Battle of Winchester, the largest engagement ever fought in the Valley, a fight involving some 40,000 Federals and 20,000 Confederates.

The Federal victory there marked the beginning of the end for the Confederacy in that war-torn valley. It was also the single bloodiest day of the war for Barbour County. Four soldiers from Barbour lost their lives, two Union and two Confederate, among them Captain Edward Corder of the Twentieth Cavalry. Shot down while leading his company in a desperate counterattack, he is said to have called out to his troops to "Go on, men, push forward and the save the day—I'm a dead man."[3] Eighteen other Barbour men were wounded, among them Moses Moats of the Fifteenth West Virginia, whose leg was blown away by canon fire. James Freeman, also of the Fifteenth, lay wounded on the field for three days, his leg shattered by shell fire. When stretcher-bearers finally brought him into a field hospital there was nothing to do except amputate the limb.

After further defeats at Fisher's Hill and Cedar Creek, Lee realized the Shenandoah Valley was a lost cause and dismantled the Confederate army there. What was left of Early's infantry boarded trains for Petersburg, leaving only remnants of Confederate cavalry to offer token resistance. Defeated at Liberty Mills and forced to abandon Staunton, Early continued to retreat south. The end finally came at Waynesboro. A small rebel army, reduced to perhaps 2,000 men and a single artillery battery, faced an onslaught of some 5,000 cavalry under George Custer. The battle, such as it was, lasted only long enough for Custer to send an entire brigade sweeping around Early's flank, routing his panic-stricken men. Half were taken prisoner.

Samuel Woods, who four years earlier had fled Philippi as Federal troops descended upon the town, was now forced to flee

Waynesboro. And, as before, his family was left behind. Isabella saw the battle unfold from her back porch. In the street in front of the house, Frank Woods and his younger sister watched as Early's men fled through the town, the Federal cavalry on their heels, shooting down the stragglers. At one point Custer himself reined up before the children and ordered them to open all their windows; his men were going to blow the bridge outside of town. They took his advice and saved their windows. Federal troopers then proceeded to ransack the house, carrying away "all the edibles they could get their hands on." The bodies of slain Confederates were laid out in their parlor.[4]

The focus of the war now moved to Richmond where Grant's army had besieged the capital since the summer of 1864. The regiments that had fought in the Shenandoah were transferred to Grant's army and joined the siege. By March, 1865, Lee concluded that he could no longer defend the city and began a withdrawal that ended at Appomattox on April 9. That morning the West Virginians in Grant's army, positioned to make a final push against the surrounded enemy, heard cheers off in the distance, cheers they would later recall as "vigorous, frantic and deep-down-from-the-heart cheering." When news of the truce reached them, the West Virginians became utterly delirious, climbing trees, throwing their hats in the air, and jumping on them.[5] The war was over, and they had survived. Across from them the Confederates also learned of the truce and surrender. James Hall sat down to record the news in the diary he had kept throughout the war:

> The die is cast. The deed is done. How strange! The Grand Old Army of Northern Virginia—the heroes of a hundred victories and of world-wide fame, surrendering to the enemy! But the Grand Old Army is not here. It is dead! From sixty or seventy thousand it is dwindled down to fifteen thousand. It is all over now![6]

Of the 145 men from Barbour who had left the county in May, 1861, to form two companies of the Thirty-First Virginia, only eight surrendered at Appomattox. Company K, the old Mountain Guards organized by Henry Sturm, had been reduced to five men. Reger's Barbour Greys numbered but two.

The next day the troops of both sides mingled freely. Former friends and neighbors from Barbour County sought one another out and exchanged news from home. After a day or so both sides parted, the Union men ordered to Richmond where they were mustered out over the next several weeks and then embarked on trains for Wheeling; the Confederates, paroled under the terms of the surrender, beginning a long walk home, a two week journey that would carry them over many of the battlefields on which they had fought. Before both Union and Confederate soldiers alike stretched a vast unknown peace.

The jubilation over the news of Lee's surrender had hardly subsided when the assassination of Lincoln sent shock waves throughout the North. This jolt to the national conscience was compounded in West Virginia with the realization that, for them, the war was not quite over. Soon after Lee's men laid down their arms, Grant issued an order that all rebels surrendering to Federal troops were to receive the same terms as those who had surrendered at Appomattox and were therefore free to return to their homes unmolested. Unionists in West Virginia were now faced with the unsettling prospect of having thousands of paroled Confederates flood into the very state they had been trying to destroy for the past four years. Governor Boreman was outraged. As soon as word of Grant's order reached him, he immediately wired Secretary of State Stanton demanding that it be rescinded. "Our situation is a peculiarly unfortunate one," he explained. Paroled Confederates were already beginning to enter the state, "wearing their rebel uniforms . . . with as much impudence and insolence as when they went away. The loyal people here feel themselves insulted by the conduct of these rebels, and are only restrained from decided action by their love of law and order."[7]

Boreman's concerns were certainly understandable. In May, 1865, nobody could say with any certainty what returning Confederates might do. A few weeks earlier, a group of Confederates had slipped into Barbour and ambushed Captain Haller and his men. Other groups of Confederates remained in arms, refusing to surrender. In early May some two dozen troopers of the Twentieth Virginia Cavalry were still lurking about the Greenbrier

Valley. Most were captured by soldiers of Ohio cavalry but their leader, Joe Harper of Randolph County, tried to make his way across the Mississippi to join Confederate troops he heard were still fighting. It was only when he learned of their surrender that he finally returned home and gave himself up.[8]

Die-hard rebels weren't Boreman's only problem. Few Unionists in West Virginia shared Grant's magnanimity toward surrendered Confederates. From across the state came a flood of petitions demanding that the government act to prevent ex-Confederates from returning home.[9] From Barbour County came the ominous demand for the prompt discharge of the county's soldiers. "They can and will do more, as citizens, to protect loyal people from depredations . . . than twice their number of soldiers from other sections of the country."[10] Left unspoken was the clear implication that such veterans, no longer subject to army control, would take matters into their own hands and deal with returning Confederates however they saw fit. The potential for widespread civil strife was thus very real and, with most of West Virginia's troops still stationed in Eastern Virginia, Boreman had scant means to preserve order should clashes occur.

Faced with the possibility their now victorious neighbors would seek retribution, a number of returning Confederates prepared for the worst. Tom Everson of Barbour carefully hid his carbine in a nearby tree when he returned home, ready for use should anyone threaten him.[11] Everson had every reason to be cautious, for many of Barbour's Union men were by no means prepared to forgive their recent enemies or to forget four years of war. When Samuel Woods reached Belington with one of his sons, he was stopped by a group of civilians and army veterans who ordered him to turn his wagon around and leave the county. Woods, ever the lawyer, brandished his parole and insisted on his right to return home. Despite threats to his life, he reached his home undisturbed.[12] Soon after this some 50 Union army veterans swept through Philippi seeking out ex-Confederates. The mob eventually dispersed, but it was only after troops from Clarksburg were ordered into town for ten days that efforts to "send the rebels back" subsided.[13]

Most Confederates who survived the war returned to Barbour County and lived out the rest of their lives. Yet there were cases of forced eviction of those perceived as having committed wrongs outside the normal bounds of warfare. Trayhern identified four of Captain Hill's men as having particularly mistreated him during his abduction and all were forced to flee the county.[14] Captain Philips was recovering from his sixth wound of the war when he surrendered and began the journey back to Barbour. When he reached Valley Furnace, "I found my home almost in ruins and briars spread over the fields. I saw wove around my affairs a web of difficulties that nothing but close attention and patient labor could untangle."[15]

Chief among the difficulties faced by Philips and other ex-Confederates was the near eradication of their civil rights. As a loyal state, West Virginia was never subjected to the dictates of Congressional Reconstruction. Nonetheless, Governor Boreman and the state legislature instituted a homegrown Reconstruction program of their own, adopting a series of laws to prevent their former enemies from winning at the ballot box a victory denied them on the battlefield.

The first of these, passed in January, 1865 and commonly called the Test Oath, required each voter to swear they had never borne arms against the United States government or the State of West Virginia, or had in any way given aid or comfort to anyone who had. Failure to give the oath resulted in one's being stricken from the voting rolls.[16] Its passage was in fact a violation of the state's constitution adopted two years earlier, which specifically entitled "all white male citizens" the right to vote. This was rectified at the beginning of 1866, when the legislature amended the constitution to conform to the law. Among the very few legislators opposing the amendment were John Keller, Barbour's representative in the House of Delegates, and Emmett O'Brien, the county's state senator. Keller, incensed at its passage as "contrary to the Constitution of the United States," unleashed a "blasphemously abusive" diatribe against his fellow legislators, singling out in particular those members of the body who were ministers unable, in Keller's mind, to extend Christian precepts of forgiveness to one-time enemies. Keller "thanked God he was not a preacher," declared he would no longer take part in further House proceedings, and promptly left for home.[17]

Keller and O'Brien had been as staunchly opposed to secession as any men in Barbour. But both were also pre-war Democrats who had refused to align themselves with the wartime Democratic opposition and continued to work within the Union Constitutional Party. Their allegiance to the Union Party abruptly ended with passage of the Test Oath. They saw the measure and the registration boards it created as nothing less than a blatant political ploy designed to perpetuate Republican control of the state.

The compromise over West Virginia's boundaries—a process in which O'Brien himself had participated—ensured that large portions of the new state would encompass territory dominated by Democratic voters. With passage of the amendment, registrars—to be appointed directly by the governor—could deny ex-Confederates the right to vote. The same fear of dictatorial rule that had sparked conservative Union Democrats to oppose measures embraced by Radical Republicans during the war was thus carried over into the immediate post-war period.

As if to confirm these fears, other proscriptive measures soon followed. Ex-Confederates were barred from holding public office, practicing law, teaching, sitting on juries, or suing in court. Confederate soldiers and civilian sympathizers who had fled to Eastern Virginia during the war now had no means of overturning judgments entered against them during their absence. Indeed, the entire judicial system became a means of retaliating against former rebels as local courts began entering judgments for damages against Confederate soldiers who had requisitioned livestock, horses, and other property during the war. John Maxwell of Philippi sued three of Porterfield's men for confiscating grain, flour, and other provisions during their brief occupation of the town in 1861. The heirs of John Shroyer, who had been killed in

1865 during one of the last raids of the war, sued Hannibal Hill for damages in 1865. John Radcliff of Barbour County was sued that year by Leonard Cole, who had been taken prisoner by Radcliff and others of his regiment. In all three cases, juries composed entirely of Union sympathizers and army veterans decided for the plaintiffs, awarding the Shroyers $225 in damages, Cole $300, and Maxwell $1,500.[18] In what became one of the most notorious cases of the post-war era, Spencer Dayton, acting as county prosecutor, obtained murder indictments against four of Hill's men for the deaths of Captain Haller and two other Home Guardsmen.[19]

Both Radcliff and those sued by Maxwell appealed the judgments entered against them all the way to the state supreme court, arguing that decisions of the United States Supreme Court had since 1862 conceded belligerent rights to Confederate soldiers and thus the requisitionings they had carried out were justifiable acts of war. The state's high court upheld verdicts in both cases and scores of similar ones brought before it.[20] Former Confederates saw all this as nothing less than acts of vengeance disguised in the mantle of law and justice. Most Unionists saw it quite differently.

At the end of the war, Republican leaders could point with pride to a fair amount of progressive legislation. They had created a free school system and had greatly democratized local government. But their principal achievement was the creation of West Virginia itself, and this they would defend against any menace, real or perceived. However much the Test Oath and other proscriptive measures they adopted may have served the interests of their party politically, it would be a misconception to characterize the very real popularity with which they were received as support for mere political chicanery. Union loyalists and army veterans did not feel threatened by a resurgence of the Democratic Party per se, but by a resurgence of Confederate political power. These fears seemed very real in 1866, when ex-Confederate officers won election to state offices and the Virginia legislature began passing resolutions seeking to reunite the two states.[21]

A convention of Unionists held in Barbour County in 1866 gave voice to sentiments held by most Unionists throughout the state. Admonishing that "eternal vigilance is the price of liberty," the meeting passed resolutions declaring "unalloyed satisfaction" with the passage of the voting rights amendment and other laws that stripped away the civil rights of ex-Confederates. While they would welcome "truly repentant rebels . . . as the returning prodigal to his father's mansion," they were determined to work diligently to prevent "the priceless heritage of Constitutional liberty" from passing into the "guardianship of unrepentant traitors":

> Too costly have been our sacrifices; too deep have flowed the streams of precious loyal life blood; too many graves of the true and brave daily meet our view; too many maimed and mutilated victims of fratricidal hate still live in our midst... for our consent to restore to places of trust and power the enemies who glory and exult in the ruin and desolation they have wrought, and now seek to accomplish by political combinations and organized disloyal factions what they have failed to achieve by force of arms.[22]

Yet in reality it was those who championed proscription who often blurred the distinction between "ex-rebel" and "Democrat." Former rebels and Confederate sympathizers aligned themselves almost to a man with the Democratic opposition, an opposition that included war-time Union Democrats. These latter, though loyal to the Union and opposed to secession, were remembered as having opposed censorship of Secessionist publications, as having worked to free imprisoned Secessionists, and above all as having jeopardized recognition of West Virginia's statehood by demanding a border scheme unacceptable to Congress and by opposing the inclusion of an emancipation clause in the state constitution. An editorial in the *Wheeling Intelligencer* in support of the Test Oath expressed sentiments shared by many Republican voters about their Democratic opponents:

It is not to be disguised that within this state of West Virginia there is a reactionary party, not only as regards National politics, but as regards the very existence of the State of West Virginia. The party calling itself "Democratic" in this state opposed the formation of the new State, and... we are not at all surprised to see men who have been in the rebellion and others who sympathized with it . . . intimating a desire to get back into the old state.[23]

The uncomfortable suspicion was that Democrats, given free rein, could easily out-poll Republicans in many local elections and most assuredly at the state level. The threat to Republican power had been evident even before the war had ended. Although Lincoln carried the state in 1864, the fact that his Democratic opponent received a third of the votes caused considerable alarm to Republican leaders. Once combined with the votes of ex-Confederates, Democrats would swamp existing Republican majorities at all levels of government. Just how this political balance worked out at the local level can be seen by examining the situation in Barbour County.

Using election returns, newspapers, and available biographical materials, it is possible to determine the post-war political affiliation for 129 of Barbour's war-time Unionists and 59 Confederates. The same sources provide party affiliation for 116 males members of the immediate families of both groups and for 45 unrelated men. While the sample is small, the trends are revealing. With but a single exception, those who supported the Confederacy during the war voted Democratic, as did the vast majority of their family members. While the majority of Unionists voted Republican, a small minority of war-time sympathizers remained loyal to The Democracy. However, support for the Republican Party appears to have been limited to those who took an active part in the war. Members of Unionist families were just as likely to vote Democratic as Republican. If these findings accurately reflect allegiances for the county as a whole, then Democratic candidates would command but a slim majority in Barbour, and one entirely dependent on the votes of former war-time Unionists. Clearly, an alliance between Union Democrats and ex-Confederates would end Republican control of Barbour. In the elections of 1866, Republican fears of just such an alliance came true.

The election that year was of paramount importance, for voters were called upon to ratify the Test Oath amendment. Democrats realized the threat its passage posed and the war-time divisions that had split their party were quickly mended. In retrospect the consummation of the alliance is not surprising. Ex-Confederates and Union Democrats shared many of the same goals. Daniel Lamb, who had led conservative Unionist opposition during the war, put it bluntly in a letter to Gideon Camden, who had served as a major in the Twenty-fifth Virginia Infantry. "However we may differ on certain points, yet in many we concur. We want a real peace—So do you. We want good government—So do you. We want to put an end to persecution and proscription & So do you; and we are going to do it."[24]

In Barbour County, as in much of the state, erstwhile enemies put the war behind them and joined together in opposition to the Republican program. Barbour's delegation to the state Democratic convention at Clarksburg was headed by Secessionist John R. Williamson and Unionist Democrats John H. Woodford, Jr. and Edwin Parsons. John Keller ran for re-election to the House of Delegates on the Democratic ticket while Nathan Taft was put forward as the party's candidate for state senator. The platform on which they ran opposed passage of the Test Oath amendment and demanded repeal of civil restrictions. And in a blatant attempt to capitalize on race prejudices, it castigated national Republicans for spending tax money on the Freedmans Bureau "to support the negro in idleness and vice" and pledged that a Democratic victory would forever ensure that voting rights would never be extended to Negroes.[25]

Republicans likewise organized a vigorous campaign in support of the amendment. The county's Republican central committee drew up resolutions declaring its passage as "essential to the preservation and existence of our beloved state of West Virginia" and labeled Democratic candidates as the men "who in early 1861 were the most zealous advocates of the secession of Virginia and the cause of the Southern Rebellion." The Barbour branch of the Soldiers and Sailors League, organized by Captain Marshall Coburn only a few months before, used its influence to get out the vote. The party's slate of candidates for local office was dominated by army veterans, among them Coburn himself, who ran for the House of Delegates, and Henson Hoff's son William, who ran for county prosecuting attorney.[26]

The election proved to be the closest one in the county's history. Democratic candidates prevailed, but only by razor-slim margins. Coburn lost to Keller by a dozen votes, Hoff to William Ice by the same number. Of six Republican candidates running for local office, only Lewis Wilson, the incumbent for county recorder, defeated his Democratic opponent. The rest lost by only a handful of votes. The vote for state offices was even more narrow. The Democratic candidate for governor, Benjamin Smith, received 699 votes in the county, against 693 for Boreman. The only Democrat to lose was Taft, whose war-time Unionism apparently alienated too many ex-Confederates. Even so, the margin by which he lost was a mere 20 votes.[27]

As resounding as the victory was for Barbour's Democrats, it was overshadowed by their losses statewide. Boreman was re-elected, and with him a majority of Republicans in the state legislature. Their victory was nonetheless a narrow one. Ten counties in the state returned majorities for Smith, while in four others Boreman prevailed by only a few votes.[28] That Republicans prevailed at all was due largely to implementation of the Test Oath even before it was ratified. Early in the year Boreman issued instructions to county election boards to enforce its provisions. Democrats protested, but to no avail.[29] While Barbour's board made no attempt to follow Boreman's instructions—and later learned a lesson for failing to do so—a sufficient number of county boards complied, ensuring Democratic defeat. Most importantly, the Test Oath was ratified and became the centerpiece of the Republican program for the next four years. The new law established Boards of Registration in each county, whose members were empowered to strike from voting lists anyone suspected of disloyalty during the war, even if they had subsequently taken the oath of allegiance. Even those who had served for a time in the Confederate army, deserted, and later joined the Federal army could be barred from voting.[30]

The registration boards created by the new law now became the focus of renewed strife. Their powers were soon extended beyond the ability simply to disenfranchise those unable to meet the requirements of the oath itself. In early 1867 a new registration law enabled board members to disqualify voters whose "loyalty" they viewed as doubtful. Appeals to board decisions could be made only to the boards themselves. A further law stipulated that suits brought against board members by those who claimed to have been illegally stricken from the rolls were to be defended at public expense.[31] Finally, to ensure the laws' mandates were strictly enforced, the registrars whom the governor appointed were to be drawn from among "those citizens most known for loyalty, firmness, and uprightness."[32] In Barbour, that translated into army veterans: Major Fenelon Howes, Captain Frederick Ford, Lieutenant William Price, and privates James Harvey and John Shomo.[33] All but Harvey had served together in the Fifteenth West Virginia Infantry, all were staunch Republicans, and all could be counted on for "firmness."

The first real test of the how ex-Confederates would react to implementation of the test oath came in the weeks preceding the 1867 elections. In October the county's Board of Registrars moved to strike from the voting lists all "rebel sympathizers, men who had been in Union prisons, and men who had broken bread and drank liquor" while in the Confederate army. The response to the notice was immediate. Crowds of Confederate veterans and their supporters gathered in Philippi, some armed with pistols, and proceded to "arrest" members of the Board. "Our streets are filled with the sansculottes of the mountains," exclaimed a Unionist eyewitness, who likened the rioting to "the noisy babble of Porterfield's reign of terror in 1861." Within a day rioting spread to three other towns in Barbour County, where Board members were physically assaulted and forced to flee polling places.[34]

Unable to quell the violence, Board chairman Fenelon Howes called upon Governor Boreman for assistance, demanding that arms be issued to loyal militiamen. Wisely, Boreman rejected the demand, and instead called upon a company of U.S. regulars stationed at Clarksburg to occupy Philippi. The riots ceased as soon as the troops entered the town, and the election proceeded without further incident.[35] With the Board now able to eliminate some 400 voters from the rolls, the election of Republican candidates was a foregone conclusion. Howes, himself a Board member, easily won election to the House of Delegates, defeating his opponent, John H. Woodford, Jr., by a vote of 405 to 279. Emmett O'Brien lost his seat in the state senate by a similar lopsided margin.[36]

Unrest continued. In July of the following year a mob of Confederate sympathizers and veterans invaded a church on Sugar Creek during Sunday services, draped the pulpit with the Confederate battle flag, and forced the presiding minister to preach a sermon praising the Confederacy. A free-for-all ensued when an even larger crowd of Union army veterans came to the preacher's rescue and succeeded in chasing out the rebels.[37] Two months later, campaign speeches by gubernatorial candidate William E. Stevenson and Francis Pierpont at Philippi were broken up by another crowd of "rebel ruffians . . . yelling and blaspheming like demons." Neither candidate was able to deliver their orations, and they left town in disgust.[38]

Rioting was by no means confined to Barbour County. The years 1867 and 1868 were marked by similar outbreaks of violence throughout the state. Registrars were attacked in Tucker and Randolph Counties and troops were called out to suppress disturbances in Greenbrier, Jefferson, Monroe, Cabell, Wayne, and Logan Counties. In Marion County Federal troops intercepted a shipment of muskets intended for a former Confederate officer.[39] Implementation of the Test Oath was securing Republican control of the state, but only at great cost. The entire concept of proscription inflamed animosities and hatreds. Disenfranchisement, designed to preserve the infant state from menace, instead served to prolong tensions and, in places like Barbour, resulted in repeated outbreaks of violence.

While stalwart Republicans were prepared to take whatever measures were necessary to enforce voting restrictions, a growing number within the party began to argue that not only was the policy unjust, but it actually threatened continued Republican control of state and local government. The movement to create West Virginia had been in large measure the direct heir of the decades-long struggle to expand democratic rights in the face of Eastern oligarchies. The incongruity of such principles with a policy denying tens of thousands the right to vote was obvious. The political reality facing the Republican Party in West Virginia was the growing resurgence of Democratic strength even in the face of voting restrictions. In 1866 the Democratic candidate for governor received 17,158 votes. Two years later he received 22,250 votes. Congressional elections revealed similar increases, with votes for Democratic candidates increasing from 16,885 in 1866 to 22,052 in 1868.[40] Horace Greeley put it succinctly in an open letter to Republican leaders in the state: "Every year one thousand of your rebels dies, and one thousand more of their sons become of age—you can't disenfranchise them. . . . I tell you that your house is built upon the sands." Greeley urged a policy of magnanimity in hopes of drawing ex-rebels into the Republican fold. "Now you can amnesty the rebels—Soon the question will be, shall they amnesty you?"[41]

Republican party caucuses in a number of counties urged repeal of the test oaths. Even the editor of the *Wheeling Intelligencer* advocated an end to disenfranchisement.[42] In 1868 and 1869 the state legislature was inundated with petitions seeking relief from civil restrictions imposed on ex-rebels. From Barbour County came petitions signed by 294 citizens requesting that Thomas Bradford be allowed to practice law. Another sought waivers for John R. Philips and Andrew Valentine so the two could teach school; 248 Barbour citizens and 178 others from Tucker and Taylor Counties asked that Samuel Woods be allowed to resume his law practice. The petitioners included many war-time Unionists and even army veterans, some of whom had been staunch supporters of voting rights restrictions only a few years before.[43] It seems people had no quarrel with proscriptive measures against "rebels" in general, but felt very differently about individuals whom they knew personally.

Some within the Republican hierarchy sensed that maintaining control of the state necessitated a reexamination of voting rights restrictions. Granville Hall, the *Wheeling Intelligencer's* editor, outlined the strategy in a letter to one of the party's leaders:

> Our only hope of perpetuating Republican ascendancy in the State is by a magnanimous policy which shall bring a portion of the ex-rebels into co-operation with us when they become voters. A very large number of them were old line Whigs before the war. They do not like the Democracy and they would come to us if we gave them the ballot. But if we wait for the Democrats to enfranchise them, they will of course fall into that party.[44]

Ironically, one of the leading figures in the movement to relax voting rights restrictions was Spencer Dayton. In 1869, Dayton ran for the state senate and shocked many of his supporters by openly campaigning for an end to test oaths and a repeal of the amendment denying ex-Confederates the right to vote. Only a year before he had publicly castigated former Confederates in Barbour, describing Samuel Woods in particular as "despised and execrated by all good citizens. . . . a traitor, whose character is the counterpart of those of Judas Iscariot and Benedict Arnold." He described William McClaskey as "one of the most unblushing rebels who have been permitted to survive the war," and William Ice as having been "imported from Marion County to improve the stock of rebels of this county." "It is very apparent," he concluded, "that neither the people of the United States or the state of West Virginia will ever submit to commit the reins of political power into the hands of such men, who at best are but driftwood that has been borne onwards and now lies lodged, seething and rotting, along the banks of the terrible and almost restless current of the late revolution."[45] Yet Dayton saw the handwriting on the wall and openly declared his support for an end to the Radical program. Democrats in Barbour actively campaigned in his favor, Woods working particularly hard for his election behind the scenes. "Mr. Dayton would have spurned that support," explained his granddaughter years later.[46]

The majority of "Let Up" Republicans sent to the legislature in the election of 1869 soon became emeshed in the issue of black suffrage. The Fourteenth Amendment guaranteeing civil rights to blacks had been ratified in 1868, and the Fifteenth, extending to them the right to vote, was set to go into effect the next year. Many Republicans and Democrats alike opposed black suffrage, and its implementation split both parties. While Democrats were united in their opposition to white disenfranshisement, they were by no means prepared to extend the same rights to former slaves, whatever Congress and the U.S. Constitution might have to say about it.[47] Others in the party were willing to swallow this blow to their deep-seated prejudices if it could be traded for the lifting of Confederate voting rights restrictions. Many within the Republican Party, among them Waitman P. Willey, the state's U.S. Senator, were adamantly opposed to black suffrage as much as their Democratic opponents, even though they stood most to gain from it.[48] The fact was that West Virginia's Republicans had done little to advance the position of blacks in the state. The constitution they promulgated in 1863 restricted voting rights to whites only. And while it included an emancipation clause—only because Congress demanded it—it would have left the status of most slaves unchanged had they not been freed by the Thirteenth Amendment at the end of 1865.

Although the legislature quickly enacted laws repealing test oaths for lawyers and teachers, the various factions in both parties became embroiled over the two controversies of white and black suffrage. Conservative Democrats demanded repeal of the Test Oath while opposing any constitutional amendments deleting the word "white" from it. Radical Republicans insisted on the preservation of restrictions on voting rights for ex-Confederates. In the end, Dayton and other liberals from both parties, led by W.H.H. Flick of Pendleton County, succeeded in formulating the Flick amendment that both repealed the Test Oath and changed the definition of those able to vote from "all white male citizens" to "all male citizens."[49] As with all amendments, this one required ratification by the electorate, and the Flick Amendment was submitted for approval in the fall elections.

Yet turmoil continued to surround the Boards of Registration. Governor Stevenson had been elected that same year on a platform that supported an end to disenfranchisement, but on his terms. Because the Test Oath remained part of the constitution, he instructed local boards to "execute the law relating to voters as formerly instructed, fearlessly and impartially."[50] However, Democrats soon found a weapon they could successfully wield against the boards, ironically one designed to give teeth to the Fifteenth Amendment many of them had so vigorously opposed. This was the Enforcement Act, which prohibited any attempt to prevent blacks from exercising their right to vote. Judge John J. Jackson, a Democrat appointed to the U.S. District Court by Lincoln in 1861, interpreted the Act as applying to all voters, regardless of their race, and instructed U.S. Marshals to arrest board members who tried to deny the vote to anyone.[51]

Some county boards continued to carry out Stevenson's edict even in the face of possible fine and imprisonment. However, the trend throughout the state was one of general relaxation of the Test Oath, due mainly to a growing sentiment that the Radicals' regime had run its course. Although it was claimed that the extension of the vote to blacks led many erstwhile Republican voters to either vote Democratic or not vote at all,[52] the party held its own in the elections. What differed this time was that thousands of former Confederates and others previously barred from voting were now able to cast their ballots and the Democrats were swept into power. Most importantly, the Flick Amendment passed by an overwhelming majority, only 6,323 of 29,869 votes cast opposing it. In Barbour, it carried by a majority of 263.[53]

It is no small measure of Dayton's convictions that he had

pushed as hard as he did for the amendment's success, for in doing so he was effectively committing political suicide for himself
and for his party. The expectation that those they had once disen-
franchised would eagerly grasp the hand of conciliation the Republicans now extended was an illusory hope. Now secure in
power, Democratic Party leaders in the legislature promptly called
for another convention to rewrite the state's constitution. For a
second time in little more than a decade, Barbour's electorate
sent Samuel Woods to a state convention, this one dominated by
conservatives and ex-Confederates bent on ensuring there would
never be a repetition of the Radical program. The new constitution specifically forbade the refusal of any citizen the right to vote
and prohibited the formation of Boards of Registration. Martial
law was declared unconstitutional and the township system abol-
ished. A strong effort was even mounted to do away with the
secret ballot, but this failed when liberal Democrats opposed the
measure on the grounds that the new constitution had no hope
of ratification if it included such a provision.[54] Conservatives also
attempted to restrict black voting rights. To his credit, Woods
vigorously opposed all such efforts and, with the aid of liberal
Democrats and the handful of Republicans sent to the convention, engineered its defeat.[55]

The framers of the new constitution also addressed the issue of the numerous judgments entered against Confederate soldiers for damages during the war. Article VII stipulated that no
citizen could be held liable for "any act done in accordance with
the usages of civilized warfare," forbade the attachment of
property to satisfy such judgments, and called upon the legislature to enact whatever laws it deemed necessary to implement
the section. The next session of the legislature promptly
complied by decreeing that those against whom such judgments
had been entered could petition local courts to set them aside,
and most of them soon were.[56]

In the end the new constitution was ratified, but by a mere
1,567 votes—just five percent of the total cast. Opposition was
intense in the Northwest and along the Ohio River, where 19
counties returned majorities against ratification. In Barbour

County the vote was dead even: 952 for ratification, 952 against.[57] Now freed from all restrictions, Democrats would retain control of the state for the next two decades. Barbour itself became once again a Democratic stronghold, many of those winning elections being Confederate veterans. Thus Jaspar Hall, a veteran of the Thirty-first Virginia, was repeatedly reelected to the state senate throughout the 1870s, as was Thomas Bradford to the House of Delegates. In state and national elections, Barbour repeatedly returned majorities for Democratic candidates for president, governor, and Congress.[58] And in recognition of Samuel Woods's legal acumen and his services on behalf of the Democratic Party, he was elevated to the state supreme court in 1883.[59]

The consolidation of Democratic power in Barbour had an immediate effect on the most noteworthy criminal case before the circuit court. The trial of the four men accused of Haller's murder had dragged on since the indictments had been first handed down, due in large part to political turmoil surrounding the office of county prosecutor. In the 1866 election William Ice had narrowly defeated the Republican William Hoff, a Union army veteran. Unionists immediately brought suit seeking to overturn the election results by charging Ice with pro-secessionist activities during the war. Although Dayton was appointed in Ice's place in 1869, he promptly resigned the office after his election to the state senate. In the next election Ice was returned to office for good. After that, no further action was taken against the four and the case was quietly dropped.[60]

The elimination of civil restrictions could not immediately sweep away countless individual animosities. Evidence of wartime divisions being carried over into the 1870s were most apparent in matters of religion and church organization. The split within the Methodist-Episcopal Church, already evident prior to the war, became final. In 1868 Abraham Hershman, arrested as a hostage for Trayhern in 1863, was licensed as a preacher of the Southern Methodist Church, the first ever in the county.[61] The first congregations of the denomination were organized in 1872 and 1873. Evidence indicates that membership was drawn almost wholly from ex-Confederates and their relatives. Of 47 persons identified by Maxwell as belonging to the denomination, 23 were veterans of the Confederate army or Secessionist sympathizers and another 15 were related to Confederates.[62]

Yet while churches may have divided along lines set down during the war, other organizations considered more sacrosanct than even religion served as vehicles for reconciliation. The Masonic Lodge at Philippi, first established in 1849, had been completely disrupted by the war. Some of its members supported the Union cause, others went South. In 1870 the lodge was reestablished by survivors of the pre-war organization. Veterans of both sides now mingled freely. Significantly, ex-Confederates like William and Isaac Johnson, James Hall, and James Knotts, all of whom had joined the Southern Methodist Church, were founding members of the new lodge and appear to have had no qualms about belonging to an organization that included veterans of the Union army. A similar mixing of veterans of the two armies occurred when a chapter of the Odd Fellows was organized at the end of 1871.[63]

The Democratic resurgence in Barbour itself acted to facilitate the healing of war-time wounds. Forced into unity by Radical post-war proscriptions, Unionist Democrats cooperated with their former enemies in organizing their party and putting forward candidates who could win elections and perform their duties, regardless of wartime sympathies. Thus James Knotts, a Confederate sympathizer, was elected sheriff in 1870. Three years later Jacob Hudkins, a Unionist Democrat, was voted into the office. Six of seven justices of the peace elected in 1872 were Democrats, two of whom had been Union loyalists, one a Secessionist sympathizer, and one a Confederate army veteran. Among constables elected during the same period, two were veterans of the Union army and three of the Confederate.[64]

Voters at Philippi, a Democratic stronghold throughout the 1870s, regularly elected both ex-Confederates and ex-Unionists for mayor, city council, and other positions. And it was not simply war-time Democrats who won the elections. John P. Thompson, a Secessionist sympathizer, and Albert G. Reger, a Confederate army veteran, served as mayors in 1873 and 1874, succeeded in 1875 by Andrew Simon and the next year by Alpheus Wilson, both war-time Union loyalists and post-war Republicans. During the same decade, while Democrats maintained large majorities on the city council, at least five men elected to the body had been Unionists who now voted Republican.[65]

One factor contributing to the process of reconciliation in Barbour was the dramatic decline in the number of war-time activists living in the county between 1865 and 1880. Of the 1,176 individuals identified as Union and Confederate sympathizers, 136 are known to have lost their lives during the war. A search of biographical material, census lists, and county records was undertaken to determine what happened to the remaining 1,040 individuals. No record could be found for 97 of them. Another 93 were verified as having died between 1865 and 1880. What is remarkable is that 355—a third of all those who survived the war on either side—are known to have left Barbour County in the fifteen-year period following the war. Most did not move very far: 111 Unionists and 58 Confederates were found to be living in neighboring Harrison, Taylor, Preston, Tucker, Randolph, and Upshur counties. Another 78 Unionists and 40 Confederates moved to other counties in West Virginia. Of the rest, six Confederates settled in Eastern Virginia and the rest moved out of state to the West.

All told, fewer than half of Barbour's Unionists and Confederates were still living in the county by 1880. To be sure, Unionists and Confederates settled in Barbour from other states and parts of West Virginia, but their numbers were few. Only 43 Unionists and 22 Confederate veterans and sympathizers could be positively identified in the 1870 and 1880 census lists as having moved to Barbour after the war.

The net effect of this migration was that there were fewer veterans and activists living in Barbour County during the post-war period—fewer people with emotional wounds to be healed, fewer people with scores to settle, and fewer people carrying the baggage of war-time animosities. Yet, however much the migration of those who had taken an active part in the war may have served to diffuse tensions within the county, it cannot by itself account for the clearly perceptible trend toward reconciliation. The co-mingling of one-time enemies in fraternal organizations and the willingness of voters to elect men to positions of responsibility without regard to their war-time backgrounds is an indication that those who remained in Barbour had begun to put the pain of the war behind them.

Perhaps the most compelling evidence that war-time animosities were subsiding in the 1870s is the growing number of marriages between members of Confederate and Union families. It will be recalled from an earlier chapter that in the years immediately prior to the war and especially during the war itself, men and women in Barbour had shown a marked preference for husbands and wives who held similar views on secession (see Table 6). War-time marriage patterns continued well into the late 1860s, clear evidence that rivalries generated by the war continued to exert personal influence. A rather touching glimpse of how these attitudes shaped the lives of men and women is revealed in an 1870 letter sent to the *Wheeling Intelligencer* at the request of William Martin of Barbour, Martin himself being unable to read or write. It seems that Martin, a veteran of the Union army, had fallen in love with one Cicely Cunningham of Randolph County. But the Cunninghams had been secession-minded during the war and the problem for Martin was that "his people was so against it that he could not marry her." The editor of the *Intelligencer* advised Martin to "forget his people" and marry her anyway, inviting them to Wheeling for the purpose. Sadly, it didn't work out for the star-crossed lovers; Cicely married another man two years later.[66]

What is noteworthy about this Romeo and Juliet-like story is not simply the influence exerted on Martin by his family, but the fact that it was Martin, a war veteran, who had no qualms about marrying someone whose relatives had sided with the enemy. Yet the chasm Martin had tried to bridge was narrowing. Beginning in the early 1870s there was an increasing tendency toward intermarriage between the two groups until, by the middle of the decade, marriage patterns had essentially returned to those that had existed in the mid-1850s (see Table 7). That it took nearly a decade for people to reach this point is testimony to just how bitter the divisions had been. Intermarriage between families divided by the war would have profound consequences for the future as well. The children and grandchildren of these unions would share a common heritage, not as descendants of Confederates or Unionists, but simply as West Virginians. The most symbolic expression of the trend came in 1916 when Ruth Woods, a granddaughter of Samuel Woods, married Arthur Dayton, a grandson of Spencer Dayton.

As the years passed, the veterans of the war grew older and passed away. In 1897 a group of veterans of both sides, seeing their dwindling numbers, held a reunion at Philippi to honor their departed comrades, swap stories, and acknowledge to themselves and everyone else that they had experienced something highly significant. The reunion was a striking success, so much so that everyone agreed they should hold another the following week—Thanksgiving Day. Significantly, Adam Coleman Bowman, whose heart still burned with the "fires of fury" over the killing of his father 34 years before, was one of the organizers of the event.[67]

-Table 7-
Marriage Patterns in Barbour: 1866-1875

Years	Unionist to Unionist	Confederate to Confed.	Unionist to Confederate	Number
1866-1867	41.4%	130.4%	28.5%	112
1868-1869	50.7%	21.3%	28.0%	75
1870-1871	38.0%	21.1%	40.8%	71
1872-1873	32.4%	22.0%	45.6%	68
1874-1875	32.4%	22.0%	45.6%	68
1876-1877	44.0%	8.5%	47.5%	59

Source: Barbour County Marriage Records, 1866-1875

Bowman's lifelong friend John R. Philips had passed away a few years previously, but almost certainly would have attended. As much as anyone, Philips had become a living symbol of changed sentiments in the county. Wounded six times, Philips had endured more than his share of hardship and could have been excused for harboring resentment. Yet years after the war he wrote a concluding entry in the diary he had kept during the conflict, remarking that his neighbors were "calmly mending their fortunes and repairing the way for a new era of prosperity." The country around him was rapidly improving, education was spreading, and people were, in general, "more refined." It is fitting that this book should conclude with his own words:

> We have lived exciting times and deplore them. Now we welcome the calm sunshine of peace... The late war has left us with better taste than it found us... The hatred begotten by the war is dying and good will is returning. This is how it should be. "Blessed are the peacemakers," let them continue the good will.

> I seemingly live over many exciting times, but I will bid adieu to the past. Let malice go, let the old prejudices sleep in the grave of forgetfulness.[68]

APPENDIX A:

NOTES ON SOURCES
AND METHODOLOGY

Adjustments for Upshur County

Any study of a particular county in West Virginia is confronted with the problem posed by the repeated formation of new counties from existing ones. Between 1800 and 1860, 37 counties were created in what is now West Virginia, and another five would be added after the war. In most instances, new counties were formed from two or more parent counties, the borders of each new county rarely coinciding with pre-existing boundaries. When Barbour was formed in 1843, it included parts of Randolph, Harrison, and Lewis Counties. In 1851 Upshur County was carved from parts of Barbour, Randolph, and Lewis. Thus the official records rarely coincide with the county borders.

To make comparisons possible for Barbour County in the years between 1843 and 1860, these records had to be carefully examined to exclude those sections covering the portion of Barbour County that was ceded to Upshur County. The Federal census and agricultural surveys for 1850 were matched to those of Upshur County for 1860. Individuals appearing in the 1860 Upshur lists were then excluded from those for Barbour in 1850. While not completely error-free, since some individuals who lived in the territory that was retained by Barbour may have moved to Upshur, the method does allow for a fairly reasonable comparison. Unlike the census records, county tax lists were compiled alphabetically. While the same method was applied to adjust the 1843 and 1850 lists, the fact that the location of each person's

landholdings was clearly designated makes the adjustment somewhat more accurate.

Land Patent Claims

The data on land patent claims were obtained from Sims'
published index for Barbour, Harrison, Randolph and Lewis
Counties. The index lists the name of each claimant, the number
of acres patented, the year the patent was filed, and the general
location of each claim. Again, only those patents claimed on land
within Barbour's 1860 boundaries were included. Residency of
patent claimants was determined by consulting the 1850 and 1860
census lists. Care had to be taken with the index. In some cases,
two or more persons would file jointly on a single tract of land,
yet were listed by Sims separately. These were considered a single
claim in this study.

Tenants and Landowners

Identifying tenants and landowning farmers posed yet another set of problems. Local enumerators at times struggled to
reduce the often complex social relations of their own localities to
the somewhat concise categories demanded by the Census Office
schedules. Some enumerators used a wide variety of terms to des-
ignate agricultural occupations – farmer, tenant, renter, share-
cropper, laborer – while others simply used the generic term
"farmer." The problem becomes evident when comparing the
terms used in the census schedules to the data set forth in the
agricultural survey. "Tenants" in the census might be listed as
landowners in the same documents, but not as such in the survey.
Historians relying solely on the Federal schedules are thus faced
with a bewildering array of contradictions when trying to determine the extent of landownership and tenancy in any given area.
One pioneering study of antebellum Georgia developed no fewer
than seven separate categories of landownership and tenants, each
with three sub-categories (see Frederick A. Bode and Donald E.
Ginter, *Farm Tenancy and the Census in Antebellum Georgia*, Athens, Ga., 1986).

Similar problems exist with the records for Barbour. The enumerator in 1850 used the term "farmer" for all persons engaged in agriculture, while his counterpart in 1860 employed the terms "farmer," "tenant," occasionally "tenant-at-will," and "laborer." On the face of it, the terms used in 1860 would appear to distinguish between tenants and landowners, and in most cases "farmers" were in fact recorded as real property owners in the census while "tenants" were not. However, "most cases" means just that, and there were enough exceptions to call into question whether this is what the enumerator intended to convey. Certainly there were far too many exceptions for a researcher to rely on the census designations as precise descriptions of actual social relations. To circumvent these problems, this study defined landowning farmers in 1850 and 1860 as those persons listed in the census as engaged in agriculture and also listed in county real property tax lists for the same years. Conversely, tenants were defined as those persons who were listed as engaged in agriculture but not listed in the county land tax records.

The discussion of the 1850 tenants who became landowners in 1860 necessarily utilized a wide range of resources. Data on each tenant were gathered from the 1850 and 1860 census schedules and agricultural surveys as well as data from the county's land tax records for the same years. Identification of the parents of each tenant required genealogical study relying on local histories, wills, death and marriage records, the latter after 1853 noting the parents of both brides and grooms. Once identified, the same sources were used to obtain information on landownership for the parents. In most cases, the death of the parents could be obtained from county death records, wills, and probates as well as the censuses themselves.

Immigration into Barbour

The tables in Appendix B provide a detailed picture of the patterns of migration into Barbour. The principle sources of this information were biographical histories, county marriage records and Federal census lists. Marriage records stating the birthplace and age of brides and grooms were of particular value in determining the area from which a family emigrated into Barbour. In many instances, family histories provide the exact date a family arrived in the county. When not available, an approximate date was obtained by comparing census lists. For example, a family listed as living in Highland or Loudoun County in 1850 and Barbour in 1860 can be said to have arrived in Barbour during the 1850s. A number of families settled in Barbour from areas just across the county line in neighboring Preston, Tucker, Randolph, Upshur, Harrison and Taylor counties. In these cases the date of arrival of the family in counties adjacent to Barbour was used.

It should be noted that the counties and states from which families migrated into Barbour do not always coincide with the county of birth. Nineteenth century Americans were far more mobile than is often believed. Many of the families that settled in Barbour did so only after having moved to other localities. The Johnsons, Robinsons, and Hoffmans, originally from New Jersey, first settled in Loudoun County, Virginia, before coming to Barbour after living for a time in Allegany County, Maryland. The Nesters, immigrants from Germany to Pennsylvania, settled later in Frederick County, Maryland, and finally in Barbour. A fairly large number of the families that came to Barbour from the Shenandoah Valley—the Zirkles, Smiths, Loughs, Sipes and Kines—had originally come from Pennsylvania and Maryland.

Pennsylvania and Maryland contributed by far the largest number of settlers from northern states, most coming from Fayette and Somerset counties in Pennsylvania, and Allegany County in Maryland. Immigrants from eastern Virginia were drawn mainly from the South Branch region and the Shenandoah Valley. The influence of road construction on migration from these regions into Barbour is readily apparent. Thus, those counties served by the Northwest Turnpike (Loudoun, Fauquier, Clarke, Frederick, Hampshire, and Hardy) and the Staunton-Parkersburg Turnpike (Augusta, Rockingham, Bath and Highland) contributed the largest number of immigrant families to Barbour.

APPENDIX B:
IMMIGRATION INTO BARBOUR

-Table 8A-
Immigration into Barbour County:
Summary of Tables 8B-8D

Place of Origin	1780s	1790s	1800s	1810s	1820s	1830s	1840s	1850s	1860s	Total
Tidewater, Va.	1	1	2	1			3			8
Piedmont, Va.	4	4	4	6	9	4	16	13	3	63
Shenandoah, Va.	3	5	8	6	1	16	28	35		102
S. Branch, Va.	11	8	4	4	2	12	26	18	2	87
Northwest, Va.	2	2	1	1		8	10	22	3	49
Northern States	17	15	30	19	13	18	27	14	2	155
Europe	2	1	5	1	2	2	4	25		42
Totals	40	36	54	38	27	60	114	127	10	506

-Table 8B-
Immigration into Barbour County: From Counties of Virginia

County of Origin	1780s	1790s	1800s	1810s	1820s	1830s	1840s	1850s	1860s	Total
Shenandoah Valley										
Alleghany						1				1
Augusta	2	1	3		1	2	3	8		20
Bath				2		2	5	1		10
Berkeley		1					1			2
Botetourt							1			1
Clarke						1		3		4
Frederick		2	1	1			2	5		11
Highland	1			2		3	1	2		9
Jefferson							1	1		2
Page						2	5	1		8
Rockbridge							1	1		2
Rockingham		1	3	1		4	7	8		24
Shenandoah			1			1	1	5		8
Total	3	5	8	6	1	16	28	35		102

-Table 8B (con't)--Table 8B (con't)-

County of Origin	1780s	1790s	1800s	1810s	1820s	1830s	1840s	1850s	1860s	Total
Northwest										
Calhoun								1	1	2
Doddridge								1		1
Kanawha								1		1
Marion						1	5	4	1	11
Momongalia	2	2	1	1		4	3	7	1	21
PLeasants								1		1
Pocahontas						3	2	4		9
Ritchie								2		2
Tyler								1		1
Total	2	2	1	1		8	10	22	3	49
Tidewater										
Fairfax	1		1							2
Hanover			1				1			2
New Kent		1								1
Prince William							1			1
Spottsylvania							1			1
Westmoreland				1						1
Total	1	1	2	1			3			8

-Table 8B (con't)-

County of Origin	1780s	1790s	1800s	1810s	1820s	1830s	1840s	1850s	1860s	Total
Northwest										
Calhoun								1	1	2
Doddridge								1		1
Kanawha								1		1
Marion						1	5	4	1	11
Momongalia	2	2	1	1		4	3	7	1	21
PLeasants								1		1
Pocahontas						3	2	4		9
Ritchie								2		2
Tyler								1		1
Total	2	2	1	1		8	10	22	3	49
Tidewater										
Fairfax	1		1							2
Hanover		1	1							2
New Kent							1			1
Prince William							1			1
Spottsylvania							1			1
Westmoreland				1						1
Total	1	1	2	1			3			8

-Table 8C-
Immigration into Barbour County: From Northern States

Place of Origin	1780s	1790s	1800s	1810s	1820s	1830s	1840s	1850s	1860s	Total
Pennsylvania	5	7	8	7	2	6	9	3		47
Maryland	9	3	15	8	8	11	10	6		70
New Jersey	2	1	3		2					8
Delaware		1	1							2
New York		2	1		1	1	3		1	9
Connecticut	1						1	2		4
Massachusetts				3						3
Maine				1						1
New Hampshire		1								1
Ohio			2				3	1	1	7
Indiana								1		1
Kentucky							1	1		2
Total	17	15	30	19	13	18	27	14	2	155

-Table 8D-
Immigration into Barbour County: From Europe

Place of Origin	1780s	1790s	1800s	1810s	1820s	1830s	1840s	1850s	1860s	Total
England	1									1
Scotland		1				2		1		4
Ireland	1		1		2		3	15		23
Germany			2	1				5		8
Switzerland								1		1
Holland			1							1
Italy								3		3
France							1			1
Total	2	1	5	1	2	2	4	25		42

APPENDIX C:

BIRTHPLACES OF BARBOUR'S SOLDIERS, THEIR FATHERS, AND THEIR GRANDFATHERS

The following lists provide a detailed breakdown of the birthplaces of Barbour's Union and Confederate soldiers and sympathizers as well as birthplaces of their fathers and grandfathers. No attempt was undertaken to carry the analysis along maternal lines due to the difficulties of determining maiden names of mothers and grandmothers.

-Table 9A-
Birthplaces of Unionists fromBarbour County

Place of Birth	Number from Barbour
Virginia	621
Georgia	1
Northern States	50
Pennsylvania	26
Ohio	9
New York	7
Connecticut	4
Illinois	2
Maine	1
New Jersey	1
Border States	36
Maryland	35
Kentucky	1
Europe	7
Ireland	5
Scotland	1
Germany	1
France	1
Total	718

-Table 9A (con't)-

Fathers of Unionists Born in Virginia

Place of Birth	Number from Barbour
Virginia	458
Northern States	91
Pennsylvania	65
New Jersey	12
Massachusetts	5
New York	4
Ohio	2
Maine	2
Illinois	1
Border States	51
Maryland	51
Europe	11
England	1
Ireland	6
Germany	2
Scotland	1
Italy	1
Birthplace Unknown	10
Total	**621**

-Table 9A (con't)-

Grandfathers of Unionists Born in Virginia with Fathers Also Born in Virginia

Place of Birth	Number from Barbour
Virginia	181
Northern States	134
Pennsylvania	80
New Jersey	47
Vermont	4
Connecticut	1
Delaware	2
"New England"	1
Border States	58
Maryland	58
Europe	49
Germany	13
England	13
Ireland	10
Scotland	10
Switzerland	3
Birthplace Unknown	36
Total	458

-Table 9B-
Birthplaces of Confederates fromBarbour County

Place of Birth	Number from Barbour
Virginia	499
Northern States	4
Pennsylvania	2
Illinois	1
New York	1
Border States	1
Maryland	1
Europe	5
Ireland	3
Canada	2
Total	509

Fathers of Confederates Born in Virginia

Place of Birth	Number from Barbour
Virginia	463
Northern States	14
Pennsylvania	14
Border States	19
Maryland	17
Kentucky	2
Europe	2
Germany	2
Birthplace Unknown	1
Total	499

-Table 9B (con't)-

Grandfathers of Unionists Born in Virginia
with Fathers Also Born in Virginia

Place of Birth	Number from Barbour
Virginia	337
Northern States	39
Pennsylvania	21
New Jersey	14
New York	2
Delaware	2
Border States	28
Maryland	28
Europe	31
England	6
Ireland	8
Germany	10
Scotland	5
Holland	1
France	1
Birthplace Unknown	28
Total	463

Appendix D:

Chronology of Enlistments

-Table 10A-
Union Army
(Federal Regiments Only)

Year	Month	First Enlistment	Second Enlistment	Total
1861	May	6		6
	June	20		20
	July			
	August	7		7
	September	17		17
	October	4		4
	November	11		11
	December	1		1
1862	January	4		4
	February	2		2
	March	5		5
	April	1		1
	May	38		38
	June	10		10
	July	1		1
	August	89	1	90
	September	38		38
	October	16		16
	November	15		15
	December	1		1
1863	January	5		5
	February	6		6
	March	3		3
	April			
	May	2		2
	June	4		4

-Table 10A (con't)-
Union Army: Federal Regiments Only

Year	Month	First Enlistment	Second Enlistment	Total
1863	July	17		17
	August	9		9
	September	1		1
	October	3		3
	November	2		2
	December	4		4
1864	January	1	10	11
	February	2	9	11
	March	7	6	13
	April	5		5
	May			
	June			
	July	2		2
	August	6	2	8
	September	23	7	30
	October	13	2	15
	November			
	December		1	1
1865	January	1	4	1
	February	24	3	28
	March	8		11
	April	7		7
Totals		441*	45	486

-Table 10B-
Confederate Army

Year	Month	First Enlistment	Second Enlistment	Total
1861	May	209		209
	June	6		6
	July	1		1
	August	2		2
	September	1		1
	October	2	1	3

-Table 10B (con't)-
Confederate Army

Year	Month	First Enlistment	Second Enlistment	Total
1862	January	1		1
	February		1	1
	March	5		5
	April	1		1
	May	2		2
	June	7	4	11
	July		1	1
	August	72	16	88
	September	5	2	7
	October	3	1	4
	November			
	December		2	2
1863	January			
	February	2	1	3
	March	3	1	4
	April	6	3	9
	May	33	9	42
	June	8	3	11
	July	4	1	5
	August			
	September			
	October	1		1
	November			
	December	1		1
1864	January	1		1
	February	2		2
	March	2		2
	April	8	5	13
	May			
	June			
	July	1		
	August			
	September			
	October			
	November			
	December			
Totals		389*	51	440

* Enlistment dates for three Federal and ten Confederate soldiers could not be confirmed.

ENDNOTES

INTRODUCTION

[1] David Poe, *Personal Reminiscences of the Civil War* (Charleston, W. Va., 1908), 35.

[2] No reliable study has yet explored the question of just how many West Virginians served in the Union and Confederate armies. Estimates have ranged from 25,000 to 35,000 Federals and between 5,000 and 20,000 Confederates. A beginning has been made with a recent study counting 15,760 Confederate soldiers serving from West Virginia. See Jack L. Dickinson, *Tattered Uniforms and Bright Bayonets: West Virginia's Confederate Soldiers* (Lexington, Va., 1995).

[3] Theodore F. Lang, *Loyal West Virginians, 1861-1865* (Baltimore, Md., 1895), 4.

[4] Granville D. Hall, *The Rending of Virginia* (Chicago, Ill., 1901), 30.

[5] James Morton Callahan, *History of West Virginia, Old and New* (Chicago, Ill., 1923), Vol. I, 332.

[6] Hall, *Rending of Virginia*, 29.

[7] Thomas Conduit Miller and Hu Maxwell, *West Virginia and Her People* (New York, 1913), 179.

[8] Callahan, *West Virginia, Old and New*, Vol. I, 333.

[9] Miller and Maxwell, *West Virginia and Her People*, 184 and 188.

[10] Charles H. Ambler, "The Cleavage Between Eastern and Western Virginia," *American Historical Review* XV (1910), 771.

[11] William Warren Sweet, *The Methodist-Episcopal Church and the Civil War* (Cincinnati, Ohio, 1912), 195 and *Wheeling Intelligencer*, March 19, 1862.

[12] Hu Maxwell, *History of Barbour County, West Virginia* (Morgantown, W.Va., 1899), 91.

[13] Lang, *Loyal West Virginians*, 3.

[14] *Ibid.*, 21.

[15] Richard Orr Curry, *A House Divided: A Study in Statehod Politics and the Copperhead Movement in West Virginia* (Pittsburgh, Pa., 1964).

[16] *Ibid.*, 13-27.

[17] Richard Orr Curry, "Crisis Politics in West Virginia, 1861-1870," in *Radicalism, Racism and Party Realignment. The Border States During Reconstruction* (Baltimore, Md., 1969), 87.

[18] John Williams, *West Virginia. A Bicentennial History* (New York, 1976), 44-47.

[19] *Ibid.*, 46; Charles H. Ambler, *Frances H. Pierpont, Union War Governor of Virginia and Father of West Virginia* (Chapel Hill, N.C., 1937), 59; *Barbour Jeffersonian*, April 5, 1861.

[20] Examples are Ambler, *Francis H. Pierpont*; Harvey Mitchell Rice, *The Life of Jonathon M. Bennett: A Study of the Virginias in Transition* (Chapel Hill, N.C., 1943); John E. Stealey, "Gideon Draper Camden: A Whig of Western Virginia," *West Virginia History* 26 (October, 1964), 13-30; Eugene Wise Jones, "Lieutenant Colonel John J. Polsley, 7th West Virginia Regiment, 1861-1865," *West Virginia History*, XI (1950), 95-159; G. Wayne Smith, *Nathan Goff, Jr.: A Biography* (Charleston, W.Va., 1959); and Craig M. Simpson, *A Good Southerner: The Life of Henry A. Wise of Virginia* (Chapel Hill, N.C., 1985).

[21] Michael F. Holt, *The Political Crisis of the 1850's* (New York, 1978).

[22] *Ibid.*, 219-238.

[23] *Ibid.*, 240-243.

[24] *Ibid.*, 248-259.

[25] Daniel W. Crofts, *Reluctant Confederates: Upper South Unionists in the Secession Crisis* (Chapel Hill, N.C., 1989).

[26] *Ibid.*, 133-135, 139-143 and 145-153.

[27] *Ibid.*, 171-175 and 363-365.

[28] Henry T. Shanks, *The Secessionist Movement in Virginia, 1847-1861* (New York, 1934). 59; William G. Brown, "John Letcher and the Slavery Issue in the Virginia Gubernatorial Contest, 1858-1859," *Journal of Southern History* 20 (1954), 22-49.

[29] Shanks, *Secessionist Movement*, 112-113.

[30] Six counties—Clay, Nicolas, Greenbriar, Fayette, Wyoming, and Monroe—returned majorities for Bell in 1860. In May, 1861 when voters were called upon to ratify the state convention's articles of secession, all six voted overwhelmingly in favor of them. In the northwest, only three counties—Hancock, Marshall and Ohio—voted for Bell in 1860. Twelve counties—Barbour, Preston, Wetzel, Marion, Doddrdge, Harrison, Ritchie, Wirt, Jackson, Brooke, Lewis, and Upshur—gave majorities for Breckenridge. In 1861 all but Barbour were officially recorded as having voted against the secession ordiance and there is good evidence Barbour did as well. For the 1860 vote, see *The Tribune Almanac for the Years 1838 to 1868* (New York, 1868), 50-51; for the vote on secession, see Curry, *A House Divided*, 141-147. Crofts makes an attempt to distinguish between eastern and western Virginia, but unfortunately draws the line at the Blue Ridge rather than the Alleghenies, thereby including several counties in southwest Virginia where support for both Breckenridge and secession predominated, Moreover, his use of the election of February 1861 as a variable for Unionism is a less significant expression of sentiment than that of the actual vote on secession itself. See Crofts, *Reluctant Confederates*, 364-365.

CHAPTER 1: BORDERLAND COUNTY

[1] George A. Shingleton, *History of Mt. Morris School, Church and Cove District* (Parsons, W.Va., 1976), 318-321.

[2] "The Civil War Journal of William B. Fletcher," *Indiana Magazine of History* 57 (1961), 71; Andrew J. Grayson, *The Spirit of 1861: History of the Sixth Indiana Regiment in the Three Months Campaign in Western Virginia* (Madison, 1875), 125; *Wheeling Intelligencer*, May 2, 1861.

[3] Thirty-five men were appointed justices of the peace between 1843 and 1851. During the same period four men were appointed sheriff, two as court clerks, two as surveyors and one as prosecuting attorney. Eight of the total were not listed in the 1850 census. Of the 36 who

were, five owned property valued in excess of $10,000, five between $5,000 and $10,000, eight between $2,500 and $5,000, sixteen between $1,000 and $2,500, and two less than $1,000. County officials taken from Maxwell, *Barbour County*, 227-231; property values derived from U.S. Census Office, *Seventh Census, 1850. Barbour County, Virginia.*

[4] A careful study of county officers and their relationship to one another reveals the extent of nepotism in local government. Of 20 new justices of the peace selected between 1843 and 1850, half were related to sitting magistrates. When William Wilson was selected to be county surveyor he chose his son Israel as his deputy; another son was given the post of court clerk. Barbour's first sheriff was Joseph McCoy, its first deputies his two sons. Charles Zinn saw to it that his brother was appointed coroner and his nephew road commissioner. Indeed, half the county's first road commissioners were directly related to the magistrates who appointed them. The list goes on and on. Fourteen new justices were elected in 1852. Of these only one had held prior office. Only three of the new justices owned property worth more than $2,500 in 1850 and only one owned property worth more than $5,000. Office holders from Maxwell, *Barbour County*, 200-211 and 227-232.

[5] Francois Andre Michaux, *Travels to Westward of the Allegheny Mountains* (London, 1805), 70.

[6] Maxwell, *Barbour County*, 285-286.

[7] *Ibid.*, 286-287.

[8] I.F. Boughter, *Internal Improvements in Northwest Virginia: A Study of State Policy Prior to the Civil War* (Pittsburgh, Pa., 1930).

[9] Callahan, *West Virginia, Old and New*, Vol. I, 182-184.

[10] *Ibid.*, 148.

[11] Henry Howe, *Historical Collections of Virginia* (Charleston, Va., 1857), 152.

[12] Netti Schreiner-Yanti, *Randolph County Tax Lists for 1787 and 1788* (n.p., 1987); on the early cattle trade in West Virginia, see Otis K. Rice, *The Allegheny Frontier: West Virginia Beginnings, 1730-1830* (Lexington, Ky., 1970), 158-160; and Richard K. MacMaster, "The Cattle Trade in Western Virginia, 1760-1830," in Robert D. Mitchell, ed., *Appalachian Frontiers: Settlement, Society and Development in the*

Pre-Industrial Era (Knoxville, Tenn., 1990), 127-149.

[13] J.R. Dodge, *West Virginia: Its Farms and Forests, Mines and Oil Wells* (Philadelphia, Pa.,1865), 161.

[14] M.F. Mauzy and William M. Fontaine, *Resources of West Virginia* (Wheeling, W.Va., 1876), 161.

[15] Howe, *Historical Collections*, 161; Callahan, *West Virginia, Old and New*, Vol. I, 149-150 and 184.

[16] Similar changes have been observed in southwestern Virginia. See Kenneth W. Noe, *Southwest Virginia's Railroad: Modernization and the Sectional Crisis* (Chicago, Ill., 1994), 43-52; and Ralph Mann, "Diversity in the Antebellum Appalachian South: Four Farm Communities in Tazewell County, Virginia," in Mary Beth Pudnup, Dwight B. Billings and Altina L. Walker, eds. *Appalachia in the Making: The Mountain South in the Nineteenth Century* (Chapel Hill, N.C., 1995), 133-162.

[17] In Randolph County, whose borders in 1800 encompassed an area that included the yet-to-be formed Barbour as well as four other counties, some 240 claims were patented on 200,000 acres in the seven years prior to 1793, the average size of the claims being between 600 and 700 acres. In 1795 another one million acres were patented by 47 claimants; by 1800 the total number of acres of patent land had risen to five million with an average size of 7,000 per claim. Lee Soltow, "Land Speculation in West Virginia in the Early Federal Period: Randolph County as a Specific Case," *West Virginia History* 44 (1983), 111-112.

[18] Wilma A. Dunaway, *The First American Frontier: Transition to Capitalism in Southern Appalachia, 1760-1860* (Chapel Hill, N.C., 1996), 56-59.

[19] One study of Tucker County (Barbour's neighbor to the east and formed from Randolph county in 1856) traced individual patent claims from their original filings through successive generations to the end of the nineteenth century. See Barbara Rasmussen, *Absentee Landowning and Exploitation in West Virginia, 1760-1920* (Lexington, Ky., 1994).

[20] By one count, 52 members of the Virginia Assembly in the 1790's held patent claims in West Virginia on tracts exceeding 10,000 acres. See Rice, *Allegheny Frontier*, 140. Between 1803 and 1827, the Assembly passed no fewer than 13 acts declaring lands on which taxes

were delinquent to be forfeited to the state. However, each law allowed owners anywhere from one to three years to redeem their lands by paying the back taxes owed on them. The redemption clauses naturally discouraged potential buyers. The 1831 law, which declared such lands "irredeemable," nonetheless extended redemption rights to 1833. In 1837 the assembly eliminated redemption rights once and for all. It also established county commissions charged with drawing up lists of delinquent land and mechanisms by which the commissioners were to dispose of the tracts. John A. Hutchinson, *Land Titles in Virginia and West Virginia* (Cincinnati, Ohio, 1887), 1-77.

[21] For the period 1827 to 1861, 40% of the patents filed were on claims of 50 acres and 100 acres. The average size of claims increased substantially after 1831. Between 1830 and 1850 only 3.7% of 186 patents were filed on claims of 500 acres or larger. In the ten-year period before the war, 12% of 192 patents were claimed on 500 acres or more.

[22] Another trend, not revealed in the figures, is the shift in the residency patterns for non-Virginians. In 1843 and 1850 virtually all land owned in this category was held by proprietors residing in Philadelphia, Washington D.C, New York, and other cities in the East. Only 350 acres in 1837 and 450 in 1850 were owned by persons living west of the Ohio River. Reflecting growing migration to the west, the 1860 list recorded 18 landowners holding nearly 3,000 acres as being residents of Iowa, Indiana, Ohio, Missouri, Kansas and Illinois, all of them former residents of Barbour.

[23] Miller and Maxwell, *West Virginia and Its People*, 262.

[24] Howe, *Historical Collections*, 153.

[25] *Ibid.*, 154.

[26] Ruth Woods Dayton, ed., *Samuel Woods and His Family* (Charleston, W. Va., 1961), 133.

[27] John Beatty, *Memoirs of a Volunteer* (New York, 1946), 22-23.

[28] Catherine Merrill, *The Soldier of Indiana in the War of the Union* (Indianapolis, Ind. 1861), 39.

[29] Festus Summers, *A Borderland Confederate. Letters of William L. Wilson* (Pittsburgh, Pa., 1962), 61.

[30] Howe, *Historical Collections*, 153.

[31] Beatty, *Memoirs*, 47.

[32] Orville Thompson, *From Philippi to Appomattox. Narrative of the Service of the Seventh Indiana Infantry in the War for the Union* (n.p., 190-), 24.

[33] Merrill, *Soldier of Indiana*, 21.

[34] Henry Clay McDougal, *Recollections, 1844-1909* (Kansas City, Mo., 1914), 214.

[35] Maxwell, *Barbour County*, 329.

[36] The literature on the alleged distinctiveness of Appalachia is large, voluminous and heavily weighted with prejudice. Two contrasting and influential examples are David Hackett Fischer, *Albion's Seed: Four British Folkways in America* (New York, 1989) and Henry D. Shapiro, *Appalachia on Our Mind: The Southern Mountains and Mountaineers in the American Consciousness* (Chapel Hill, N.C., 1978).

[37] John R. Philips, "History of Valley Furnace," *Barbour Democrat*, August 7, 1968.

[38] Howe, *Historical Collections*, 155.

[39] *Barbour Circuit Court Order Books, 1855-1861*. It should be noted that the man found guilty of manslaughter was not a resident of Barbour. Adam Minear, who attacked his wife, was committed to the state insane asylum. Peyton Booth, charged with felony assault in 1860 and never tried, joined the Confederate army, was captured and died in prison.

[40] *Probate Records, 1843-1868, Barbour County Court Records.*

[41] Schreiner-Yanti, *Randolph County Tax Lists*. The estimate is based on the identification of individuals known to have settled in what is know Barbour. Forty families would have roughly translated to a population of about 200 people.

[42] While many speculators withheld large tracts of land from the market in the hopes of cashing in on future mineral and logging rights, others actively disposed of their lands to pioneer settlers. See Rice, *Allegheny Frontier*, 143.

CHAPTER 2: WELLSPRINGS OF LOYALTY

[1] Crofts, *Reluctant Confederates*, passim,; Richard Lowe, "The Republican Party in Antebellum Virginia, 1856-1860," *Virginia Magazine of History and Biography* 81 (July, 1973), 259-279; and James Alexander Baggett, "Origins of Upper South Scalawag Leadership," *Civil War History* 29 (March, 1983), 53-73.

[2] Whig Unionists were Lewis Wilson, Edgar Parsons, Joseph Teter, Moore McNeil, and John Keller. Wilson ran for a seat in the House of Delegates in 1859, Teter in 1861. Keller served in the state senate in 1835. Secessionist Whigs were William and Samuel Elliott, John H. Woodford, Sr., John W. Woodford, and Henry Barron. Samuel Elliott served in the House of Delegates in 1840 and represented Barbour at the Whig Party convention in 1852, Barron and Woodford at the party's 1859 convention. Sources: *Richmond Whig and Public Advertiser*, April 20, 1852, March 11 and June 1, 1859; Maxwell, *Barbour County*, 380 and 500; Callahan, *West Virginia, Old and New*, Vol. III, 437-438; Henry H. Sims, *The Rise of the Whigs in Virginia, 1824-1840* (Richmond, 1929), 167-192.

[3] Lang, *Loyal West Virginians*, 7-11.

[4] Isabella Woods to Samuel Woods, September 26, 1862, in Dayton, *Samuel Woods*, 41.

[5] Maxwell, *Barbour County*, 504.

[6] U.S. Census Office, *Eighth Census, 1860. Slave Schedules. Barbour County, Virginia.*

[7] *Boner vs. Boner* in John M. Hagans (comp.), *Supreme Court of Appeals of West Virginia 1863-1874* (Morgantown, W.Va., 1906), Vol. 6, 1873, 377.

[8] Hall, *Rending of Virginia*, 74.

[9] Dayton, *Samuel Woods*, 23.

[10] Lang not only opposed slavery, but voted against the ordinance of secession. Winfield Lang, "The Career of D.B. Lang," *Confederate Veteran* XIII (1905), 37.

[11] Callahan, *West Virginia Old and New*, Vol. II, 557.

[12] Barbour County Historical Society, *Barbour County, West Virginia: Another Look*, Dallas, TX, 1979, 328.

[13] *Ibid.*, 122.

[14] Thompson, *Philippi to Appomattox*, 24.

[15] Isabella Woods to Samuel Woods, September 16, 1861, in Dayton, *Samuel Woods*, 37.

[16] Maxwell, *Barbour County*, 268.

[17] Miller and Maxwell, *West Virginia and Her People*, 291.

[18] The breakdown of church membership as noted by Sturm was: Methodist-Episcopal—201; Baptist—50 families; Methodist-Protestant—37 families; United Brethren—31 families; Catholic—15 families; German Baptist—9 families; Lutheran—7 families; Campbellite—3 families; Presbyterian—2 families.

[19] John N. Norwood, *The Schism in the Methodist-Episcopal Church, 1844* (New York, 1923), 19.

[20] Sweet, *Methodist-Episcopal Church*, 34-26.

[21] When the West Virginia Conference of the Methodist-Episcopal Church, South was established in 1850, it claimed a membership of 5,000 served by 23 preachers. By 1857, 66 preachers were ministering to over 8,300 members. Its strength lay in the southwestern counties with less than 10% of its members belonging to the northernmost circuit at Clarksburg. C.F. Deems, *Annals of Southern Methodism* (New York, 1856-1860), Vol. I, 22 and Vol. VII, 95. By comparison, the West Virginia Conference of the Methodist-Episcopal Church claimed 12,300 members and 2,500 probationers in 1865. C.C. Goss, *Statistical History of the First Century of American Methodism* (New York, 1866), 108.

[22] Sweet, *Methodist-Episcopal Church*, 34-36.

[23] *Ibid.*, 48.

[24] The preacher was Dr. Abraham Hershman, arrested in 1863 by order of Governor Pierpont. Isabella Woods to Samuel Woods, January 27, 1863, in Dayton, *Samuel Woods*, 79.

[25] Sarah Rider Bird, *Following the Upward Trail* (n.p., n.d.), 28 and 33; Dayton, *Samuel Woods*, 69.

[26] Although Southern Methodists had established circuits at Clarksburg and Rowlesburg prior to the war, there is no record of any

ministers practicing in Barbour until 1867 when the first minister of the denomination is recorded as having performed a marriage in the county. Its first churches were organized in Barbour in the early 1870s.

[27] Miller and Maxwell, *West Virginia and Her People*, 274.

[28] Isaac A. Barnes, *The Methodist-Protestant Church in West Virginia* (Baltimore, Md., 1926), 289-294.

[29] Donald G. Mathews, *Religion in the Old South* (Chicago, Ill., 1977), 66-81 and 150-184.

[30] *Ibid.*, 161-163; Mary Burnham Putnam, *The Baptist and Slavery, 1840-1845* (Ann Arbor, Mich., 1913), 21-23.

[31] Ancel H. Bassett, *A Concise History of the Methodist-Protestant Church* (Baltimore, Md., 1882), 124-196; Barnes, *Methodist-Protestant Church*, 285-297.

[32] Rev. A.P. Funkhouser and Oren F. Morton, *History of the Church of the United Brethren in Christ, Virginia Conference* (Dayton, Va., 1921), 113-115.

[33] Donald F. Durnbaugh, *The Brethren Encyclopedia* (Philadelphia, Pa., 1983-1984), Vol. II, 728-729; 831-832 and 1189-1190; Rufus D. Bowman, *The Church of the Brethren and War, 1708-1941* (New York, 1971), 114-156.

[34] In addition to notations by Sturm in the 1860 census and individual biographies, sources on church membership included: H.H. Hardesty, "Hardesty's Historical and Geographical Encyclopedia,: in James Comstock, ed., *West Virginia Encyclopedia* (Richwood, W.Va., 1974), Vol.3, 214-221; Shingleton, *History of Mt. Morris*, 84-88; *Barbour County, Another Look*, 18-23; Barnes, *Methodist-Protestant Church*, 284-307; Benjamin Funk, *Life and Labors of Elder John Kline, The Martyr Missionary* (Elgin, Ill., 1900), 356, 375, 400, 423 and 435; Philips, "Valley Furnace," *Barbour Democrat*, August 7, 1968; and *Barbour County Church Records*.

[35] Maxwell, *Barbour County*, 231.

[36] Bird, *Following the Upward Trail*, 28-33.

[37] There is no single source listing all churches in Barbour prior to the war. From the sources noted above, Maxwell, *Barbour County*, 321,

327, and 329, and David Benedict, *A General History of the Baptist Denomination of America* (New York, 1848), 672-680, twenty-one churches could be identified: four Methodist-Episcopal, five Methodist-Protestant, four Baptist, and one each for the United Brethren and German Baptist. Five were established in the four decades before 1830, eight during the next two decades, and eight in the ten years prior to the war.

[38] Most of the Irish were former construction workers hired to the build the Staunton-Parkersburg road. Callahan, *History of West Virginia, Old and New*, Vol. I, 150-151. The nearest Lutheran Church was Saint Pauls in Preston County. In 1820 Lutherans in Barbour established the Old Dutch Church; a decade later most of its members had converted to Methodism. Shingleton, *History of Mt. Morris*, 107.

[39] Philips, "Valley Furnace," *Barbour Democrat*, August 7, 1968. See also Shingleton, *History of Mt. Morris*, 84 and 86; and Funk, *Elder John Kline*, 400 and 423.

[40] John Henry Cammack, *Personal Recollections of a Soldier of the Confederacy* (Huntington, W.Va., 1920), 5.

[41] Beatty, *Memoirs*, 22.

[42] Ruth Dayton Woods, ed., *The Diary of James E. Hall* (Charleston, W.Va., 1962), 11, 31, 35 and 47.

[43] Maxwell, *Barbour County*, 419.

[44] Philips, "Valley Furnace," *Barbour Democrat*, August 21, 1968.

[45] Cited in Curry, *A House Divided*, 50.

CHAPTER 3: DARK CLOUDS GATHER

[1] John R. Philips, "History of Valley Furnace," *Barbour Democrat*, August 21, 1968.

[2] Maxwell, *Barbour County*, 367-372.

[3] The 1850 census schedules for Barbour list the value of Woods' real property at $700, that of Dayton's at $1,300. In 1860, the value of real and personal property owned by Woods was $15,754, for Dayton $12,840. Of the seven other lawyers listed in 1860, one owned prop-

erty valued at $5,730, another at $3,610. None of the other lawyers owned property worth more that $1,400 and three owned property worth less than $500.

[4]Dayton, *Samuel Woods*, 111-115; Maxwell, *Barbour County*, 367-372 and 487-498.

[5] *Tribune Almanac*, 50.

[6] *Ibid.*, 63. Of 1,929 votes cast for Lincoln in Virginia, only 1,526 were listed by county. On votes for Lincoln in Barbour, see Callahan, *West Virginia, Old and New,* Vol. II, 557 and Vol. III, 500. As in Barbour, no votes for Lincoln were officially recorded in neighboring Harrison County despite several having been cast for him. *Wheeling Intelligencer,* April 15, 1863 and Cammack, *Personal Recollections*, 8.

[7]In 1856 Barbour cast 938 votes for Buchanan against 325 for Fillmore. In the 1859 gubernatorial elections, John Letcher, the Democratic candidate, received 818 votes against 425 for Goggin, his Whig opponent. Barbour's delegates to the state legislature in the 1850s, Albert G. Reger and William Johnson, were both Democrats. *Richmond Whig and Public Advertiser,* June 1 and 3, 1859; *Tribune Almanac*, 50.

[8]Shanks, *Secessionist Movement*, 107, 112, and 115-118; *Richmond Whig and Public Advertiser*, June 1 and 3, 1859; *Tribune Almanac*, 50.

[9]Shanks, *Secession Movement*, 115-119; a quantitative analysis of voting patterns in the border states is set forth in Crofts, *Reluctant Confederates*, 55-65; the same pattern was noted in early studies of the region. See Edward Conrad, *The Borderland in the Civil War,* (New York, 1927).

[10]Dayton, *Samuel Woods*, 119.

[11]Philips, "Valley Furnace," *Barbour Democrat*, September 11 and 18, 1968.

[12]Maxwell, *Barbour County*, 238.

[13] *Wheeling Intelligencer*, February 29, 1864.

[14] *Ibid.*, April 23, 1863.

[15]Maxwell, *Barbour County*, 239.

[16] *Ibid.*, 239.

17 *Ibid.*, 242.

18 Beatty, *Memoirs*, 33.

19 Philips, "Valley Furnace," *Barbour Democrat*, August 21, 1968.

20 Maxwell, *Barbour County*, 237; Philips, "Valley Furnace," *Barbour Democrat*, August 21, 1968.

21 Callahan, *West Virginia, Old and New*, Vol. I, 395.

22 Merrill, *Soldier of Indiana*, 39.

23 *Barbour County Marriages, 1853-1865.* In addition to residents of Barbour, the figures take into account non-residents who married in Barbour and who could be identified as either Union or Confederate soldiers or sympathizers.

24 Maxwell, *Barbour County*, 237-238; Philips, "Valley Furnace," *Barbour Democrat*, August 21, 1968.

25 *Wheeling Intelligencer*, January 11, 1868.

26 Shanks, *Secessionist Movement*, 107.

27 *Ibid.*, 163.

28 Maxwell, *Barbour County*, 239-240.

29 *Ibid.*, 241.

30 *Ibid.*, 240.

31 Hall, *Rending of Virginia*, 163.

32 The figures are those for the initial vote taken on April 17. On that day 88 delegates voted in favor of secession. One delegate refused to vote. Eight others were absent, six of whom later voted for the ordinance. Of the 55 who initially voted against it, nine switched their votes to the affirmative. Shanks, *Secessionist Movement*, 204-205; Hall, *Rending of Virginia*, 539-541.

33 Hall, *Rending of Virginia*, 149 and 152.

34 On the reaction in Virginia to the Peace Conference and the other efforts at compromise preceding it, see Crofts, *Reluctant Confederates*, 208-213; and Shanks, *Secession Movement*, 170-171.

35 According to Curry's detailed analysis of election returns on the May 24 vote, the 35 counties of the Northwest voted 30,536 against

and 10,021 in favor of the ordinance. Curry points out that in the counties of the Shenandoah Valley and the Southwest the returns were heavily in favor of secession. Thus for West Virginia as a whole the vote was somewhat closer, 34,677 opposed, 19,121 in favor. Curry, *A House Divided*, 141-147.

[36] *Wheeling Intelligencer*, May 31, 1861. Curry acknowledged the existence of conflicting returns for Barbour, but elected to rely on the figure of a 231 majority in favor of the ordinance, explaining that "Available evidence... definitely places Barbour in the Secessionist camp." Curry, *A House Divided*, 142. Maxwell, citing no figures at all, claimed the vote in Barbour favored secession, but only by a slight margin. Maxwell, *Barbour County*, 237.

[37] *Wheeling Intelligencer*, June 20, 1861. In fact, governor Letcher had specifically authorized troops to vote outside their home counties. F.N. Berry, *John Letcher of Virginia* (University, Al., 1966), 336.

[38] Maxwell, *Barbour County*, 239-240.

[39] *The War of the Rebellion. A Compilation of the Official Records of the Union and Confederate Armies*, Series 1, Vol., L, 848; Colonel Robert White, *Confederate Military History: West Virginia*, (Atlanta, 1899), 7 and 15.

[40] Maxwell, *Barbour County*, 249.

[41] Philips, "Valley Furnace," *Barbour Democrat*, August 28, 1968.

[42] Maxwell, *Barbour County*, 249; Philips, "Valley Furnace," *Barbour Democrat*, August 21, 1968; David B. Kuhl, "Christian Kuhl of the Gilmer Rifles," http://www.rootsweb.com/~/hcpd/kuhl.htm, December 7, 1997.

[43] Dayton, *Diary of James E. Hall*, 11.

[44] Philips, "Valley Furnace," *Barbour Democrat*, August 21, 1968.

[45] Maxwell, *Barbour County*, 255-256; Grayson, *The Spirit of 1861*, 21-25.

[46] Maxwell, *ibid.*, 257-258 and 336.

[47] Frank Moore, ed., *The Rebellion Record* (New York, 1866), Vol. I, 336; C.J. Rawlings, *History of the First Regiment West Virginia Infantry* (Philadelphia, 1887), 27.

[48]Grayson, *Spirit of 1861*, 24; Thompson, *Philippi to Appomattox*, 19-23.

[49]Hall, *Rending of Virginia*, 151.

[50]Poe, *Personal Reminiscences*, 5; Cammack, *Personal Recollections*, 21.

CHAPTER 4: PATTERNS OF ENLISTMENT

[1] Of 19 counties ordered to furnish troops to Porterfield, only nine organized companies and all but Barbour organized only one. Other than Barbour's three companies, only four managed to even reach him. The rest of Porterfield's army was comprised of troops sent from the Shenandoah Valley.

[2] Poe, *Personal Reminiscences*, 4.

[3] The Thirty-first Virginia was comprised of companies raised in Barbour, Gilmer, Harrison, Lewis, Marion, Randolph, Pocahontas and Highland counties. The Twenty-fifth Virginia included only four companies raised west of the Alleghenies in Taylor, Braxton, Upshur and Webster counties. John M. Ashcraft, *31st Virginia Infantry* (Lynchburg, Va., 1988), 2-13; Richard L. Armstrong, *25th Virginia Infantry* (Lynchburg, Va. 1990), 8-11.

[4] Dayton, *Diary of James E. Hall*, 35.

[5] For first-hand accounts of Confederate recruiting behind Federal lines, see Poe, *Personal Reminiscences*, 14-18; Cammack, *Personal Recollections*, 72-83; and T.E. Fox, "Leaving West Virginia Home for Dixie," *Confederate Veteran* XIV (1906), 25.

[6] The Confederates who were killed were apparently summarily executed. McDougal, *Recollections*, 219.

[7] Armesy's case gained considerable notoriety. His harsh sentence was in fact given in retaliation for a similar sentence against Major Nathan Goff of the Fourth West Virginia Cavalry. Armesy was exchanged in 1864. John Harper Dawson, *Wildcat Cavalry: A Synoptic History of the Seventeenth Virginia Cavalry* (Dayton, Ohio, 1982), 84-85; G. Wayne Smith, "Nathan Goff, Jr., and the Civil War," *West Virginia History* XVI (1953), 126-131.

[8] Haviland Harris Abbott, "General John D. Imboden," *West Virginia History* XXI (1960), 94.

[9] National Archives, *Record Group 109. War Department Collection of Confederate Records. Company H, 62nd Virginia Mounted Infantry (formerly Company F, 1st Partisan Rangers). Muster Roll, September 1, 1862.*

[10] *Official Records*, Series 2, Vol. IV, 899.

[11] *Wheeling Intelligencer*, August 27, 1862.

[12] *Confederate Records. Company E, 62nd Virginia Mounted Infantry (formerly Company C, 1st Partisan Rangers). Muster Roll, August 29, 1862.*

[13] A.J. Boreman to Governor Pierpont, September 4, 1862; William A. Harrison to Governor Pierpont, September 4, 1862; D.D.F. Farnsworth to Governor Pierpont, September 4, 1862, in H. W. Flournoy, *Virginia State Papers* (Richmond, Va., 1893), Vol. XI, 388-389.

[14] *Wheeling Intelligencer*, September 3, 1862.

[15] *Ibid.*, August 27, 1862.

[16] *Official Records*, Series 1, Vol. XXV, 653.

[17] In all, only 30 men were recruited into the 31st Virginia during the raid. See compiled service records in Ashcraft, *31st Virginia Infantry*, 114-165. On Corder's company, see *Confederate Records. Company D, 20th Virginia Cavalry. Muster Roll, May 3, 1863.*

[18] Dr. Albert S. Bosworth, *A History of Randolph County, West Virginia* (Elkins, W.Va., 1975), 155-157.

[19] *Confederate Records. Company D, 20th Virginia Cavalry. Payroll, August 31 to October 31, 1864.*

[20] U. S. Congress, Sixty-first Congress, Second Session, *Senate Document 378, Federal and State Military Organizations*, 48-50. Local commanders like General Robert Milroy had long urged the creation of such units. "Our large armies are useless here," he complained to Governor Pierpont. "They cannot catch guerrillas in these mountains any more than a cow can catch fleas." R.H. Milroy to the Governor, October 27, 1862, in Flournoy, *Virginia State Papers*, Vol. XI, 399-400.

[21] *Wheeling Intelligencer,* February 20, 1864.

[22] Maxwell, *Barbour County,* 271.

[23] Perhaps to spur enlistments, the *Wheeling Intelligencer* printed the names of each volunteer between February and June as well as the county to which he was credited. Most of the non-resident volunteers credited to Barbour that spring were members of Company N, 6th West Virginia Infantry who re-enlisted while stationed at Philippi after their initial three-year terms had expired.

[24] *Wheeling Intelligencer,* February 7, 1865.

[25] The names of those drawn were published in the *Wheeling Intelligencer* March 25 and 26, 1865.

[26] Forty-four men were inducted into the army between February and April, 1865. Of these, 15 were substitutes hired by draftees, seven of whom had seen prior service in the army.

[27] Maxwell, *Barbour County,* 336.

[28] Philips, "Valley Furnace," *Barbour Democrat,* August 21, 1968

CHAPTER 5: WAR IN THE MOUNTAINS

[1] Dayton to Pierpont, August 24, 1861, quoted in Curry, *A House Divided,* 50.

[2] Hu Maxwell, *History of Tucker County, West Virginia* (Kingwood, W.Va., 1881), 327-339.

[3] National Archives. *Compiled Service Records of Confederate Soldiers Serving in Organizations from the State of Virginia. Thirty-first Virginia Infantry.*

[4] Cammack, *Personal Recollections,* 38; Dayton, *Diary of Jams E. Hall,* 22.

[5] Herman Edmund Matheny, *Major General Thomas Maley Harris* (Parsons, W.Va., 1963), 34-35; Genevieve Brown, "History of the Sixth regiment, West Virginia Volunteers," *West Virginia History* IX (1948), 315-368; National Archives. *Record of Events, Company B, 2nd West Virginia Infantry.*

[6] Matheny, *General Thomas M. Harris*, 34-35 and 39-41; *Wheeling Intelligencer*, July 21, 1862 and December 7, 1863; National Archives, *Record of Events, Company B, 2nd West Virginia Infantry*.

[7] *Barbour County Marriages, 1861-1863*. In addition to the 19 Barbour soldiers who married during this period, 24 soldiers from outside the county married local girls while stationed in Barbour.

[8] *Barbour County, Another Look*, 418.

[9] Isabella Woods to Samuel Woods, October 6, 1861, in Dayton, *Samuel Woods*, 76.

[10] Ashcraft, *31st Virginia Infantry*, 150.

[11] Maxwell, *Barbour County*, 418.

[12] Philips, "Valley Furnace," *Barbour Democrat*, October 23, 1968.

[13] *Barbour County, Another Look*, 107.

[14] *Ibid.*, 433.

[15] *Official Records*, Series 1, Vol. XXXIII, 1167-1168 and Vol. XXL, Part 2, 658.

[16] Clifford Dowdey, ed., *The Wartime Papers of R.E. Lee* (Boston, Mass., 1967), 650-651.

[17] *Ibid.*, 650.

[18] Of 136 men of the Thirty-first Virginia who later served in Imboden's or Jackson's brigade, only 48 transferred formally; the rest deserted. Compiled Service Records for the Thirty-first Virginia Infantry in Ashcraft, *Thirty-first Virginia Infantry*, 114-165.

[19] Cammack, *Personal Recollections*, 140.

[20] Dayton, *Diary of James E. Hall*, 54.

[21] *Official Records*, Series 1, Vol. XIX, 156-150.

[22] Inspecting officers in 1864 rated the discipline of many of the companies of the 62nd as "limited." See also Marshall M. Brice, *Conquest of a Valley* (Charlottesville, Va., 1965), 23-24.

[23] *Official Records*, Series 1, Vol. XII, 951.

[24] *Wheeling Intelligencer*, February 20, 1863.

[25] *Ibid.*, January 17, 1863.

[26] *Ibid.*, January 23, 1863.

[27] Frank S. Reader, *History of the Fifth West Virginia Cavalry, Formerly the Second West Virginia Infantry, and Battery G, First West Virginia Light Artillery* (New Brighton, Pa., 1890), 52.

[28] *Wheeling Intelligencer*, February 20, 1863.

[29] *Ibid.*, April 21, 1863.

[30] *Ibid.*, February 25, 1863.

[31] *Official Records*, Series 3, Vol. II, 944; Maxwell, *Tucker County*, 345.

[32] *Official Records*, Series 3, Vol. II, 943-944.

[33] *Ibid.*, Series, 3, Vol. III, p.8.

[34] *Ibid.*, p.11.

[35] *Ibid.*

[36] Maxwell, *Tucker County*, 345.

[37] *Official Records*, Series 1, Vol. XXI, 1102.

[38] The events of that night are set forth in detail by Spencer Dayton in a letter to the *Wheeling Intelligencer,* January 25, 1863.

[39] McDougal, *Recollections*, 219.

[40] Sarah Jane Holt to Isabella Woods, April 6, 1863, in Dayton, *Samuel Woods*, 98.

[41] Isabella Woods to Samuel Woods, February 7, 1863, in *ibid*, 84.

[42] J. Reily [sic] Philips to A. Coleman Bowman, January 29, 1863, on Fournoy, *Virginia State Papers*, Vol. I, 244.

[43] A. Coleman Bowman to Governor Letcher, n.d., in *ibid.*, 243-244; Maxwell, *Barbour County*, 337-338.

[44] *Wheeling Intelligencer*, January 17 and 24, 1863.

[45] *Ibid.*, January 24, 1863.

[46] J.D. Imboden to R.H. Milroy, January 20, 1863, in Flournoy, *Virginia State Papers*, Vol. IX, 405-406.

[47] R.H. Milroy to J.D. Imboden, January 27, 1863, in *ibid.*, 407.

[48] *Wheeling Intelligencer*, January 24, 1863.

[49] *Ibid.*

[50] Isabella Woods to Samuel Woods, January 27, 1863, in Dayton, *Samuel Woods*, 79.

[51] *Official Records*, Series 2, Vol. V, 612 and 691.

[52] *Ibid.*, Series 1, Vol. XXI, 1102.

[53] *Barbour County, Another Look*, 304.

[54] Isabella Woods to Samuel Woods, January 27, 1863, in Dayton, *Samuel Woods*, 80.

[55] *Official Records*, Series 1, Vol. XXV, 652-653.

[56] *Ibid.*, Part 1, 99-102.

[57] *Ibid.*, 115-119.

[58] *Ibid.*, Series 1, Vol. XXV, 104.

[59] Isabella Woods to Samuel Woods, February 7, 1863, in Dayton, *Samuel Woods*, 98; *Official Records*, Series 1, Vol. XXV, Part 2, 198, 225 and 250; Cammack, *Personal Recollections*, 64-65.

[60] Betty Hornbeck, *Upshur Brothers of the Blue and the Grey* (Parsons, W.Va., 1967), 124.

[61] Isabella Woods to Samuel Woods, May 14 and 17, 1863, in Dayton, *Samuel Woods*, 108.

[62] Callahan, *West Virginia, Old and New*, Vol. III, 594.

[63] Eva Margaret Carnes, *The Centenniel History of the Philippi Covered Bridge* (Philippi, W.Va., 1952), 21.

[64] Isabella Woods to Samuel Woods, May 14, 1863, in Dayton, *Samuel Woods*, 108.

[65] *Official Records*, Series 2, Vol. VI, 10.

[66] John D. Sutton, *History of Braxton County* (Suttton, W.Va., 1919), 172-174.

[67] *Wheeling Intelligencer*, October 26, 1863.

[68] On Averell's campaign, see Andrew Price, "Plain Tales of Mountain Trails," *West Virginia Blue Book* 13 (1928), 323-511; Reader, *Fifth West Virginia*, 213-219; and Lang, *Loyal West Virginians*, 362-364.

[69] Pocahontas County Historical Society, *Pocahontas County History* (Dallss, Tx.,1982), 28.

[70] *Wheeling Intelligencer*, January 23, 1864.

[71] Cammack, *Personal Recollections*, 78; Charles B. Waggoner, et al., to Boreman, August 20, 1863; T.F. Sturms and F. Parish to Boreman, November 12, 1863, in Works Progress Administration, Historical Records Survey, *Calendar of Arthur I. Boreman Letters in the State Department of Archives and History* (Charleston, W.Va., 1939).

[72] Captain Michael Haller to Governor Boreman, March 30, 1864; Callahan, *West Virginia, Old and New*, Vol. III, 124.

[73] Poe, *Personal Recollections*, 37; on the killing of Lieutenant Stewart, see *The Wheeling Daily Register*, March 28, 1863.

[74] Maxwell, *Barbour County*, 272.

CHAPTER 6: KEEP THE HOME FIRES BURNING

[1] Isabella Woods to Samuel Woods, February 19, 1862, in Dayton, *Samuel Woods*, 7 and 66-67.

[2] *Barbour County, Another Look*, 82.

[3] Maxwell, *Barbour County*, 98, 355, 469.

[4] *Ibid.*, 241.

[5] *Wheeling Intelligencer*, May 2, 1861.

[6] James Morton Callahan, *Genealogical and Personal History of the Upper Monongahela Valley* (New York, 1912), 1112.

[7] Grayson, *Spirit of 1861*, 25; Orville Thompson, *Narrative of the Services of the Seventh Indiana Infantry* (n.p., n.d.), 24. Thompson, a private in the Seventh Indiana, described Philippi as a "secessionist hole."

[8] Grayson, *Spirit of 1861*, 25. The soldier, one John Lott, was

described by Grayson as "the first colored man that shouldered a musket in the Union army." Lott was immediately arrested and jailed at Wheeling. A month later his commanding officer secured his release when the regiment returned to Indiana. However, Lott is not listed as a member of the regiment in its official history.

[9] *Wheeling Intelligencer*, June 26, 1861.

[10] *Ibid.*, September 20, 1861.

[11] Maxwell, *Barbour County*, 288; Isabella Woods to Samuel Woods, July 18, 1861, in Dayton, *Samuel Woods*, 6 and 27.

[12] Grayson, *Spirit of 1861*, 25.

[13] Maxwell, *Barbour County*, 302.

[14] *Ibid.*, 506. Ironically, Wilson's partners in the oil venture were Lair D. Morrall and John W. Payne, both Secessionists who fled with Porterfield.

[15] Isabella Woods to Samuel Woods, October 8, 1861, in Dayton, *Samuel Woods*, 46.

[16] Isabella Woods to Samuel Woods, July 18, 1861 and February 2, 1862, in *ibid.*, 27 and 67.

[17] Isabella Woods to Samuel Woods, January 3, 1863, in *ibid.*, 61.

[18] Isabella Woods to Samuel Woods, January 27, 1863, in *ibid.*, 79-80.

[19] Sarah Jane Holt to Isabella Woods, April 6, 1863, in *ibid.*, 98.

[20] William Hewitt, *History of the Twelfth West Virginia Volunteer Infantry* (Steubenville, Ohio, 1892), 101-103.

[21] Hardesty, "Historical and Geographical Encyclopedia," in Comstock, *West Virginia Heritage Encyclopedia*, Vol. 3, 28.

[22] Rush, West and Company, *Biographical and Portrait Cyclopedia of Monongalia, Marion and Taylor Counties* (Philadelphia, Pa., 1895), 68-69.

[23] *Wheeling Intelligencer*, January 12, 1863.

[24] Poe, *Personal Reminiscences*, 16-18.

[25] Shingleton, *History of Mt. Morris*, 170.

[26] *Wheeling Intelligencer*, July 10, 1863.

[27] Moore, *The Rebellion Record*, Vol. IV, 82.

[28] Brown, "Sixth Regiment West Virginia Infantry," 327.

[29] *Wheeling Intelligencer*, June 26, 1861.

[30] Reader, *Fifth West Virginia Cavalry*, 51.

[31] Colonel George R. Latham to the Gov., April 14, 1862, in Flournoy, *Virginia State Papers*, Vol. IX, 372. On the activities of the Harper brothers, see Maxwell, *Tucker County*, 238-249.

[32] *Wheeling Intelligencer*, August 29, 1862.

[33] *Ibid.*, September 7, 1863.

[34] *Ibid.*, December 13, 14, and 23, 1864. Murphy died of typhoid fever while in prison.

[35] *Wheeling Intelligencer*, July 8 and 22, 1863. Reed's fate is unknown, no further record of her being found.

[36] *Wheeling Intelligencer*, May 6 and September 3, 1862; January 8, 1864.

[37] Isabella Woods to Samuel Woods, May 16, 1862, in Dayton, *Samuel Woods*, 70-71.

[38] *Barbour County, Another Look*, 227.

[39] Isabella Woods to Samuel Woods, May 18, 1862, in Dayton, *Samuel Woods*, 73.

[40] *Ibid.*, 462; George H. Cross to Pierpont, August 20, 1861; Brigadier General Benjamin F. Kelley to Pierpont, September 10, 1862 and October 9, 1862, in *Pierpont Letters and Papers*.

[41] Maxwell, *Barbour County*, 267.

[42] *Wheeling Intelligencer*, June 26, 1861.

[43] Philips, "Valley Furnace," *Barbour Democrat*, August 21, 1968.

[44] Dayton, *Diary of James E. Hall*, 35.

[45] *Wheeling Intelligencer*, September 3, 1862.

[46] Charles J. Harrison to Adjutant General Samuels, August 17, 1862, in *Calendar of Pierpont Papers*. On Shoemaker's trial after the war, see *Wheeling Intelligencer*, September 20, 1865.

[47] *Wheeling Intelligencer*, September 3, 1862.

[48] Richard Ellsworth Fast and Hu Maxwell, *The History and Government of West Virginia* (Morgantown, W.Va., 1901), 260-284, 310-315, and 404-409.

[49] *Tribune Almanac*, Vol. II, 50-51.

[50] Dayton was lambasted for bolting the Whigs. "It would amuse you to hear Spencer Dayton, Esq. making Democratic speeches," reported one local Whig. "In fact, it is said that he told his late Whig friends that he hardly knew how to make a Democratic speech, as he had not been over long enough to see the difference." *Richmond Whig and Public Advertiser*, April 2, 1859.

[51] Callahan, *History of West Virginia, Old and New*, Vol. III, 406.

[52] *Richmond Whig and Public Advertiser*, June 1, 1859.

[53] Isabella Woods to Samuel Woods, January 3, 1862, in Dayton, *Samuel Woods*, 61.

[54] Maxwell, *Barbour County*, 241 and 482.

[55] While Dayton was attending the convention in Wheeling, Taft was in Philippi where he was elected to the House of Delegates. Taft then promptly presented his credentials to the convention and demanded he be seated as Barbour's representative according to the convention's rules. Dayton was forced to resign when the Committee on Credentials supported Taft. Virgil A. Lewis, ed., *How West Virginia Was Made. Proceedings of the First Convention of the People of Northeastern Virginia at Wheeling* (Wheeling, W.Va., 1909), 93-95.

[56] Curry, *A House Divided*, 106-119 and 131-140.

[57] Lewis, *How West Virginia Was Made*, 269. See also Curry, *A House Divided*, 86-89.

[58] Charles H. Ambler, ed., *Debates and Proceedings of the First Constitutional Convention of West Virginia* (Huntington, W.Va., 1939), Vol. III, 429-436.

[59] Curry, *A House Divided*, 100-119.

[60] The clause freed all slaves born after July 4, 1863. Children of slaves under 10 years of age on that date were declared free when they reached the age of 21 and children of between the ages of 10 and 21 were free when they reached 25. Thus any slaves over the age of 21 in 1863 would never gain their freedom and their children would only many years later.

[61] Curry, *ibid.*, 131-140; and "Crisis Politics in West Virginia, 1868-1870," 80-104.

[62] Maxwell, *Barbour County*, 267-268.

[63] On Taft's attendance, see Lewis, *How West Virginia Was Made*, 128, 131, 132, and 135; on his petition to the governor of Ohio and his representation of Secessionists in civil suits, see Isabella Woods to Samuel Woods, September 16, 1861 and May 16, 1861, in Dayton, *Samuel Woods*, 56 and 70.

[64] *Wheeling Intelligencer,* January 31, 1863.

[65] Maxwell, *Barbour County*, 504.

[66] *Ibid.*, 245.

[67] *Wheeling Intelligencer*, April 23, 1863, August 2 and 9, 1864.

[68] *Ibid.* Hoff's new-found prominence proved to be distinctly detrimental for his son William, an officer in the Fifteenth West Virginia who was taken prisoner in 1864. When Confederate authorities realized who he was, they promptly slapped him in irons and sentenced him to hard labor in retaliation for the same treatment handed out to two Confederate agents captured in West Virginia. Hoff was released in an exchange worked out in early 1865. *Wheeling Intelligencer*, February 15, 1865.

[69] *Ibid.*, February 4, 1863.

[70] *Ibid.*, February 20, 1863.

[71] *Ibid.*, June 6 and 7, 1863; Maxwell, *Barbour County*, 235.

[72] Henry Mahoney to Spencer Dayton, November 12, 1863; Robert Adams to Dayton, November 30, 1863; Dayton to D.D.F. Farnsworth, January 23, 1864; Lewis Wilson to General Benjamin Kelley, n.d., in W.P.A., *Boreman Papers*.

[73] Yeager had served as Woodford's secretary at recruitment rallies in 1862; see *Wheeling Intelligencer*, September 3, 1862; M.T. Haller to Boreman, August 12, 1863; Spencer Dayton and Lewis Wilson to Boreman, August 17, 1863; I. Smith to Boreman, August 17, 1863, in *ibid.*

[74] A total of 777 votes were cast in Barbour at the May, 1863 elections. Wilson received 100% of the votes cast, Dayton 82%. Joseph Teter, Jr. was elected to the House of Delegates with only 56% and Spencer Glascock sheriff with 58%. *Wheeling Intelligencer*, June 7, 1863.

[75] George W. Atkinson, *Prominent Men of West Virginia* (Wheeling, W.Va., 1890), 108-109 and 118-119.

[76] *Wheeling Intelligencer*, June 16, 1863.

[77] Small state proponents had sought to limit West Virginia to 38 counties of the northwest. Conservatives repeatedly tried to extend the new state deep into Virginia. O'Brien voted with the majority in extending the boundary to the "natural borders" of the Allegheny Mountains, but consistently opposed the inclusion of counties in the Shenandoah Valley and Virginia's Piedmont. The closest that proponents of a free state came to eliminating slavery occurred in February, 1862 when Gordon Battelle sought to include a gradual emancipation clause in the constitution. The motion was tabled by a vote of 28 to 27, O'Brien voting with the minority. Ambler, *First Constitutional Convention*, Vol. I, 215, 316, 372, 546, and 557; Vol. III, 406, 415 and 423.

[78] *Wheeling Intelligencer*, February 9 and 14, 1866.

[79] Isabella Woods to Samuel Woods, no date, but probably July or August, 1861; and September 16, 1861, in Dayton, *Samuel Woods*, 31 and 37.

[80] Hewitt, *Twelfth West Virginia Infantry*, 10; see also Robert H. Milroy to Mary Milroy, March 25, 1862, in Margaret B. Paulus, ed., *The Papers of General Robert Huston Milroy* (n.p., 1965), Vol., I, 23.

[81] Isabella Woods to Samuel Woods, January 3, 1862, in Dayton, *Samuel Woods*, 63. The 1860 slave schedules for Barbour listed 95 slaves and black freemen. The census of 1870 counted only 45 blacks, only eight of whom were old enough to have been alive during the war. Postwar race relations were further transformed by court decree. Several mixed-race families had lived in Barbour since the 1790's. Maxwell,

Barbour County, 310-311. Continued intermarriage with whites had, by the time of the war, made them virtually indistinguishable from caucasians. Indeed, several men from these families served in West Virginia regiments during the war. Immediately prior to and soon after the war, most successfully petitioned the county court to declare them legally white. *Petitions of George W. Male and James Male, January Session, 1861; Petitions of Hiram Male, Stephen Newman, Richard Male, Stephen A. Male, Levi Collins, Franklin Male, George W. Collins, Elisha Male, Hezekiah Male and William Male, November Session, 1866, Barbour County County Circuit Court Records.*

[82] *Wheeling Intelligencer*, September 3, 1862.

[83] Lieutenant John E. Parkinson to Governor Pierpont, October 20, 1862, in Flournoy, *Virginia State Papers*, Vol. XI, 397.

[84] *Wheeling Intelligencer*, April 21, 1863.

[85] Hewitt, *Twelfth West Virginia Infantry*, 60.

[86] *Ibid.*, 61.

[87] Charles J. Rawlings, *History of the First Regiment, West Virginia Infantry* (Philadelphia, Pa., 1887), 233.

[88] Hewitt, *Twelfth West Virginia Infantry*, 35-37.

[89] David E. Long, *The Jewel of Victory: Abraham Lincoln's Re-Election and the End of Slavery* (Mechanicsville, Pa., 1994), 218-220.

[90] *Wheeling Intelligencer*, September 7 and 23, October 21, 1864.

[91] Rutherford Hayes to his mother, September 13, 1864, and to his uncle, October 12, 1864, in Charles R. Williams, ed., *Diary and Letters of Rutherford B. Hayes* (Columbus, Ohio, 1922, 504 and 524.

CHAPTER 7: STRANGERS IN A STRANGE LAND

[1] *Official Records*, Series 3, Vol. I, 417-418; Vol. III, 111-112.

[2] Isabella Woods to Samuel Woods, n.d., in Dayton, *Samuel Woods*, 30.

[3] Isabella Woods to Samuel Woods, May 16, 8162, in *ibid.*, 69.

[4] Isabella Woods to Samuel Woods, June 18, 1862, in *ibid.*, 74.

[5] Isabella Woods to Samuel Woods, June 11, 1862, in *ibid.*, 74.

[6] *Ibid.*

[7] Isabella Woods to Samuel Woods, February 7, 1862, in *ibid.*, 84.

[8] Mary Elisabeth Massey, *Refugee Life in the Confederacy* (Baton Rouge, La., 1964), 244-245.

[9] Isabella Woods to Samuel Woods, April 16, 1863, in Dayton, *Samuel Woods*, 100.

[10] *Ibid.*

[11] Isabella Woods to Samuel Woods, January 18, February 1 and 7, 1863, in *ibid.*, 78, 81 and 83.

[12] Isabella Woods to Samuel Woods, February 12, 1863; Samuel Woods to Isabella Woods, February 15, 1863, in *ibid.*, 85 and 88-89.

[13] Samuel Woods to Isabella Woods, February 14, 1863, in *ibid.*, 87-88.

[14] Isabella Woods to Samuel Woods, February 23, 1863, in *ibid.*, 92.

[15] *Barbour County, Another Look*, 293.

[16] Ashcraft, *31st Virginia Infantry*, 156.

[17] *Official Records*, Series 4, Vol. I, 1061-1062 and 1094-1100.

[18] Cammack, *Personal Recollections*, 20.

[19] Ashcraft, *31st Virginia Infantry*, 158; Callahan, *West Virginia, Old and New*, Vol. II, 499-500.

[20] Dayton, *Diary of James E. Hall*, 5.

[21] Data obtained from service records published in Armstrong, *25th Virginia Infantry*, 121-257, and Ashcraft, *31st Virginia Infantry*, 114-165.

[22] Five former captains and 19 lieutenants of the 31st Virginia Infantry became officers in Imboden's brigade. Data from service records in Armstrong, *25th Virginia Infantry*, 121-257; Ashcraft, *31st Virginia*

Infantry, 115-165; Roger U. Delauter, *18th Virginia Cavalry* (Lynchburg, Va. 1988), 55-100; and Delauter, *62nd Virginia Mounted Infantry* (Lynchburg, Va., 1989), 56-117.

[23] Philips, "Valley Furnace," *Barbour Democrat*, October 30, 1968; "A Confederate Journal," West Virginia History 22, No. 7 (July, 1961), 215.

[24] Poe, *Personal Reminiscences*, 45-46; Philips, "Valley Furnace," *Barbour Democrat*, August 28, 1968; "A Confederate Journal," 208 and 215.

[25] Philips, "Valley Furnace," *Barbour Democrat*, September 18, 1968.

[26] *Ibid.*

[27] Dayton, *Diary of James E. Hall*, 34 and 125-127; Maxwell, *Barbour County*, 282; "A Confederate Journal," 211-216.

[28] Philips, "Valley Furnace," *Barbour Democrat*, October 30, 1968.

[29] *Ibid.*, October 23, 1968.

[30] Dayton, *Diary of James E. Hall*, 62.

[31] *Ibid.*, 125-127.

[32] Isabella Woods to Samuel Woods, February 7, 12, and 17, 1863, in Dayton, *Samuel Woods*, 85 and 91.

[33] Isabella Woods to Samuel Woods, January 14 and 27, 1863, in *ibid.*, 77 and 79.

[34] Dayton, *Diary of James E. Hall*, 71.

[35] Philips, "Valley Furnace," *Barbour Democrat*, September 18, 1968.

[36] James M. McCann, "Scouting in West Virginia," *Confederate Veteran* I, No. 7 (July, 1894), 214.

[37] Dayton, *Diary of James E. Hall*, 125-127.

[38] Isabella Woods to Samuel Woods, April 1, 1863, in Dayton, *Samuel Woods*, 97.

[39] Massey, *Refugee Life*, 127-128.

[40] *Official Records*, Series 4, Vol. II, 472. An example of the level of participation in such elections is the vote for Marion County's representative to the House of Delegates in 1861. A total of 34 votes were cast, 29 by soldiers serving with the Thirty-first Virginia. "A Confederate Journal," 208.

[41] Dayton, *Diary of James E. Hall*, 128.

[42] Carle H. Scheele, *A Short History of the Mail Service*, (Washington, D.C., 1970), 89.

[43] *Official Records*, Series 1, Vol. XXII, Part 3, 864.

[44] Sarah Jane Holt to Isabella Woods, April 6, 1863; Isabella Woods to Samuel Woods, January 27, 1863, in Dayton, *Samuel Woods*, 79-80 and 99.

[45] Philips, "Valley Furnace," *Barbour Democrat*, August 28, 1986.

[46] Isabella Woods to Samuel Woods, September 5, 1861; October 27, 1861; December 31, 1861; and May 16, 1862, in Dayton, *Samuel Woods*, 35, 50, 59, and 70.

[47] Federal authorities had been after Sturm for several weeks before he was arrested in December, 1861. Although he took an oath of allegiance in 1863, he was still held at Camp Chase despite the urging of several citizens in Barbour that he be released. Isabella Woods to Samuel Woods, December 20, 1861 in *ibid.*, 59; Henson Hoff to Governor Boreman, July 14, 1864 in W.P.A., *Boreman Letters*.

[48] Isabella Woods to Samuel Woods, October 6, 1861 and May 16, 1862, in *ibid.*, 46 and 70-71.

[49] McCann, "Scouting in West Virginia," 215.

[50] *Barbour County, Another Look*, 301-302.

[51] Philips, "Valley Furnace," *Barbour Democrat*, August 38, 1968.

[52] Isabella Woods to Samuel Woods, October 27, 1861, November 30, 1861 and December 23, 1861, in Dayton, *Samuel Woods*, 48, 55 and 59.

[53] Dayton, *Diary of James E. Hall*, 32 and 35. Hall's problems with getting mail from home were finally solved after he was taken prisoner at Gettysburg. During his twenty-month confinement, his diary

entries recorded receiving no fewer than 61 letters from friends and relatives in Barbour, an average of three letters a month. See 83-124.

[54] Philips, "Valley Furnace," *Barbour Democrat*, October 23, 1968.

[55] Dayton, *Diary of James E. Hall*, 68.

[56] Philips, "Valley Furnace," *Barbour Democrat*, September 18, 1968.

[57] Isabella Woods to Samuel Woods, February 7, 1863, in Dayton, *Samuel Woods*, 82.

[58] Philips, "Valley Furnace," *Barbour Democrat*, September 18, 1968.

[59] Dayton, *Diary of James E. Hall*, 22 and 47.

[60] Philips, "Valley Furnace," *Barbour Democrat*, November 13, 1968.

[61] Dayton, *Diary of James E. Hall*, 22, 24 and 35.

[62] Isabella Woods to Samuel Woods, April 16, 1863, in Dayton, *Samuel Woods*, 99-100.

[63] Dayton, *Diary of James E. Hall*, 26.

[64] Philips, "Valley Furnace," *Barbour Democrat*, September 18, 1968.

[65] Samuel Woods to Isabella Woods, February 15, 1863, in Dayton, *Samuel Woods*, 87-100.

[66] Isabella Woods to Samuel Woods, November 30, 1861, in *ibid.*, 56.

[67] Isabella Woods to Samuel Woods, February 1, 1863, in *ibid.*, 80-81.

[68] Isabella Woods to Samuel Woods, February 17, 1863, April 19, 1863, and May 14, 1863, in *ibid.*, 99, 101 and 101; Philips, "Valley Furnace," *Barbour Democrat*, October 23, 1968; and Cammack, *Personal Recollections*, 65.

[69] Isabella Woods to Samuel Woods, May 14 and 17, 1863, in Dayton, *Samuel Woods*, 108 and 110.

[70] Data derived from compiled service records in Delauter, *The 62nd Virginia Infantry*, 56-117; and Richard L. Armstrong, *The 19th and 20th Virginia Cavalry* (Lynchburg, Va., 1994), 189-254. As the number of surrendering Confederates increased, Federal commanders in West Virginia reported "great dissatisfaction among the rebels" and urged that if word could be gotten to others that they would be sent home simply by surrendering and taking an oath of allegiance, "thousands would come into our lines." *Official Records*, Vol. XXIX, Part 1, 590.

[71] Cammack, *Personal Recollections*, 112.

CHAPTER 8: LET MALICE GO

[1] At the beginning of 1864, West Virginia had 19 Home Guard companies under arms and would add another 10 by the end of the year. U.S. Senate, *Federal and State Military Organization*, 48-49.

[2] General studies dealing with the 1864 campaign in the Shenandoah Valley are: Brice, *Conquest of a Valley*; Sanford C. Kellogg, *The Shenandoah Valley and Virginia: A War Study* (New York, 1903); Thomas A. Lewis, *The Shenandoah in Flames: The Valley Campaign of 1864* (Alexandria, Va., 1987); George E. Pond, *The Shenandoah Valley* (New York, 1883); and Edward J. Stackpole, *Sheridan in the Shenandoah—Jubal Early's Nemesis* (Harrisburg, Pa., 1961).

[3] Callahan, *West Virginia, Old and New*, Vol. III, 593-594.

[4] Dayton, *Samuel Woods*, 14-15.

[5] Hewitt, *Twelfth West Virginia Infantry*, 213.

[6] Dayton, *Diary of James E. Hall*, 136.

[7] *Official Records*, Series 2, Vol. VIII, 533-534.

[8] Hu Maxwell, *History of Randolph County, West Virginia* (Morgantown, W.Va., 1889), 407-408.

[9] *Wheeling Intelligencer*, April 20, May 2, 16 and 18, 1865.

[10] *Ibid.*, May 5, 1865.

[11] Calhoun County Historical and Genealogical Society, *History of Calhoun County, West Virginia* (Waynesville, N.C., 1989), 187.

[12] Dayton, *Samuel Woods*, 16.

[13] *Ibid.*, 17.

[14] Maxwell, *Barbour County*, 267.

[15] Philips, "Valley Furnace," *Barbour Democrat*, November 13, 1968.

[16] Charles H. Amber, *Disenfranchisement in West Virginia* (n.p., 1905), 41.

[17] The vote in the State Senate was 14 to 4 in favor; in the House, 38 to 13. *Wheeling Intelligencer*, February 2, 9, 14 and March 2, 1866.

[18] *Shroyer vs. Hill, Barbour County Circuit Court, Law Orders, Book 4, 1865.*

[19] Indicted were Adam Moore, Silas Harris and William Fitzwater of Barbour and William Dadisman of Taylor County. *State vs. Harris, et. al., Barbour County Circuit Court, Law Orders, Book 4, 1866-1870.*

[20] *Cole Vs. Radcliff, et. al., Maxwell vs. Hood, et. al., in Hagans, Supreme Court of Appeals*, Vol. 4, 1870; See also Milton Gerofsky, "Reconstruction in West Virginia, Part II," *West Virginia History* 7 (October, 1945), 10.

[21] Curry, "Crisis Politics in West Virginia," 93-96.

[22] *Wheeling Intelligencer*, March 19, 1866.

[23] *Wheeling Intelligencer*, January 27, 1866.

[24] Lamb to Camden, April 17, 1866, quoted in Curry, *A House Divided*, 143.

[25] *Wheeling Intelligencer*, April 14, 1866.

[26] *Ibid.*, February 28, April 14 and May 17, 1866.

[27] *Ibid.*, November 2, 1866.

[28] Majorities for Smith were recorded in Calhoun, Clay, Hardy, Barbour, Greenbrier, Tucker, Randolph, and Ohio Counties. Boreman prevailed by only a handful of votes in Braxton, Pleasants, Brooke, and Gilmer Counties. Atkinson, *Prominent Men of West Virginia*, 110-111.

[29] Ambler, *Disenfranchisement*, 49.

[30] *Wheeling Intelligencer*, February 8, 1866.

[31] Gerofsky, "Reconstruction, Part I, *West Virginia History* 6 (July, 1945), 317-318.

[32] Ambler, *Disenfranchisement*, 48.

[33] *Barbour County Circuit Court. Law Orders, 1867.*

[34] *Wheeling Intelligencer,* October 24, 1867.

[35] *Ibid.,* January 25, 1868.

[36] *Ibid.,* November 11, 1867.

[37] *Ibid.,* January 22, 1868.

[38] *Ibid.,* September 8, 1868.

[39] *Ibid.,* September 8 and November 30, 1868; Ambler, *Disenfranchisement,* 51; Callahan, *West Virginia, Old and New,* Vol. II, 406.

[40] Atkinson, *Prominent Men of West Virginia,* 110-111.

[41] *Wheeling Intelligencer,* May 21, 1869.

[42] *Ibid.,* May 12, 1869.

[43] *Ibid.,* January 27, February 8, 24 and 25, 1869. A number of those listed as petitioners were also listed as previously endorsing resolutions urging strict compliance with the Test Oath and other civil restrictions. See Wheeling *Intelligencer, May 17, 1866.*

[44] Granville Hall to Charles Summer, September 14, 1869, quoted in Curry, "Crisis Politics in West Virginia," 98-99.

[45] *Wheeling Intelligencer,* January 11, 1868.

[46] Dayton, *Samuel Woods,* 114.

[47] Gerofsky, "Reconstruction, Part I," 327.

[48] *Ibid.*

[49] *Ibid.,* 332-341.

[50] *Ibid.,* 348.

[51] *Ibid.,* 343-348; Curry, "Crisis Politics in West Virginia," 100-102.

[52] Gerofsky, "Reconstruction, Part I," 354.

[53] In the 1868 gubernatorial election, Stevenson polled 27,348 votes; in 1870 the vote for him was 26,683, a decline of only 665 votes. In the latter election, Democratic voting strength increased by nearly 6,000 votes. See Curry, "Crisis Politics in West Virginia," 102-103; on the vote in Barbour, see Atkinson, *Prominent Men of West Virginia*, 116-117.

[54] Callahan, *West Virginia, Old and New*, Vol. II, 413-418.

[55] Gerofsky, "Reconstruction, Part II," 20-30.

[56] William L. Wilson, "Reconstruction in West Virginia," in Hillary A. Herbert, ed., *Why the Solid South?* (Baltimore, Md., 1890), 276-278.

[57] Counties voting against ratification were Berkeley, Brooke, Doddridge, Grant, Hancock, Hardy, Harrison, Kanawha, Lewis, Marshall, Mason, Monongalia, Morgan, Pleasants, Preston, Taylor, Tyler, Upshur, and Wood. Atkinson, *Prominent Men of West Virginia*, 116-117.

[58] *Ibid.*, 108-111 and 120-123.

[59] Maxwell, *Barbour County*, 493-494. The animosity between Woods and Dayton nonetheless continued to the end of their lives. Yet Woods never lost his respect for the legal abilities of his one-time law partner. It is said that while serving on the bench, a lawyer appearing before him questioned a motion made by Dayton, to which Woods responded, "Why, that cannot be so! Spencer Dayton wrote this paper, and in matters of law and forms he is as infallible as the Apostle Paul." *Ibid.*, 371.

[60] *Barbour County Circuit Court, Law Orders, Books 1-4, 1866-1873*. Court records show the case as being continued through session after session. In September, 1867, the charges against Adam Moore were dropped in exchange for his testimony against Dadisman, Harris and Fitzwater. After then, there are no further references to the case. Moore, Harris and Fitzwater all left the county soon after.

[61] *Ibid., Book 4, May Term*, 1868.

[62] Maxwell, *Barbour County*, 349, 367, 379-389, 387, 397-398, 401, 407-409, 416, 420, 425, 427, 430, 435, 438-439, 441-442, 448, 456, 469, 479 and 514.

[63] Maxwell, *Barbour County*, 301-309.

[64] *Ibid.*, 227-231.

[65] *Ibid.*, 280-281.

[66] *Wheeling Intelligencer*, August 23, 1871. Cunningham's marriage to John Haney—who had served with Martin in the 3rd West Virginia—is recorded in Barbour's Marriage Book in 1872.

[67] *The Philippi Republican*, November 4, 1897.

[68] Philips, "Valley Furnace," *Barbour Democrat*, November 13, 1968.

BIBLIOGRAPHY

PRIMARY SOURCES

I. United States Government Documents

U. S. Bureau of the Census. *Eleventh Census, 1890*. Schedule of Surviving Soldiers, Sailors and Marines and Widows, West Virginia.

U. S. Census Office. *First Census, 1790*. Maryland, Pennsylvania and Virginia.

_____. *Third Census, 1810*. Harrison, Lewis and Randolph Counties, Virginia.

_____. *Fourth Census, 1820*. Harrison, Lewis and Randolph Counties, Virginia.

_____. *Fifth Census, 1830*. Harrison, Lewis and Randolph Counties, Virginia.

_____. *Sixth Census, 1840*. Harrison, Lewis and Randolph Counties, Virginia.

_____. *Seventh Census, 1850*. Albemarle, Augusta, Barbour, Bath, Clarke, Doddridge, Gilmer, Fairfax, Fauquier, Fluvanna, Frederick, Hampshire, Hardy, Harrison, Highland, Jackson, Lewis, Loudoun, Louisa, Marion, Monongalia, Pendleton, Pocahontas, Preston, Randolph, Rappahannock, Ritchie, Rockbridge, Rockingham, Shenandoah, Taylor and Tyler Counties, Virginia; Allegany County, Maryland. *Agriculture*, Barbour County, Virginia.

_____. *Eighth Census, 1860*. Barbour, Harrison, Preston, Randolph, Taylor, Tucker and Upshur Counties, Virginia. *Agriculture*, Barbour County, Virginia. *Slave Schedules*, Barbour County, Virginia.

_____. *Ninth Census, 1870*. Barbour County, West Virginia.

_____. *Tenth Census, 1880.* Barbour County, West Virginia.

U.S. Senate Executive Doc. 84, Pt. 5, *List of Pensioners on the Roll, January 1, 1883. West Virginia.* 47th Cong., 2d sess., 1883.

U. S. Senate Doc. 378, *Federal and State Military Organization.* 61st Cong., 2d sess., 1910.

War Department. *Compiled Service Records of Confederate Soldiers Who Served in Organizations from the State of Virginia.* 11th Virginia Cavalry, 18th Virginia Cavalry, 14th Virginia Cavalry, McClanahan's Battery, 19th Virginia Cavalry, 17th Virginia Cavalry, 62nd Virginia Mounted Infantry, 31st Virginia Infantry, 20th Virginia Cavalry, 25th Virginia Infantry.

_____. *Confederate Records.* Muster and Payrolls of the 62nd Virginia Mounted Infantry, Muster and Payrolls of the 31st Virginia Infantry, Muster and Payrolls of the 20th Virginia Cavalry.

_____. *Record of Events.* Co. F, 15th W. Va. Infantry; Co. B, 2nd W. Va. Infantry; 6th W. Va. Infantry.

_____. *Register of Prisoners,* Camp Chase, Ohio, 1861-1865.

II. West Virginia State Documents

Barbour County: Cemetery Records, Church Records, Circuit Court, Law Books, 1853-1873; County Court, Law Books, 1853-1866; Death Records, 1853-1875; Estate Settlements and Probates Records, 1843-1870; Marriage Records, 1843-1849, 1853-1888; Tax Lists, 1843-1860; Wills, 1843-1899.

Harrison County: Marriage Records, 1784-1888.

Pierpont, Francis H. *Annual Report of the Adjutant General of the State of West Virginia for the Year 1864.* Wheeling, 1865.

_____. *Annual Report of the Adjutant General of the State of West Virginia for the Year 1865.* Wheeling, 1866.

Randolph County: Marriage Records, 1787-1899.

Tucker County: Marriage Records, 1856-1888.

III. Newspapers

The Barbour Jeffersonian, April 5, 1861; April 20 and May 7, 1884.

Clarksburg Patriot, 1861-1863.

The Jeffersonian Plaindealer, May 21, July 16 and 23, 1896.

The Philippi Plaindealer, 1900 - 1906.

The Philippi Republican, 1882 - 1906.

The Old Flag, April 7 and December 2, 1869.

The Richmond Whig and Public Advertiser, 1852-1862.

Wheeling Daily Register, 1860-1865.

Wheeling Intelligencer, 1860-1875.

IV. Published Diaries, Letters and Memoirs

Dayton, Ruth Woods, ed. *The Diary of James E. Hall*. Charleston, WV, 1961.

_____. *Samuel Woods and His Family*. Charleston, WV, 1939.

Bird, Sarah Rider. *Following the Upward Trail*. n.p., 1925.

Brigham, Lorimar S., ed. "The Civil War Journal of William B. Fletcher," *Indiana Magazine of History* 57 (March, 1961), pp. 41-76.

Cammack, John Henry. *Personal Recollections of a Soldier of the Confederacy, 1861-1865*. Huntington, WV, 1920.

Cresswell, Stephen, ed. "A Civil War Diary from French Creek: Selections from the Diary of Sirene Bunten," *West Virginia History* 48 (1989), pp. 131-141.

De Forrest, William. *A Volunteer's Adventures*. New Haven, CT, 1946.

Durham, James A. "The Battle of Belington," *Indiana Magazine of History* 7 (September, 1911), pp. 119-122.

Early, Jubal. *War Memoirs: Autobiographical Sketch and Narrative of the War Between the States*. Bloomington, IL, 1960.

Egan, Michael. *The Flying, Gray-Haired Yank*. Philadelphia, PA, 1888.

Ford, Harvey S., ed. *Memoirs of a Volunteer, 1861-1863*. New York, NY, 1947.

Fox, T. E. "Leaving West Virginia Home for Dixie," *Confederate Veteran* 14 (1906), p. 25.

Grayson, Andrew J. *History of the 6th Indiana Regiment in the Three Months Campaign in West Virginia*. Madison, WI, 1875.

Harris, Jaspar W. "The Sixty-Second Virginia at New Market," *Confederate Veteran* 16 (1908), pp. 461-462.

Hewitt, William. *History of the Twelfth West Virginia Volunteer Infantry*. Steubenville, OH, 1892.

Hooten, James. "Diary of James Hooten, 6th West Virginia Infantry," *Preston County Journal* October 10, 1957 - February 27, 1958.

King, John R. *My Experience in the Confederate Army and the Northern Prisons*. Clarksburg, WV, 1917.

Knauss, William H. *The Story of Camp Chase*. Nashville, TN, 1906.

Kuhl, David B. "Christian Kuhl of the Gilmer Rifles," Online. <http://www.rootsweb.com/~hcpd/kuhl.htm>. December 7, 1997.

Leib, Charles. *Nine Months in the Quartermaster's Department; or, The Chances for Making a Million*. Cincinnati, OH, 1862.

McCann, James M. "Scouting in West Virginia," *Confederate Veteran* 2 (July, 1894), 213-214.

McDougal, Henry C. *Recollections, 1844-1909.* Kansas City, MO, 1910.

"A Confederate Journal," *West Virginia History* 22 (1960), pp. 207-216.

Philips, John R. "History of Valley Furnace," *Barbour Democrat*, July 31 - November 13, 1968.

Poe, David. *Personal Reminiscences of the Civil War.* Charleston, WV, 1908.

Rawlings, Charles J. *History of the First Regiment, West Virginia Infantry.* Philadelphia, PA, 1887.

Reader, Frank S. *History of the Fifth West Virginia Cavalry, Formerly the Second Infantry, and of Battery G, First West Virginia Light Artillery.* New Brighton, PA, 1890.

Schmitt, Martin F., ed. *General George Crook: His Autobiography.* Norman, OK, 1946.

Summer, Festus P., ed. *A Borderland Confederate: Letters of William L. Wilson.* Pittsburgh, PA, 1962.

Thompson, Orville. *From Philippi to Appomattox: Narrative of the Services of the Seventh Indiana Infantry.* n.p., n.d.

Williams, Charles R., ed. *Diary and Letters of Rutherford B. Hayes.* 2 vols. Columbus, OH, 1922.

V. Other Published Source Material

"Abstracts of Wills, Appointments and Estates," *Randolph County Historical Society, Magazine of History and Biography* 9 (1937), pp. 38-57.

Ambler, Charles H., ed. *Debates and Proceedings of the First Constitutional Convention of West Virginia.* 3 vols. Huntington, WV, 1939.

Brodine, Helen, ed. "Early Marriages, Monongalia County," *National Genealogical Society Quarterly*, XLII (1954), pp. 7-12, 73-76, 142-145.

Brumbaugh, Gaius Marcus, ed. *Maryland Records. Colonial, Revolutionary, County and Church Records from Original Sources.* 2 vols. Baltimore, MD, 1975.

Challenger, Marian Waters, Charles Gilchrist, and Joy Gilchrist, eds. *1870 Barbour County, West Virginia Census.* West Lafayette, OH, 1985.

Chalkey, Lyman, ed. *Chronicles of Scotch-Irish Settlement in Virginia. Extracts from Court Records of Augusta County, Virginia 1745-1800.* 3 vols. Rosslyn, VA, 1912.

Crickard, Madeline W., ed. *1860 Census of Randolph County, Virginia.* Beverly, WV, 1872.

Crozier, William A., ed. *Early Virginia Marriages.* Baltimore, MD, 1986.

Cupler, Margaret Curst, ed. *Allegany County, Maryland. 1800 Census.* Baltimore, MD, 1971.

_____. *Early Allegany County Records.* n.p., 1970.

Curry, Richard Orr, ed. "Ideology and Perception: Democratic and Republican Attitudes on Civil War Politics and the Statehood Movement in West Virginia," *West Virginia History* 44 (Winter, 1983), pp. 135-155.

Davis, Eliza T., ed. *Frederick County Marriages, 1771-1825.* Baltimore, MD, 1973.

Dickison, Jack L. *Tattered Uniforms and Bright Bayonets: West Virginia's Confederate Soldiers.* Lexington, VA, 1995.

Dorman, John Frederick, ed. *Culpepper County, Virginia: Deeds.* Washington, DC, 1975.

Dowdey, Clifford, ed. *The Wartime Papers of R. E. Lee.* Boston, MA, 1967.

Flourney, H. W., ed. *Calendar of Virginia State Papers, Vol. XI, 1836-1869.* Richmond, VA,1893.

Fothergill, Augusta B., ed. *Virginia Tax Payers, 1782-1787, Other Than Those Published by the U. S. Census Bureau.* Richmond, VA, 1940.

_____. *Wills of Westmoreland County, Virginia.* Baltimore, MD, 1973.

Garner, Grace, ed. *Early Marriages, Western Frederick County, Virginia, Eastern Hampshire County, West Virginia.* n.p., 1975.

Gower, Karl K., ed. *The Aurora Documents.* Oakland, MD, 1983.

Hagans, John M., ed. *Supreme Court of Appeals of West Virginia, 1863-1874.* 7 vols. Morgantown, WV, 1906.

Harter, Mary, ed. *Pendleton County, Virginia. Marriage Records, 1791-1853.* Key West, FL, 1979.

Hawkins, Paul C. and Judith Hawkins, eds. *Upshur County Death Records 1853-1928.* Bowie, MD, 1993.

Hutchinson, John A., ed. *Land Titles in Virginia and West Virginia.* Cincinnati, OH, 1887.

Ingmire, Frances and Carolyn Ericson, eds. *Confederate POWs. Soldiers and Sailors Who Died in Federal Prisons and Military Hospitals in the North.* n.p., 1984.

Jackson, Ronald Vern, ed. *Mortality Schedules, West Virginia. 1850.* Bountiful, UT, 1979.

Jewell, Aurelia M., ed. *Loudoun County, Virginia, Marriage Records to 1881.* Berryville, VA, 1975.

Johnston, Ross B., ed. *West Virginia Estate Settlements, 1753-1850.* Baltimore, MD, 1978.

_____. *West Virginians in the American Revolution.* Baltimore, MD, 1977.

King, J. Estelle Stewart, ed. *Abstracts of Wills, Conventions and Administrations of Frederick County, Virginia.* Berryville, VA, 1973.

_____. *Abstracts of Wills, Inventories and Administration Accounts of Loudoun County, Virginia, 1757-1800.* Baltimore, MD, 1978.

_____. *Abstracts of Wills, Administrations and Marriages of Fauquier County, Virginia, 1759-1800.* Baltimore, MD, 1978.

Knorr, Catherine Lindsay, ed. *Marriages of Culpepper County, Virginia, 1781-1815.* Pine Bluff, AR, 1954.

Lewis, Virgil A., ed. *How West Virginia Was Made: Proceedings of the First Convention of the People of Northwestern Virginia at Wheeling.* Wheeling, WV, 1909.

Liggett, Thomas J., ed. *Census of Upshur County, West Virginia, 1860.* n.p., n.d.

Marsh, William A., ed. *1880 Census of West Virginia : Compiled Alphabetically by Counties.* 12 vols. Parsons, WV, 1979-1993.

Moore, Frank, ed. *The Rebellion Record: A Diary of American Events, with Documents, Narratives, Illustrative Incidents, Poetry, Etc.* New York, NY, 1861-1863.

Paulus, Margaret B., ed. *Papers of General Robert Huston Milroy.* 2 vols. n.p., 1965.

Ross, Clara Moe., ed. *1850 Federal Census Hardy County, West Virginia.* Colfax, NC, 1983.

Sage, Clara McCormack and Jones, Laura Sage, eds. *Early Records of Hampshire County, Virginia.* Delava, WI, 1939.

Schreiner-Yantis, Netti, ed. *Harrison County Tax Lists for 1787 and 1788.* n.p., 1987.

_____. *Randolph County Tax Lists for 1787 and 1788.* n.p., 1987.

Sims, Edgar, ed. *Sims Index to Land Grants in West Virginia.* Charleston, WV, 1952.

Tetrick, William Guy, ed. *Census Returns of Barbour and Taylor Counties, West Virginia, for 1850.* Clarksburg, WV, 1932.

_____. *Census Returns of Doddridge, Ritchie and Gilmer Counties, West Virginia, for 1850.* Clarksburg, WV, 1933.

_____. *Census Returns of Lewis County, West Virginia, for 1850.* Clarksburg, WV, 1930.

_____. *Census Returns of Harrison County, West Virginia, for 1850.* Clarksburg, WV, 1930.

_____. *Obituaries from Newspapers of Northern West Virginia.* 2 vols. Clarksburg, WV, 1933.

The Tribune Almanac and Political Register, 1856-1865. New York, NY, 1966.

Vogt, John and T. William Kethley, eds. *Frederick County Marriages, 1738-1850.* Athens, GA, 1984.

_____. *Loudoun County Marriages, 1760-1850.* Athens, GA, 1985.

_____. *Augusta County Marriages, 1748-1850.* Athens, GA, 1986.

_____. *Orange County Marriages, 1747-1850.* Athens, GA, 1984.

_____. *Rockingham County Marriages, 1778-1850.* Athens, GA, 1984.

_____. *Shenandoah County Marriages, 1772-1850.* Athens, GA, 1984.

_____. *Fluvanna County Marriages, 1788-1849.* Athens, GA, 1984.

The War of the Rebellion. Official Records of the Union and Confederate Armies. Prepared under the direction of the Secretary of War by Robert N. Scott. 69 vols. in 127, Washington, DC, 1880-1900.

Worrell, Anne Lowrey, ed. *Early Marriages, Wills and Some Revolutionary War Records, Botetourt County, Virginia.* Hillsville, VA, 1958.

Wulfeck, Dorothy Ford, ed. *Culpepper County, Virginia. Will Books.* Naugatuck, CT, 1965.

West Virginia. State Service Commission. *Report for 1902.* Charleston, WV, 1903.

Works Progress Administration. *Historical Records Survey. Calendar of the Francis Harrison Pierpont Letters and Papers in West Virignia Depositories.* Charleston, WV, 1940.

_____. *Calendar of the Arthur I. Boreman Letters in the State Department of Archives and History.* Charleston, WV, 1939.

_____. *Calendar of Wills in West Virginia. Upshur County.* Charleston, WV, 1940.

Zinn, Melba Pender, ed. *Monongalia County (West) Virginia: Records of the District, Superior and County Courts.* 3 vols. Bowie, MD, 1990-<2000>.

SECONDARY SOURCES

Abbott, Haviland H. "General John D. Imboden," *West Virginia History* XXI (1960), pp. 88-122.

Ambler, Charles H. *West Virginia, Stories and Biographies.* New York, 1937.

_____. *Sectionalism in Virginia from 1776 to 1861.* Chicago, 1910.

_____. *Disenfranchisement in West Virginia.* New Haven, Conn., 1905.

_____. *Francis H. Pierpont, Union War Governor of Virginia and Father of West Virginia.* Chapel Hill, 1937.

_____. "The Cleavage Between Eastern and Western Virginia," *American Historical Review* 15 (1910), pp. 726-780.

_____. "General Lee's Northwest Virginia Campaign," *West Virginia History* 1 (1939), pp. 15-29.

Armstrong, Richard L. *The 11th Virginia Cavalry*. Lynchburg, VA, 1989.

_____. *The 25th Virginia Infantry*. Lynchburg, VA, 1991.

_____. *The 19th and 20th Virginia Cavalry*. Lynchburg, VA, 1994.

_____. *The 26th Virginia Cavalry*. Lynchburg, VA, 1994.

Ashcroft, John M. Jr. *The 31st Virginia Infantry*. Lynchburg, VA, 1989.

Atkinson, George W. and Alvaro F. Gibbens. *Prominent Men of West Virginia*. Wheeling, 1890.

_____. *Bench and Bar of West Virginia*. Charleston, WV, 1919.

Baggett, James Alexander. "Origins of Upper South Scalawag Leadership," *Civil War History* 29 (March, 1983), pp. 53-73.

Baillet, Stephen Clay. *The Baillet, Bailliett, Bailliette, Balyeat, Bolyard and Allied Families*. Baton Rouge, LA, 1968.

Barbour County Historical Society. *Barbour County, West Virginia ... Another Look*. ?Phillipi, WV, 1979.

Barnes, Isaac A. *The Methodist-Protestant Church in West Virginia*. Baltimore, MD, 1926.

Bassett, Ansel Henry. *A Concise History of the Methodist-Protestant Church*. Pittsburgh, PA, 1878.

Bean, William G. "John Letcher and the Slavery Issue in Virginia's Gubernatorial Contest, 1858-1859," *Journal of Southern History* 20 (1954), pp. 22-49.

Benedict, David. *General History of the Baptist Denomination in America*. New York, NY, 1848.

Bishop, William H. *History of Roane County, West Virginia.* Spencer, WV, 1927.

Bittinger, Foster Melvin. *A History of the Church of the Brethren in the First District of West Virginia.* Elgin, IL, 1945.

Bode, Frederick A. and Donald E Ginter. *Farm Tenancy and the Census in Antebellum Georgia.* Athens, GA, 1986.

Boney, F. N. *John Letcher of Virginia: The Story of Virginia's Civil War Governor.* University, AL, 1966.

Bosworth, Albert S. *A History of Randolph County, West Virginia.* Elkins, WV, 1916.

Boughter, I. F. *Internal Improvements in Northwest Virginia: A Study of State Policy Prior to the Civil War.* Pittsburgh, PA, 1930.

Briant, Charles C. *History of the Sixth Regiment Indiana Volunteer Infantry.* Indianapolis, IN, 1891.

Brick, Gertrude N. and Ridgeway, Thurman. *Ridgeways in the U.S.A.* Baltimore, MD, 1980.

Brice, Marshall M. *Conquest of a Valley.* Charlottesville, VA, 1965.

Brown, Dec Alexander. *The Galvanized Yankees.* Urbana, IL, 1963.

Brown, Genevieve. "A History of the Sixth Regiment, West Virginia Infantry Volunteers," *West Virginia History* 9 (1948), 315-368.

Brumbaugh, Martin G. *A History of the German Baptist Brethren in Europe and North America.* Mt. Morris, IL, 1899.

Calhoun County Historical Society. *History of Calhoun County.* Grantsville, WV, 1989.

Callahan, James Morton. *Genealogical and Personal History of the Upper Monongahela Valley.* New York, 1912.

_____. *The Semi-Centennial History of West Virginia.* Morgantown, WV, 1913.

____. *History of West Virginia, Old and New*. 3 vols. Chicago, IL, 1923.

Carnes, Eve Margaret. *Centennial History of the Philippi Covered Bridge*. Philippi, WV, 1952.

Cartmell, Thomas K. *Shenandoah Valley Pioneers and Their Descendants: A History of Frederick County, Virginia*. Winchester, VA, 1909.

Coffman, Mary Stemple. *Footsteps of Our Forefathers: Early Settlers of Tacy*. Baltimore, MD, 1978.

Cohen, Stan. *The Civil War in West Virginia: A Pictorial History*. Missoula, MT, 1976.

_____. *A Pictorial Guide to West Virginia's Civil War Sites and Related Information*. Charleston, WV, 1990.

Cole, Arthur Charles. *The Whig Party in the South*. Gloucester, MA, 1962.

Comstock, James. *West Virginia Heritage Encyclopedia*, Supplemental Series. 25 vols. in 23, Richwood, WV, 1974.

_____. *Lewis County in the Civil War, 1861-1865*. Charleston, WV, 1924.

Conley, Phil. "The First Land Battle of the Civil War," *West Virginia History* (1959), 120-123.

Coontz, Violet Gadel. *The Western Waters: Early Settlers of Eastern Barbour County*. Denver, 1991.

Corder, Lyle K. "William Cole and John Cole," Online. <http://www.rootsweb.com/~cole.fam.htm>. December 8, 1997.

Core, Earl L. *The Monongalia Story: A Bicentennial History*. 3 vols. Parsons, WV, 1974.

Crofts, Daniel W. *Reluctant Confederates: Upper South Unionists in the Secession Crisis*. Chapel Hill, NC, 1989.

Current, Richard Nelson. *Lincoln's Loyalists: Union Soldiers from the Confederacy*. Boston, 1992.

Curry, Richard Orr. *A House Divided: A Study of Statehood Politics and the Copperhead Movement in West Virginia.* Pittsburgh, PA, 1964.

_____. *Radicalism, Racism and Party Realignment: The Border States During Reconstruction.* Baltimore, MD, 1969.

_____. and F. Gerald Ham. "The Bushwacker's War: Insurgency and Counter-Insurgency in West Virginia," *Civil War History* 10 (Dec., 1964), 416-433.

Cutright, William B. *History of Upshur County, West Virginia.* Buckhannon, WV, 1907.

Davis, Dorothy. *History of Harrison County, West Virginia.* Clarksburg, WV, 1970.

Davisson, Russell Lee. *The History and Genealogy of the Davissons.* Parson, WV, 1996.

Dawson, John Harper. *The Wildcat Cavalry: A Synoptic History of the 17th Virginia Cavalry Regiment of the Jenkins-McCausland Brigade.* Dayton, OH, 1982.

Dayton, Ruth Woods. "The Beginning - Philippi, 1861," *West Virginia History* 13 (1952), 254-266.

Deems, C. F. *Annals of Southern Methodism.* New York, NY, 1856-1860.

Delauter, Roger U., Jr. *The 18th Virginia Cavalry.* Lynchburg, VA, 1985.

_____. *The 62nd Virginia Infantry.* Lynchburg, VA, 1989.

Doddridge, Joseph. *Notes on the Settlement and Indian Wars, 1763-1783.* Wellsburg, VA, 1824.

Dodge, J. R. *West Virginia: Its Farms and Forests, Mines and Oil Wells, with a Glimpse of Its Scenery, a Photograph of its Population, and an Exhibit of Its Industrial Statistics.* Philadelphia, PA, 1865.

Driver, Robert J. *The 14th Virginia Cavalry.* Lynchburg, VA, 1989.

_____. *The Staunton Artillery, McClanahan's Battery*. Lynchburg, VA, 1988.

Dunaway, Wilma A. *The First American Frontier: Transition to Capitalism in Southern Appalachia, 1760-1860*. Chapel Hill, NC, 1996.

Durnbaugh, Donald F. *The Brethren Encyclopedia*. 2 vols. Philadelphia, PA, 1984.

Elliott, Charles. *History of the Great Secession from the Methodist-Episcopal Church in the Year 1845, Eventuating the Organization of the New Church Entitled the Methodist-Episcopal Church, South*. Cincinnati, OH, 1855.

Fansler, Homer Floyd. *History of Tucker County, West Virginia*. Parsons, WV, 1962.

Fast, Richard E. and Hu Maxwell. *The History and Government of West Virginia*. Morgantown, WV, 1901.

Fischer, David Hackett. *Albion's Seed: Four British Folkways in America*. New York, NY, 1989.

Frame, Katherine Hart. *The Harts of Randolph*. Parsons, WV, 1976.

Funk, Benjamin. *Life and Labors of Elder John Kline, the Martyr Missionary*. Elgin, IL, 1900.

Funkhauser, A. P. *The United Brethren in Christ, Virginia Conference*. Dayton, VA, 1921.

Gardiner, Mabel H. and Ann H Gardiner. *Chronicles of Old Berkeley*. Durham, NC, 1938.

Gerofsky, Milton. "Reconstruction in West Virginia," *West Virginia History* 6 (July, 1945), pp. 295-360 and 7 (October, 1945), pp. 5-39.

Goss, C. C. *Statistical History of the the First Century of American Methodism*. New York, NY, 1966.

Gray, Lewis C. *History of Agriculture in the Southern United States to 1860.* 2 vols. Washington, DC, 1933.

Green, Raleigh Travers. *Genealogical and Historical Notes on Culpepper County, Virginia.* Baltimore, MD, 1958.

Gross, Alexander. *A History of the Methodist-Episcopal Church, South, in the United States.* New York, NY, 1894.

Hall, Granville D. *The Rending of Virginia.* Chicago, IL, 1902.

_____. *The Two Virginias, Genesis of Old and New.* Glencoe, IL, 1915.

Hall, Septimus. *Genealogy of Thomas Hall, His Children and Grandchildren.* Parsons, WV, 1967.

Hardesty, H. H. *Hardesty's Historical and Geographical Encyclopedia.* Chicago, IL, 1883.

Haymond, Henry. *History of Harrison County, West Virginia.* Morgantown, WV, 1909.

_____. *History of Hampshire County, West Virginia.* Morgantown, WV, 1910.

Herbert, Hillary A., ed. *Why the Solid South?* Baltimore, MD, 1890.

Hinshaw, William W. *Encyclopedia of American Quaker Genealogy.* Vol. 6, *s.v.* "Virginia." Ann Arbor, MI, 1950.

Hitchcock, William S. "The Limits of Southern Unionism: Virginia Conservative and the Gubernatorial Election of 1859," *Journal of Southern History* 47 (February, 1981), 57-72.

Holt, Michael F. *The Political Crisis of the 1850's.* New York, NY, 1978.

Hornbeck, Betty. *Upshur Brothers of the Blue and the Gray.* Parsons, WV, 1967.

Howe, Henry. *Historical Collections of Virginia.* Charleston, SC, 1852.

Howell, Robert Boyle C. *The Early Baptists of Virginia*. Philadelphia, PA, 1857.

Hungerford, Edward. *The Story of the B & O, 1827-1927*. 2 vols. New York, NY, 1928.

Hutter, Paul Andrew. *Phil Sheridan and His Army*. Lincoln, NE, 1985.

Jones, Eugene Wise. "Lieutenant-Colonel John J. Polsey, 7th West Virginia Regiment, 1861-1865," *West Virginia History* 11 (1950), 95-159.

Jones, Virgil Carrington. *Gray Ghosts and Rebel Raiders*. New York, NY, 1956.

Judy, E. L. *History of Grant and Hardy Counties*. Charleston, WV, 1951.

Kellogg, Sanford C. *The Shenandoah Valley and Virginia, 1861-1865: A War Study*. New York, NY, 1903.

Kercheval, Samuel. *A History of the Valley of Virginia*. Woodstock, VA, 1902.

Keyes, Charles M. *The Military History of the 123rd Regiment Ohio Volunteer Infantry*. Sandusky, OH, 1874.

Kirk, John W. *Progressive West Virginians*. Parkersburg, WV, 1935.

Kuykendall, George B. *History of the Kuykendall Family Since It Settled in Dutch New York in 1646*. Portland, OR, 1919.

Lafferty, John J. *Sketches of the Virginia Conference, Methodist Episcopal Church, South*. Richmond, VA, 1880.

Lang, Theodore F. *Loyal West Virginians, 1861-1865*. Baltimore, MD, 1895.

Lang, Winfield. "The Career of Col. D. B. Lang," *Confederate Veteran* 13 (1905), 129

Leach, Elias. "A Sketch of the Leach Family," *Indiana Magazine of History* 30 (1934), 171-181.

Lewis, Thomas A. *The Shenandoah in Flames: The Valley Campaign of 1864*. Alexandria, VA, 1987.

_____. *The Guns of Cedar Creek*. New York, NY, 1988.

Lewis, Virgil. *The Soldiery of West Virginia*. Baltimore, MD, 1967.

Linger, James Carter. *Confederate Military Units of West Virginia*. Tulsa, OK, 1990.

Long, David E. *The Jewel of Victory: Abraham Lincoln's Re-Election and the End of Slavery*. Mechanicsville, PA, 1994.

Lowe, Richard. "The Republican Party in Antebellum Virginia, 1856-1860," *Virginia Magazine of History and Biography* 81 (July, 1973), pp. 259-279.

Lowther, Minnie Kendall. *History of Ritchie County, West Virginia*. Wheeling, 1911.

Maddox, Robert Franklin. "The Presidential Election of 1860 in West Virginia," *West Virginia History* 25 (April, 1864), 211-227.

Markeley, Ruth. *John Markeley Descendants*. Baltimore, MD, 1908.

Massey, Mary Elisabeth. *Refugee Life in the Confederacy*. Baton Rouge, LA, 1964.

Matheny, Herman Edmund. *Major General Thomas Maley Harris*. Parsons, WV, 1963.

Mathew, Donald G. *Religion in the Old South*. Chicago, IL, 1977.

Maury, Mathew F. and Fontaine, William. *Resources of West Virginia*. Wheeling, WV, 1876.

Maxwell, Hu. *History of Barbour County, West Virginia*. Morgantown, WV, 1899.

_____. *History of Randolph County, West Virginia*. Morgantown, WV, 1889.

_____. *History of Tucker County, West Virginia*. Kingwood, WV, 1884.

_____. *History of Hampshire County, West Virginia*. Morgantown, WV, 1897.

McGregor, James J. *The Disruption of Virginia*. New York, NY, 1922.

McKinney, Gordon B. *Southern Mountain Republicans, 1865-1900*. Chapel Hill, NC, 1978.

McWhorter, Lucullus Virgil. *The Border Settlers of Northwestern Virginia from 1768 to 1795*. Richwood, WV, 1974.

Merrill, Catherine. *The Soldier of Indiana in the War for the Union*. Indianapolis, 1864.

Mering, John V. "The Slave-State Constitutional Unionists and the Politics of Consensus," *Journal of Southern History* 43 (August, 1977), 395-410.

Michaux, Francois Andre. *Travels to the Westward of the Allegheny Mountains*. London, 1805.

Miller, Thomas C., and Hu Maxwell. *West Virginia and Its People*. New York, NY, 1913.

Mitchell, Robert D., ed. *The Appalachian Frontier: Settlement, Society and Development in the Pre-Industrial Era*. Knoxville, TN, 1990.

Moore, George Ellis. *A Banner in the Hills: West Virginia's Statehood*. New York, NY, 1963.

Morton, Oren F. *History of Highland County, Virginia*. Monterrey, VA, 1922.

_____. *A History of Pendleton County*. Dayton, VA, 1910.

_____. *A History of Preston County*. Kingwood, WV, 1914.

_____. *History of Rockbridge County, Virginia*. Staunton, VA, 1920.

_____. *Annals of Bath County, Virginia*. Staunton, VA, 1907.

_____. *History of Alleghany County, Virginia*. Dayton, VA, 1923.

_____. *History of the United Brethren in Christ, Virginia Conference*. Dayton, VA, 1921.

Murphy, Robert E. *Progressive West Virginians: Some of the Men Who Have Built Up and Developed the State of West Virginia*. Wheeling, WV, 1905.

Myers, Edward H. *The Disruption of the Methodist Episcopal Church, 1844-1845*. Nashville, TN, 1875.

Noe, Kenneth W. *Southwest Virginia's Railroad: Modernization and the Sectional Crisis*. Chicago, IL, 1994.

Norris, J. E. *History of the Lower Shenandoah Valley: Counties of Frederick, Berkeley, Jefferson and Clarke*. Chicago, IL, 1890.

Norman, Don. "Descendants of Jacob Bowman," Online. <http://www.rootsweb.com/~hcpd/norman/norman/htm>.

_____. "Descendants of Rutger Johnson." Online. http://www.rootsweb.com/~hcpd/norman/norman/htm.

Norwood, John N. *The Schism in the Methodist Episcopal Church, 1844: A Study of Slavery and Ecclesiastical Politics*. New York, NY, 1923.

Osborne, Randall, and Weaver, Jeffrey C. *The Virginia State Rangers and State Line*. Lynchburg, VA, 1994.

Parker, Granville. *The Formation of the State of West Virginia and Other Incidents of the late Civil War*. Wellsburg, WV, 1875.

Pemberton, Robert L. *A History of Pleasant County, West Virginia*. St. Mary's, WV, 1929.

Pocahontas County Historical Society. *History of Pocahontas County, West Virginia, 1981, Birthplace of Rivers*. Marlinton, WV, 1982.

Pendleton, William C. *Political History of Appalachian Virginia, 1776-1927.* Dayton, VA, 1927.

Pond, George E. *The Shenandoah Valley in 1864.* New York, NY, 1883.

Preston County Historical Society. *Preston County History.* Kingwood, WV, 1979.

Price, William T. *Historical Sketches of Pocahontas County, West Virginia.* Marlington, WV, 1911.

Price, Andrew. "Plain Tales of Mountain Trails," *West Virginia Blue Book* 13 (1928), 323-511.

Pudnup, Mary Beth; Dwight B. Billings,; and Altina L. Walker, eds. *Appalachia in the Making: The Mountain South in the Nineteenth Century.* Chapel Hill, NC, 1995.

Putnam, George W. *The Baptists and Slavery, 1840-1845.* Ann Arbor, MI, 1913.

Rasmussen, Barbara. *Absentee Landowning and Exploitation in West Virginia, 1760-1920.* Lexington, VA, 1994.

Redford, A. H. *History of the Organization of the Methodist Episcopal Church, South.* Nashville, TN, 1879.

Rice, Harvey M. *The Life of Jonathon M. Bennett: A Study of the Virginias in Transition.* Chapel Hill, NC, 1943.

Rice, Otis K. *The Allegheny Frontier: West Virginia Beginnings, 1730-1830.* Lexington, KY, 1970.

Roane County Family History Committee. *Roane County, West Virginia Family History.* Spencer, WV, 1990.

Rorabaugh, James D. *John R. Rohrbach (Rohrabaugh), 1728-1821: Descendants and Marriage Connections.* Parsons, WV, 1966.

Rush, West and Co. *Biographical and Portrait Cyclopedia of Monongalia, Marion and Taylor Counties.* Philadelphia, PA, 1895.

Sappington, Roger E. *The Brethren in Virginia: History of the Church of the Brethren in Virginia.* Harrisonburg, VA, 1973.

Scharf, J. Thomas. *History of Western Maryland.* Baltimore, MD, 1968.

Scheele, Carl H. *A Short History of the Mail Service.* Washington, DC, 1970.

Shaffer, John W. "Loyalties in Conflict: Union and Confederate Sentiment in Barbour County, " *West Virginia History* 50 (1991), 109-128.

Shanks, Henry T. *The Secessionist Movement in Virginia, 1847-1861.* Richmond, VA, 1934.

Shapiro, Henry D. *Appalachia On Our Mind: The Southern Mountains and Mountaineers in the American Consciousness, 1870-1920.* Chapel Hill, NC, 1978.

Shawkey, Morris Purday. *West Virginia History, Life, Literature and Industry.* 5 vols. Chicago, IL, 1928.

Shingleton, George A. *History of Mt. Morris School, Church and Cove District.* Parsons, WV, 1976.

Sims, Henry H. *The Rise of the Whigs in Virginia, 1824-1840.* Richmond, WV, 1929.

Smith, Edward Conrad. *The Borderland in the Civil War.* New York, NY, 1927.

_____. *History of Lewis County, West Virginia.* Weston, WV, 1920.

Smith, Mariwyn M. *And Live Forever: A Compilation of Senior Citizens Articles from the Parsons Advocate.* Parsons, WV, 1974.

Smith, G. Wayne. *Nathan Goff, Jr.: A Biography.* Charleston, WV, 1959.

_____. "Nathan Goff, Jr. in the Civil War," *West Virginia History* 16 (1953), 108-135.

Smith, H. C. *A History of the Yoakum Family*. Glendale, CA, 1963.

Soltow, Lee. "Land Speculation in West Virginia in the Early Federal Period: Randolph County as a Specific Case," *West Virginia History* 44 (1983), 111-134.

Spindel, Donna J. "Women's Legal Rights in West Virginia, 1863-1984," *West Virginia History* 51 (1992).

Stackpole, Edward J. *Sheridan in the Shenandoah - Jubal Early's Nemesis*. Harrisburg, VA. 1961.

Stalnaker, Cecil E. *A Chronology of the Stalnaker Family in America*. Baltimore, MD, 1982.

Stutler, Boyd B. "The Civil War in West Virginia," *West Virginia History* 22 (1961), 76-82.

_____. *West Virginia and the Civil War*. Charleston, WV, 1966.

Summer, Festus P. *Johnson Newlon Camden: A Study in Individualism*. New York, NY, 1937.

_____. "The Jones-Imboden Raid," *West Virginia History* 1 (1939), 15-29.

Sutton, John D. *History of Braxton County and Central West Virginia*. Sutton, WV, 1919.

Swaney, C. B. *Episcopal Methodism and Slavery With Sidelight on Ecclesiastical Politics*. Boston, MA, 1926.

Sweet, William W. *Virginia Methodism: A History*. Richmond, VA, 1955.

_____. *The Methodist Episcopal Church and the Civil War*. Cincinnati, OH, 1912

Torbet, Robert G. *A History of the Baptists*. Chicago, IL, 1950.

Van Meter, Benjamin F. *Genealogies and Sketches of Old Families Who Have Taken a Prominent Part in the Development of Virginia and Kentuckty*. Louisville, 1901.

Waddell, Joseph Addison. *Annals of Augusta County*. Bridgewater, VA, 1958.

Wayland, John W. *A History of Rockingham County, Virginia*. Dayton, VA, 1912.

_____. *The German Element in the Shenandoah Valley*. Charlottesville, VA, 1907.

_____. *The Bowmans: A Pioneering Family in Virginia, Kentucky and The Northwest*. Staunton, VA, 1943.

_____. *A History of Shenandoah County, Virginia*. Strasburg, VA, 1927.

The West Augusta Historical and Genealogical Society. *The History of Wood County, West Virginia*. Parkersburg, WV, 1990.

Williams, John. *West Virginia: A Bicentennial History*. New York, NY, 1976.

White, Robert. *Confederate Military History: West Virginia*. Atlanta, GA , 1899.

Wiley, Samuel T. *History of Preston County, West Virginia*. Kingwood, WV, 1882.

_____. *History of Monongalia County, West Virginia*. Kingwood, WV, 1883.

Wooster, Ralph A. *Politicians, Planters and Plain Folk: Courthouse and Statehouse in the Upper South, 1850-1860*. Knoxville, TN, 1975.

Zigler, D. H. *History of the Brethren in Virginia*. Elgin, IL, 1914.

INDEX